Under the Guns

Under the Guns

New York: 1775–1776

☆

BRUCE BLIVEN, JR.

HARPER & ROW, PUBLISHERS

New York, Evanston, San Francisco, London

FIRST EDITION

LIBRARY OF CONGRESS CATALOG CARD NUMBER: 69-15299

STANDARD BOOK NUMBER: 06-010379-5

For Naomi and Fred

Contents

☆

Introduction

☆

British and American soldiers had been fighting for almost fifteen months before the Second Continental Congress told the world that the colonies' purpose was a total dissolution of the connection between themselves and Great Britain. Yet the Declaration of Independence was not belated. The announcement came fairly quickly after the colonies had made up their minds that they were no longer protesting but rebelling. It had been difficult for most of the colonies to arrive at that decision. For one thing, the war had not gone well and there was no reason to believe that the Americans, even if they remained united, could win it. Then, too, although British policy toward America seemed to get steadily worse instead of better, many sensible Americans could not help believing that a negotiated settlement of some sort was possible.

The fifteen-month-long decision-making process called on countless Americans, especially those males who met the property qualifications for voting, to explain more about themselves in public, not always voluntarily, than they ever had before, and what was true of individuals was also true of villages, towns, cities, counties, and whole colonies. As the months went by, there was less and less middle ground between yes and no, and consequently fewer kinds of refuge for those who honestly saw some merit on both sides of the argument. By persuasion or by fear; because of economic or family relationships—and some-times despite them—whether they wished to or not, Americans were forced to take sides.

This book watches New York, and New York City especially, during this time, as independence changes from an unthink-able—or perhaps only unmentionable—concept to a political necessity, and as the province reveals itself, painting its own portrait in fine, but not necessarily flattering, detail. New Yorkers considered their set of problems unique, but few of New York's difficulties were as peculiar to New York as New Yorkers imagined. What was hard for them was hard for all the other colonies, and many of New York's crises, quandaries, doubts, and confusions had their counterparts, or at least their parallels, else-where in the country. To a large extent, New York's experience during these fifteen months was the experience of the United Colonies as a whole.

New York's situation was unique in only one way: its delibera-tions and its actions took place directly under the guns of British warships, and for most of the fifteen months the New York Provincial Congress feared that the city was a hostage for the Congress' own good behavior, since by firing a few firebombs into the highly inflammable town the British could easily start a fire that would destroy New York City. The city was never again vulnerable to sudden, physical obliteration until the Soviet Union's intercontinental missiles became operational, but now-adays the nuclear bomb appears to be only an intellectual reality. New Yorkers have to be reminded to worry about it, and it seems to have little effect on their political thinking. In 1775 and 1776, on the other hand, New Yorkers could not get the firebombs out of their minds. The bombs filled them with fear, even though the danger was mostly to their buildings, not to their lives. The warships' inhibiting effect on the province's

conduct of its affairs was obvious, preposterous, and under-
standable, all at once, for New Yorkers had no idea how much
rebellion the British would tolerate, and no way to find out
except by going too far. With some exceptions, historians have
not been sympathetic to New York on this account: if New York
had not had the ships' guns for an excuse, the argument goes, it
would have found another explanation for its timidity. This
common view seems to me to echo the eighteenth-century
opinion of New York, which was the least trusted of the thirteen
colonies in the Continental Association. New Englanders,
Southerners, and good Associators in the other middle colonies
believed that, if any province were to break the agreement to act
together in protest against British policies, New York would
doubtless be the first to try to make separate terms. While that
opinion was unjust—New York's faithful cooperation in the
protest movement was a matter of record—the province's poor
reputation was far from new. New York City was largely to
blame. Something about the place rubbed strangers the wrong
way, and it hardly mattered whether New York was really
wickeder than Boston, Providence, New Haven, Philadelphia,
Charleston, or any other town. It was *believed* to be wickeder—
more sinful, that is, and entirely preoccupied with making
money. For this reason, I think, the warships' menacing presence, as a factor influencing New York, was not and has not
usually been given enough weight. In any case, since my purpose
is to explore how people made up their minds to support the
American Revolution, this book refrains, as far as possible, from
saying what New Yorkers should or should not have done. My
interest is in what they did do.

Some children, by the time they can crawl, seem to be essentially who they are going to be for the rest of their lives. New
York is like that—not only Manhattan, but the other four

boroughs, too—and New York City's character was distinct and apparently fully formed at least one hundred years before the Revolutionary War. New York in 1775 and 1776 met its problems in an unmistakably New York style, with large numbers of the citizens preferring to escape history rather than to make it, and with an odd but persistent, ingrained New York indifference to out-of-towners' opinions. The smallness of the town helps the historian discover what New Yorkers were thinking. The whole population of New York in 1775 could be seated in Madison Square Garden, and the main action is confined to a space much smaller than the present Wall Street area. I have tried, within limits, to put the old places in terms of present-day landmarks—a fool's game, because the district is undergoing more changes, more rapidly, than almost any other part of the city.

New York has always treated its Revolutionary War sites, and most of its other historical places, like dirt—as ground on which bigger and taller buildings can be built. (St. Paul's Chapel is the one authentic Revolutionary War shrine standing in the neighborhood, but you can spend some time beside it without seeing anyone pause to pay his respects to brave Montgomery, whose tomb is just a few feet from Broadway.) It is too late for New York to change its ways: the price of Manhattan real estate prohibits shrine-building as it prevented shrine-preservation. It is better to think of the entire city, if not the whole United States, as a monument to the Revolution, and a monument that is primarily its people, for there is no one in New York, as there is no one in the United States, except heirs to the decisions, good and bad, that were made by men like the men in the New York Provincial Congress. Their wisdom was mixed with foolishness; their generosity was occasionally marred by meanness; and their bravery sometimes wavered:

they were our spiritual if not our literal fathers, and they were human. I think we owe them respect—a Roman *pietas*, if you like. They left us a large legacy.

New York City

BRUCE BLIVEN, JR.

Some Facts About the Illustrations

THE illustration on the jacket, "A View of New York from the Northwest," is often called "The Wooded Heights View." It shows the west shore of New York City from about Cortlandt Street to the Battery, in late 1772 or early 1773. It was originally printed in *The Atlantic Neptune*, which was the first marine atlas of the east coast of North America, from Quebec to the Gulf of Mexico. The atlas was prepared and published by the British Admiralty during the years 1763 to 1784 under the direction of Joseph F. W. Des Barres. The atlas is in the Phelps Stokes Collection of the New York Public Library.

Visible in the illustration is Trinity Church, on the bluff at the left. The other steeples from left to right are the Lutheran Church, the Middle Dutch Church, the Wall Street Presbyterian Church, the French Church du St. Esprit, the cupola and flag of City Hall, and the South Dutch Church. Fort George and the Governor's House, behind the ramparts of the Grand Battery, are at the right.

The map, whose formal title is "Plan of the City of New York, in North America: Surveyed in the years 1766 and 1767," was originally published in London on January 12, 1776. The map was drawn by a British army officer named Bernard Ratzer, whose name was misspelled by the engraver, one Thomas Kitchen, and was thus immortalized as Ratzen. The map shows changes as late as 1774 and is the most useful and accurate map of the City and its surroundings during the Revolutionary War period. The original is also in the Stokes Collection of the New York Public Library.

The book's endpapers are a middle section of the view of New York, from Governor's Island, which appears as a frieze at the bottom of the Ratzer map.

Under the Guns

I. June to December, 1775

☆

WHEN, in the late spring of 1775, New York City heard that British and American troops had fought at Lexington and Concord, two villages not far from Boston, some New Yorkers were delighted. Indeed, judging by appearances, the entire city was overjoyed, for the parades, bonfires, street meetings, and fireworks lasted for the better part of three days—a celebration more appropriate to the end of a war than to its beginning. Yet there were New Yorkers, temporarily less conspicuous than the revelers, who were not happy. Supporters of the Royal Government were appalled, not realizing that the reports, which had been sent by Massachusetts rebels, exaggerated the British defeat. And even some militant members of the anti-British protest movement were dismayed by uncertainties. If a war had begun in Massachusetts, they wondered what New York could and should do to help, and they were far from sure that New York City itself was safe from attack.

New York Province, which in size and shape approximated what is now New York State, and the city, its capital, a pleasant seaport of slightly more than twenty thousand persons, were fully engaged in the Continental Association, as the protest movement called itself. Throughout the ten or twelve years in which the disputes with Great Britain had been simmering, New York had cooperated with the twelve other colonies in every formal objection to British policy. Informally, New York had produced a full share of tea parties, Stamp Act riots, mass rallies, and ridings on rails. Like the other colonies, New York was fairly well controlled by a Provincial Congress, an upstart body that functioned as both a provincial legislature and a provincial executive in defiance of, and in competition with, the established order: the Governor and the Lieutenant Governor, the Governor's appointed Council, and the elected New York Assembly. New York's record gave out-of-province patriots elsewhere no just reason to doubt that, in war or rebellion, New York would do its part.

Yet all twelve of the other colonies did doubt New York's devotion to the American cause. The fact was that most New Yorkers preferred to think that loyalty to the king and loyalty to the Continental Association were not entirely exclusive. Some leaned this way, some that, but the majority could agree that only the extremists on both sides, of whom there were more than a few, were wrong. The Provincial Congress, whose very existence, in London's view, was proof of rebellion, was dominated by New York lawyers, merchants, and property owners, many of whom were active in the radical movement for a conservative reason: because they had thought it better to serve as delegates than to hang back and let the Liberty Boys have things their way.

On Sunday, June 25, New York City was confronted by an embarrassment that summed up its quandary with the blunt economy of a political cartoon. It was required to stage, simultaneously, official welcomes for George Washington, who had just been chosen Commander-in-Chief of the new Continental Army, and for William Tryon, the Royal Governor of New York Province, who was returning from England after more than a year's absence. Washington was passing through New

York on his way from Philadelphia to Cambridge, Massachusetts, to take up his new command. He was not expected to be in town long. Tryon, on the other hand, would presumably stay indefinitely, resume official residence in the city, and at least try to go on governing the province as before. The immediate difficulty was practical: the city was too small to handle two first-class receptions—two parades, along two routes of march, both thronged with cheering citizens—at once, and no street except Broadway, which ran from Fort George on the south (where the Custom House Building stands today) to just north of the Commons, or Fields (now City Hall Park), was suitable for a parade; the others were all too narrow, too crooked, or too short. Besides, the entire built-up area was so small that wherever one man's parade went the other man would be almost certain to hear the cheering for his rival. Furthermore, the city had only one militia unit, Colonel John Lasher's Independent Battalion, adequate to, and properly uniformed for, ceremonial duty. And then, even if it had been possible to hold both receptions at the same time, doing so would upset the plans of the many New Yorkers who wished to attend both.

Washington had been in New York before, but he was not widely known. Now that he had become America's most talked-about leader, New Yorkers, whatever their enthusiasm for the Continental cause, wanted to see what he looked like, and, in view of his new influence, many men imagined that an acquaintance with the General might do them good. As for Governor Tryon, he had been, and still was, genuinely popular. Even his political enemies, for the most part, admired him as a fine, bluff, soldierly fellow. And since Tryon was still New York's chief administrator—if only according to law—the hundreds of New Yorkers who worked for the British government, either full- or part-time, felt they were obliged to welcome their employer.

The Provincial Congress, reflecting the city's politically biga-
mous affections, wanted to impress Washington, but hoped that
it could please the General without offending the Governor. The
delegates to the Congress had worked out a desperate plan to
keep Washington's welcome uptown and Tryon's downtown,
thinking that at least the celebrations could be kept from clash-
ing in midtown. Early in the morning, with this maneuver in
mind, the Congress met and ordered Colonel Lasher to commit
two of his battalion's ten companies. One company was posted at
the south end of Broad Street, beside Coenties Slip, the pier
where Tryon was expected to land. The second accompanied
John Sloss Hobart, Thomas Smith, Gouverneur Morris, and
Richard Montgomery, a four-man subcommittee of the Provincial Congress, across the Hudson to Newark. They were to meet
Washington on the road and steer his party north, on a one-mile
detour, past the Paulus Hook Ferry, which ran between what is
now Jersey City and Cortlandt Street, Manhattan, to the Hoboken Ferry, which docked well above the built-up section of the
West Side. (The landing was near what is now the west end of
Canal Street.) It was as far away from Coenties Slip as one could
get and remain in the city. The rest of Lasher's battalion—the
eight companies in reserve—was stationed near the Commons,
about halfway between the two landing places, with orders to
keep alert and to proceed, on the double, to greet whichever
dignitary arrived first.

Only Tryon's tact enabled this shaky arrangement to succeed.
While he waited on board his ship, the *Juliana*, in the Bay for
New York to prepare its greeting, some of his friends, and his
son-in-law and secretary, Edmund Fanning, sailed out to visit
him. They told him the whole story. Tryon postponed his landing time, which he had scheduled for 4 P.M., by four hours. That
took the worst of the pressure off New York, and when Wash-

ington and his party, including two other newly elected Continental generals, Charles Lee and Philip Schuyler, their aides and staff officers, along with a troop of Philadelphia light horse that had ridden to New York as an honorary escort, arrived on time, an impressive crowd was waiting. If Washington noticed that the reception was short of uniformed men, he said nothing. After a round of introductions and handshaking, Washington's officers and the members of the New York Provincial Congress, the New York City Committee, the Continental Association's local body, and a few ministers stopped at Leonard Lispenard's country house, a handsome mansion on an eight-acre estate, which was only a few hundred yards from the Hoboken ferry landing. The eight companies of Lasher's reserve hurried up from the Commons and, finding that the dignitaries were inside, took this chance to catch their breaths and get set for the parade. The New York crowd, in a holiday mood, waited patiently out of doors.

Lispenard was a successful brewer, a New York County delegate to the Provincial Congress, and a hard-working, cautious member of its moderate bloc. He was delighted that the reception arrangements gave him an unexpected chance to entertain so many distinguished visitors. But the brief stop at his house was not just a party. The Provincial Congress, on its own initiative, had earlier in the day stopped an express rider carrying a letter from the Massachusetts Provincial Congress addressed to John Hancock, the President of the Continental Congress, at Philadelphia. The New Yorkers thought that Washington ought to open it and read it—the sooner the better, for they were not quite sure they had done the correct thing. They imagined it contained a reliable report of the fighting on Charlestown Neck which, they already knew, had taken place a week earlier. Scraps of gloomy news about the battle had been arriving in New York for several days. Washington hesitated to open Hancock's mail. The New Yorkers persuaded him it was the only sensible thing to do. After Washington had read the letter, he confirmed what they feared—the battle had been bloody; Breed's Hill, Bunker's Hill, and all the rest of Charlestown Neck were lost; the only cheerful note was that the Americans had forced the British to pay a high price in soldiers' lives.

The Massachusetts Congress also reported, not for the first time, that the Continental Army's gunpowder shortage was acute, and begged the Continental Congress to find some way to relieve it. This gave the New Yorkers a modest opportunity to boast about their devotion to the cause. They told Washington that, three days earlier, on June 22, New York had shipped almost every pound of its gunpowder to Massachusetts. The amount—a mere thousand pounds—was trivial compared to the need. Still, by doing so, New York had almost completely disarmed itself. As long as the city could not fire the cannon at the Battery, it could be cowed by one British warship of even the smallest class. The city was highly vulnerable to fire, as all its residents were constantly aware. A firebomb or two could start a conflagration that might burn New York to the ground. And, just lately, the British battleship *Asia*, which had sixty-four guns, had joined the *Kingfisher*, a sloop of war, at New York. The *Asia* was riding at anchor in the East River, not far north of Nutten (now Governor's) Island, towering over all the other vessels in sight, her almost vertical sides punctuated with gunports. As everyone was aware, she had plenty of powder and shot stored in her capacious ammunition lockers. New York City's existence depended on the chance that the *Asia* or, for that matter, the *Kingfisher* would not choose to destroy it.

An hour later, at almost five o'clock, Washington's parade got under way. The General had taken time to draft a note to Hancock, apologizing for having opened the letter and adding his hope that something (beyond New York's contribution) could be done about gunpowder. After it was written, the party still had to wait while one of the General's military secretaries made a fair copy. Then the procession headed south, down Greenwich Road, along the riverbank, with Lasher's battalion (minus one company) in the lead. The soldiers were followed, in order, by the New York Congress- and Committee-men, the three Continental generals, their staffs, the Philadelphia light horse, and, bringing up the rear, a cheering swarm of spectators who, as soon as the parade had passed them, got merrily into the line of march themselves. A block or two south of Read's (now Reade) Street, the West Side's northernmost crosstown thoroughfare, the parade turned east toward the Commons, then south onto Broadway, and down that handsome, tree-lined boulevard to Hull's Tavern, at No. 115, on the west side of the street, not far north of Trinity Church. Hull's Tavern, which was run by a man named George Burns, was the best hotel in New York—high praise, for, as a seaport, the city catered to transients, and there were a dozen other hotels, as well as boardinghouses, private houses with a room or two for rent, fifty licensed bars, two or three coffeehouses, and countless unlicensed establishments where a stranger could buy a drink and, perhaps, something to eat. For the past several years, Hull's Tavern's management had been especially hospitable to New York Associators—provided they could afford its prices. It was the logical place for the Commander-in-Chief to stay.

Washington's large, happy crowd had not completely dispersed by eight o'clock, the hour set for Tryon's postponed arrival. Even so, those who felt like it were able to leave the General without seeming to hurry and walk the few blocks to

the foot of Broad Street in time to meet the Governor. A substantial number of New Yorkers did exactly that. Added to a
small group of men who had boycotted Washington's reception,
and to Lasher's one company, which had stood there all day,
they formed a respectably large gathering. Tryon came up the
slip's steps to street level (today, the intersection of Broad and
Front streets), looked the crowd over, and felt gratified by New
York's showing. But no reception, least of all a noisy parade,
could have cheered him much. He had grown somber—his
greeters noticed that his face looked uncharacteristically glum—
listening to the reports of the friends who had gone out to talk
to him on his ship. All he wanted was to say a brief hello to the
crowd and then get on to Hugh Wallace's town house, where he
was going to spend the night. As Governor, Tryon was entitled
to live in a governor's mansion, but the old one, which had stood
inside the open rectangle of Fort George, had burned down in
1773. Since then, Tryon had been living in various rented houses
and dickering with London for an appropriation for a new mansion. Possibly because, as Governor of North Carolina from 1765
to 1771, he had built a governor's palace, at New Bern, that was
more luxurious than any other residence in North America,
London had been dilatory.

Tryon and his party—which included Wallace, who was a
member of the Governor's twelve-man Council and one of the
group who had been complaining all the way from Gravesend
Bay—made their way on foot up Broad Street for a few blocks,
past the Royal Exchange, an imposing two-story meeting hall in
the middle of the roadway between Dock Street (now Water
Street) and Pearl Street (still Pearl Street) past Fraunces'
Tavern (where the reconstructed Fraunces' Tavern stands), and
then west toward Bowling Green. Broad Street was second only
to Broadway in elegance. It was three times as wide as the

average street in New York—it had once been two roads flanking a canal, long since filled in and cobbled over. It was lined by private houses, retail stores, and warehouses, a mixture that characterized nearly all the city's streets. There were newer sections and older sections, fashionable and less fashionable districts, but the city was not divided, except for a stretch of a block or two here and there, into residential and commercial neighborhoods. A few of the older Broad Street buildings, in Dutch style, had their gable ends, rather than their fronts, to the street. But Broad Street had seen a lot of new construction—mostly three-story red-brick buildings with shuttered windows, handsome doorways, and symmetrical façades that would not have seemed out of place in London. They were, in fact, models of the latest English architectural fashions. The town houses on lower Broadway—from Bowling Green, a small oval park north of Fort George, up the hill to the high ground opposite the western end of Wall Street, where Trinity Church stood—were even bigger and more beautiful than those on Broad Street. Wallace's house was one of these.

Tryon supped at Wallace's, and, for an hour or two after, he received callers. His visitors included a surprise guest: Oliver De Lancey, the most active member of what had been for generations New York's most powerful—and probably still was its richest—family. From the beginning of Tryon's governorship, in 1771, De Lancey had been a member of Tryon's Council—as he had been a member of every Governor's Council since 1760. No New York governor would dare exclude the leading De Lancey from his cabinet. But De Lancey and Tryon had quarreled over many things, and considering the bad blood between them, it was remarkable that De Lancey should pay his respects, however insincerely, and more remarkable that, on the whole, he seemed affable. (One of the other councillors, William

Smith, Jr., did notice, on the other hand, that De Lancey occasionally hummed a tune to himself—a sure sign he was in a foul temper.) The visit confirmed everything that Wallace had been telling the Governor, for nothing short of revolution would have induced De Lancey to seek peace with Tryon.

De Lancey and all the rest of Tryon's callers that night hoped the Governor could do something about New York's affairs. Most New Yorkers felt exactly the other way—they hoped Tryon would do nothing. With the exception of a few radicals, the city's residents had little or no objection to going through the motions of acknowledging Tryon's authority, provided that he did not try to exercise it. They simply took it for granted that they could not rely on the Crown's representative to protect New York from punishment by the Crown. It was greatly to Tryon's political credit that men on both sides of the argument imagined, for what they thought were good reasons, that the Governor would do, or not do, as they wanted. Besides his personality, the catalog of Tryon's assets contained something for almost everybody.

To the conservatives, he was a hero because, as Governor of North Carolina, shortly before his transfer from New Bern to New York, Tryon, with a small army, had routed a band of up-country farmers who called themselves the "Regulators"; the lively skirmishing, later named the Battle of the Alamance, had taken place at Alamance Creek in May, 1771. Those New Yorkers who were most frightened by the activities of the Sons of Liberty cheered themselves up by remembering that their Governor had put down one rebellion with musket fire. (Like most historical analogies, the comparison was precarious. The Regulators had been almost completely insulated from the anti-British movement, but they were furious because their local county register's office, which Tryon had entrusted to his protégé, Fanning, was a mess; and Tryon had been so reluctant to use force against the farmers that he had hesitated for three years before giving the command to shoot.) New Yorkers all across the political spectrum—everywhere except within the De Lancey camp—recalled with pleasure Tryon's audacity, when he first came to New York, in telling the De Lanceys that he really intended to govern the province instead of taking orders from De Lanceys. (The second most powerful family faction, the Livingstons, had been especially appreciative.) Tryon had even won the respect of some of New York's most ardent Associators because of his evident distress over Great Britain's policies toward the American colonies. Within his limits as a Crown-appointed official, he had done his best to report, both by letter and in person, that Americans would not accept parliamentary taxation. Apart from what Tryon had done or what he believed, New Yorkers liked him as a man. He was forty-six, which seemed pleasantly young, if only in contrast to Lieutenant Governor Cadwallader Colden's eighty-seven years. Tryon was a professional soldier who wanted to do any job well, as a good soldier should. The attraction of his earnest eagerness outweighed his fault of being vain and his tendency to be pompous, even by the standards of a job in which some pomposity was expected.

Tryon's widespread popularity was an achievement that hardly anyone could measure—except, perhaps, Lord Dartmouth, the Secretary of State for the Colonies, and Lord North, the Prime Minister. They realized that Tryon hated being Governor of New York. He did not want a job in the colonies at all. His ambition was a regimental command or an appointment as one of the King's military aides. He found New York winters unbearably cold and New York summers unbearably hot; about the best he could say for his assignment was that New York was better than North Carolina, which he had loathed. His health was bad—his doctor's diagnosis was "the gout"—and he had returned to his post only because he had been ordered back. He had no troops at his command, no objective in view, no new instructions that made any sense, and apart from soldierly habit, no ambition to succeed.

At Hull's Tavern, three blocks north of Wallace's house, the mood of the evening's conversations was considerably brighter. Although the Continental Army's unsolved problems began with the fact that Washington lacked experience in commanding large units, and continued with a list of shortages that included nearly everything required to wage a war, Washington, Lee, and Schuyler were optimistic. Their sense of purpose accounted for some of the difference. Washington, for instance, was completely free from one of Tryon's bothersome doubts. The General had stopped wondering whether the American cause was right, and so he could concentrate on the multitude of practical difficulties before him. Lee was temporarily happy—he was far too neurotic to be satisfied with anything for long—because his rank was high.

He was a small man, thin, wiry, and as casual about his dress and bearing as Washington was careful. Lee was English, a professional soldier turned soldier of fortune. He had arrived in America in 1773, and, after a two-year campaign of energetic self-promotion, Lee and his new friends had persuaded the Continental Congress to make him the third-ranking general officer (Artemas Ward was second), mostly on the strength of Lee's own opinion that he knew more about the arts of war than any of the other candidates, including the Commander-in-Chief. It was fortunate that Lee was brilliant and almost as knowledgeable as he claimed, for he was serving as Washington's senior subordinate and technical adviser, and Washington could do with some help. Never, in all Lee's forty-four years, had so many important persons held him in such esteem. Even his favorite dog, Spada— Lee was always accompanied by a small pack of hounds—was sharing in Lee's glory and was enjoying an unusual amount of petting at the hands of patriotic ladies.

Schuyler, a man esteemed from birth, was pleased with his assignment, too. He was to take command of the Continental Army's New York Department. Schuyler's election, like that of Connecticut's Israel Putnam, had been one of the Congress' geographical choices, intended to rally every section of the country by recognizing its local hero, and Schuyler was delighted with the honor, both for himself and for New York Province. He was forty-one years old, a frail-looking man of medium height, with a florid complexion and mobile features, and a keen, snapping glance that suggested he would put up with no nonsense. He was the squire of Albany County, by far the richest man in the area, the owner of several mansions, and he was connected by family and by marriage to many of New York's other landowning aristocrats (his mother was a Van Cortlandt, and his wife a Van Rensselaer). He had been a soldier, on and off, for twenty years, had fought with the British, had served in the French and Indian War, and had been a colonel in the New York militia since then. Schuyler had also been active in the Association movement for a long time—the chance that such activity might lead to his sacrificing everything he owned did not concern him at all. He had been chosen as a delegate to both the First and the Second Continental Congresses—although he had not been able to attend the First because of poor health—and, in everything connected with the anti-British campaign, Schuyler had been his country's first spokesman. He knew Tryon quite well. Schuyler had been a member of the Assembly, and when Tryon had visited Albany,

Schuyler had been his host. But their friendship had been largely formal—Schuyler resented, among other things, the fact that Tryon, in 1773, had carved a new county, Tryon County, out of land that Schuyler felt belonged to Albany—and Schuyler relished becoming, as military commander of New York, Tryon's direct rival.

Since the next battle, if any, would probably be at Boston, Washington and Lee were eager to get on with their journey to Cambridge, and Schuyler was anxious to reach Albany, for his first task was to raise and equip a force that could take control of Lake George and Lake Champlain, those strategically important links in the water route between New York Bay and the St. Lawrence River. But the New Yorkers were in no hurry to see the generals go. The Provincial Congress wanted to stage another ceremony before they departed. The next morning, two of its members, William Morris and Isaac Low, called on Washington right after breakfast and asked him to delay his departure long enough to allow the Congress to present the generals with a set of three short testimonial addresses. Washington could hardly reject the request without wounding New York's feelings. Since he was waiting, anyhow, for his aide, Colonel Thomas Mifflin, to return from buying him some wine, stationery, a trunk, and a few other odds and ends, Washington agreed to stay, provided the ceremony began promptly at 2:30 P.M.

After the congressmen left, Washington conferred with his subordinates about what should be done if Governor Tryon caused trouble. The three generals were agreed that, until Tryon commanded more strength than two warships, he was not likely to do much. But he might try, for instance, to arrest the leaders of the Continental Association or to keep the Provincial Congress from meeting. In such a case, should Schuyler on his own initiative order the Governor's arrest? Should he wait for permission from the Continental Congress? The wait might be long, for in good weather, with solid footing on the roads, it took at least forty-eight hours to deliver a letter from New York City to Philadelphia; and if Schuyler happened to be at Albany at the time of an emergency, a request for instructions could not be acted upon in much less than two weeks. Yet Washington was not as worried about Tryon's aggressiveness as he was about Schuyler's. Schuyler's hot temper was notorious, and Washington feared that he might be pricked into ordering Tryon's arrest before it was a clear military or political necessity. A precipitate act might alienate Tryon's many friends, Associators among them, and seriously hurt the Continental cause. Washington put his decision in writing, so that there could be no doubt about it. No matter what the provocation, Schuyler was not to use force against the Governor's person without explicit permission from Philadelphia. "The seizing of a Governor [is] quite a new thing," Washington explained, "and of exceeding great importance."

That decision made, it was time for Washington to compose his reply to the Provincial Congress' forthcoming address. (He had asked to see an advance copy of the text.) What New York was going to say was so feeble that most of the good effect of the Sunday-afternoon reception was undone. In Philadelphia, the General had been bombarded with warnings against New York, mostly predictions that the province was likely to break with the Association and make a separate peace. The address, which attempted to include all shades of opinion within the Congress, and to balance every affirmation with a negation, did little to belie these unfair comments. Its introduction, for example, began with a masterpiece of compromise: "At a time when the most loyal of His Majesty's subjects, from a regard to the laws and constitution by which he sits on the throne, feel themselves reduced to the unhappy necessity of taking up arms to defend their dearest rights and privileges; while we deplore the calamities of this divided Empire, we rejoice in the appointment of a gentleman from whose abilities we are taught to expect both security and peace. . . ."

And so it wound along, heading first this way and that, until it made an insulting request. The Provincial Congress asked Washington for his word that when the fighting was over he would resign "cheerfully" as Commander-in-Chief and "reassume the character of our worthiest citizen."

This was not only impolite, but naïve, for if Washington had ambitions to become a postwar military dictator, he was unlikely to confess them publicly. The General took advantage of the blunder, and at the afternoon ceremonies, which began right on time, when it came his turn to thank New York for his welcome, Washington gave the Provincial Congress exactly the answer it wanted, in a sentence that was quoted repeatedly thereafter: "When we assumed the soldier, we did not lay aside the citizen; and we shall most sincerely rejoice with you in that happy hour when the establishment of American liberty, upon the most firm and solid foundations, shall enable us to return to our private stations in the bosom of a free, peaceful, and happy country."

The meeting ran longer than Washington had hoped, and there was a further loss of time because a number of New Yorkers wanted to escort Washington's party out of town, but had to go and get their horses. With one thing and another, Washington's cavalcade rode no farther that night than a tavern near the King's Bridge across the Harlem River, at Manhattan's northern tip.

It sometimes seemed as if New York City were fated to be misunderstood by out-of-town visitors. In this respect, Washing-

ton's short stay, though it included the biggest public demonstration he had ever received, was typical: the General came
away disliking and mistrusting New York City. The commonest
complaint, apart from politics, was morals. New York was supposed to be the most sinful city in America, according to those
who did not live there. New Yorkers were willing to admit that
prostitution was a civic problem, especially on the upper West
Side, in the neighborhood of King's College (now Columbia
University) on Murray Street between Church Street and
Chapel Street (now West Broadway). It was also true that New
York took Sabbath-breaking lightly (by comparison with, say,
Boston), and that New Yorkers were fond of many amusements
—or had been until, in a recent burst of austerity inspired by
resolutions of the Continental Congress, the city had banned
theatergoing, dancing, gambling, horse racing, cock fighting and
bull baiting for the duration of the emergency. But most residents did not think of New York as sinful, and some of them
wondered whether the city's so-called moral laxity could not be
more accurately described as polish or urbanity. New York was
undeniably a city of the world, and though it was smaller than
Philadelphia, and not much bigger than Boston or Charleston, it
seemed far less provincial than they.

In many ways, New York's variety was unmatched. Its population, predominantly Dutch a hundred years earlier, had become polyglot, an assemblage of people from all over, with the
English infusion, to be sure, the most conspicuous. One group of
New Yorkers or another was almost certain to furnish an exception to any generalization about New Yorkers. That in itself
annoyed visiting generalizers. New York was constantly scolded
for not being sufficiently religious, for instance, and yet the city
supported seventeen churches, whose spires, along with the
towering masts of the sailing ships tied up at the East River

docks, dominated the city's low skyline. The trouble—at least from the point of view of some transients—was that the seventeen churches belonged to fourteen different denominations. No one denomination was strong enough to dominate local manners or morals, and, anyway, the Anglicans, who were the strongest numerically (in the province as a whole they were outnumbered by the Presbyterians) had no great interest in blue laws. There were three Anglican churches—Trinity, St. Paul's, and St. George's. There were also three Dutch churches (but they belonged to three different sects) and two Presbyterian meeting houses. There was one French church, a synagogue, and a Quaker meeting house; and the Lutherans, the New Lutherans, the Calvinists, the Moravians, the Anabaptists, and the New Scots each had a church. Roman Catholicism was not tolerated by law, but for some years past a priest had come up from Maryland from time to time to say Mass in private houses. Nobody minded. What New York lacked, in short, was not religion, but religious conformity.

Whatever the justness of their accusations, New York's detractors were everywhere from northern Massachusetts (now Maine) to southern South Carolina. Their concentration in Connecticut was perhaps heaviest of all. Whether they had recently visited the city or not, they were all convinced that New York was a hotbed of inimicality, filled with secret and overt enemies of the Continental cause, and as unreliable as it had always been lax. The truth was infinitely more complicated than New York's critics realized, but, for the most part, New Yorkers felt no obligation to defend their town's reputation. The city's and the province's apparent indifference to out-of-province criticism made the scolds still angrier.

No sooner had the generals and their escorts ridden away than the Provincial Congress met for a late-afternoon session.

The delegates had already been through a very long day, and yet every man, except those who were riding as far as the King's Bridge with Washington, attended. Hard work and long hours were no novelty. For several weeks, the Provincial Congress had been rushing through business, and, what with subcommittee meetings and official decisions to be executed in hours apart from the debates proper, some of the busiest delegates had been putting in sixteen hours a day, seven days a week—lending substance to the complaint that New Yorkers were Sabbath-breakers. Time had been lost—the delegates hoped it had not been wasted—and the Provincial Congress wanted to make it up.

The Provincial Congress met at City Hall (at the head of Broad Street, on the present site of the Federal Hall Museum) in a handsome chamber built for the New York Assembly, the colonial legislature. The Assembly was not using the room because it had been sitting out the recent series of crises in discreet adjournment, and had not met since March, when it had formulated its own protests and forwarded them to London. No one had told Washington how hard the Provincial Congress was working, and from what he had seen, he may not have appreciated the extent of its local prestige. If he had not, the General could hardly be blamed. The delegates themselves did not know how popular or powerful the Provincial Congress was, and they would not know until its authority had been tested. Its members had all been elected quite recently, but the convening of such a body was unprecedented, and none of them was certain what his constituents expected of him. To make matters more vague, the county voting lists—for its election the Provincial Congress had used the same lists as the Assembly—were limited to men who owned property worth at least forty pounds, or one of several equivalents to that amount. That disqualified about half of New York's free males over the age of twenty-one. But the Provincial Congress could not afford to ignore the views of the voteless 50 percent. The Congress' most urgent business was to raise an army. If recruiting was to succeed, the Congress would have to persuade New York's poor as well as her voters to enlist.

The recruiting drive started on Tuesday, June 27, the day after Washington left. The Continental Congress had assigned each colony a quota of men to raise for the Continental Army; New York's was four regiments of ten companies apiece. A company, besides a captain and four lieutenants, consisted of seventy-two "able-bodied and sober men of good reputation," including three sergeants, three corporals, a drummer, and a fifer. New York, in other words, was expected to enlist more than three thousand officers and men. The number seemed large before the recruiting began, and larger after it started. Recruiting was the job of the company officers, who were given temporary warrants of authority, which were exchangeable for commissions after they had signed up a company-size group of volunteers. The Provincial Congress anticipated that the recruiters might encounter some hesitancy, and therefore, in its first set of recruiting instructions, addressed to the County Committees, had emphasized the virtue of sobriety. In the past, recruiting officers had been known to ply young men with so much liquor that they did not know or care what they were signing. Although the Continental enlistment period was short—only until December 31—the Provincial Congress had hoped to raise regiments of men with some clear notion of what they were getting into. Before the recruiting drive was one week old, the Congress was ready to forget its scruples, give recruiting officers an allowance to buy drinks for prospects, and publish an official list of New York City taverns designated for use as "places of rendezvous and the encouragement of volunteers." In the time a shocking shortage of volunteers had been discovered. The city's militia units, which might have been sources for numbers of semitrained men, were of little help. Peacetime amateur soldiering had never been especially popular in the city, and many men—a majority of Lasher's battalion, for example—were extremely reluctant to run any risk of being ordered to march away from home. The Provincial Congress was even having trouble trying to find qualified New Yorkers to accept nominations as company officers. This difficulty appeared to confirm one nasty accusation against the city. It had been said that the sons of New York's most prominent families, the sort of young men who were considered the likeliest Continental Army officer material in every colony, lacked confidence in the American cause. To the Provincial Congress' distress, a few New York scions admitted that if they had to join an army they would prefer the British. Two members of the Provincial Congress, the merchants Isaac Roosevelt and Abraham Walton, were assigned to call on reluctant officer nominees to try to change their minds, and, in one or two cases, the congressmen succeeded. Nonetheless, as the officer roster of New York City's own regiment, the First New York, filled up, there were few well-known local names. The regiment did include a Varick, a Platt, a Beekman, and a Bleecker, but these tokens of the regiment's social respectability were more than offset by names identified with the extreme radical wing of anti-British agitation: three McDougalls (Colonel Alexander McDougall, commanding the First, and two of his sons), two Hugheses (the sons of Hugh Hughes, a firebrand and an ardent member of the Sons of Liberty), a Goforth, a Mott, and a Willett. (There were some landowning Willetts on Long Island, but this young man, Marinus, was a cabinetmaker.) The captain of the Tenth Company of the First, David Lyon, was not even a New Yorker, but a New Jersey man, from Elizabeth.

While New York was still trying to find officers, Connecticut finished its recruiting drive, having taken only ten days to fill its quota. To make the contrast between New York and Connecticut obvious in both provinces, the New York Provincial Congress was compelled to borrow some Connecticut militiamen to protect New York City, in case the British had any hostile acts in mind. Connecticut's willingness to oblige struck some New Yorkers as excessive. The fifteen hundred men Connecticut sent, parts of two different militia regiments, began to arrive on June 28. The units had been ready for some time, and they did not have far to march, because their regular stations were in the vicinity of Stamford, thirty-five miles from the city. Still, when New York learned that the commander of the Connecticut force, a self-important, middle-aged farmer, Brigadier General David Wooster, had secured his provincial government's permission to go to New York before Tryon's return and before New York had requested reinforcement, the city wondered just what mission Wooster had in mind. The rumor was that Wooster had been thinking of arresting New York inimicals, something that, in New York's opinion, only the New York Provincial Congress and its subordinate local committees were qualified to do. But that was only gossip. The facts were that New York had asked for help and that help had arrived with uncommon speed. The Connecticut men were sturdy-looking young fellows who appeared forceful, despite their lack of uniforms, and the city was pleased to have them.

New York did its best to make Wooster's men welcome and comfortable in their encampment, which was on the west side of the Bowery Road (not far south of Cooper Square, in present-day terms), a half-hour's march, at the double, from Fort George. The New York Military Club, which was socially if not militarily impeccable, gave a splendid dinner in honor of all the Connecticut officers. Yet, inevitably, the benevolent occupation of Manhattan by Connecticut troops caused friction. In return for the loan, New York had agreed to feed Wooster's men. Some members of the Provincial Congress could hardly believe the returns on how much fifteen hundred soldiers, mostly teen-agers, could eat. But that annoyance was trivial compared with a second discovery: some of Wooster's men, off duty and in town looking for recreation, were recognized as New Yorkers' missing apprentices and indentured servants. The young men had run away across the Connecticut border and had taken refuge in the ranks of the Connecticut militia—a superb hiding place as long as the Connecticut regiments stayed in Connecticut. The New York City jail, a handsome, three-and-a-half-story brick structure on the Commons, immediately northeast of the site of today's City Hall, was soon filled with these runaways, arrested on their masters' complaints. Among the several bothersome legal and diplomatic questions their cases raised, the most immediate was: Who should feed them?

Despite these and other difficulties, the presence of the Con-necticut soldiers—all but a few were genuine Connecticut citi-zens—left the Provincial Congress some time to think about another urgent military matter, fortifications. Except for old Fort George, facing out across the Bay, New York had none. At best, the fort's military effectiveness was nothing to boast about, and until the city procured gunpowder replenishments to fire the cannon mounted along a promenade-battlement, the Grand Battery, the fort was as good as useless. New York knew that it needed ammunition, more cannon, other gun positions, entrenchments, breastworks, and barricades. But defense fortifi-cation was the highly technical specialty of a military engineer, and for the time being, no such man was available. General Schuyler, who was now responsible for the city's defense, might have helped find one, but he was on his way north, and the problems there were occupying all his attention. Schuyler had to

delegate his responsibility to his subordinates, particularly to
Colonel McDougall. Since McDougall's hands were more than
full with the task of recruiting his First Regiment, fortifications,
like a thousand and one other subjects, fell to the non-experts in
the Provincial Congress. The more these businessmen and lawyers—with help from the few delegates, like McDougall, who
had a little military knowledge—thought about defensive works
for the city, the more difficult the problem appeared. Neither the
city nor the province (nor, for that matter, the continent) yet
had a single warship. Logic therefore demanded that New York
concede control of the Bay, the Hudson River, the East River,
and the Harlem River to the British. But that led directly to the
realization that Manhattan Island's entire perimeter, except for a
few places where the banks were very steep, was vulnerable to a
British landing force. Since New York could hardly fortify the
entire shoreline, the situation looked hopeless. Yet military
hopelessness was not politically acceptable.

It was anything but strange that the New Yorkers, guarded
by borrowed militiamen and with no fortifications worthy of the
name, felt exposed and apprehensive. Still, the city did have
something to be grateful for; Tryon, after he had finished
taking stock of his own situation, seemed to be in a surprisingly
benign mood, and if he had any thought of using the warships'
guns to restore his power, he gave no hint of it. Those residents
who were disappointed—some of them, at least—promptly had
the shutters nailed closed on the windows of their houses and
packed up their belongings. They intended to take the next boat
to England, following the examples of men like John Watts and
Henry Cruger, both rich merchants and members of the Governor's Council, who had not waited to see what Tryon might be
able to accomplish. Myles Cooper, President of King's College,

was another non-Associator who had decided—and not a moment too soon—that New York was temporarily no place to stay. If Cooper had not fled in the middle of one night and taken refuge on a ship in the East River, he would have been manhandled by an obstreperous mob of patriotic ruffians. James De Lancey, Oliver's older brother, had also moved to England. He had been gone since April and had left in such a state of discouragement that, before sailing, he had sold his dearest possession, his fine stable of race horses. But for every New Yorker who felt dismayed by Tryon's attitude, scores were relieved. No matter how they felt about politics, New Yorkers did not want to see their houses, shops, and warehouses bombarded or burned.

Tryon made an unaggressive move on July 3, when he extended the Assembly's adjournment to August 9. (This postponed the day when the Assembly and the Provincial Congress might have to contend for possession of the meeting room in City Hall.) Tryon did so because he was convinced that the "general revolt," as he called it, had robbed him of all his civil power—everything except a few remnants of authority that the Provincial Congress had been too busy to take away. (The New York courts, for instance, were still in the hands of Tryon's judges, who were busy, and, for the most part, happy, dispensing English justice.) Tryon saw no purpose in issuing orders that would not be obeyed. That left him with no immediate course of action.

As it happened, inaction was what Lord Dartmouth, the British Colonial Secretary, wanted. British intentions, as of July, were to smash the rebellion around Boston before it could spread south. Small naval squadrons, which were being formed, were to take stations at New York Harbor, the Bay of Delaware, Chesapeake Bay, and off the Carolina coast. The British ships were supposed to cut off sea communications among the colonies, intercept any shipments of aid to New England, and serve as places of refuge for Crown officers who might be in danger on shore. If any of the middle or southern colonies, undaunted by the demonstrations of British seapower, should still go ahead with "actual rebellion," the warships were to "proceed" against it—as far as naval gunfire could reach. Because news took six or seven weeks to cross the ocean, Dartmouth, writing these instructions in July, did not know that all the American colonies, including New York, had already rebelled, by his definition. That is, New York was raising troops (however slowly), erecting military works (when it could think where they ought to go), and stealing British arms and ammunition (or at least was strongly suspected of doing so).

There was no doubt about New York's being twice guilty, but the third charge had yet to be proved. Somebody had indubitably broken into the King's magazine, a warehouse at the Turtle Bay Cove, on the East River, in the vicinity of what is now the foot of Forty-eighth Street, and plundered it, early on the morning of June 12. That was the day after the British Army garrison, a hundred-man detachment, had been transferred from the barracks to the battleship *Asia*. The Provincial Congress had not ordered the robbery, could not understand it, and was distressed by it. A committee had been trying to find the booty and return it, but had not succeeded. New York was inclined to believe that the theft had been the work of Connecticut men, operating by boat from Stamford. That hypothesis accounted for the otherwise inexplicable coincidence that some of Wooster's soldiers' equipment exactly fitted the descriptions of the stolen property.

Since Tryon had not yet received Dartmouth's instructions and his definitions of rebellion, the Governor observed, reported, and restricted himself to the minimum of official routine. When he first heard there was a plot to kidnap him, he could hardly believe it. The majority of the members of the Provincial Congress were equally incredulous. There was such a scheme, however, and the chief plotter was a member of the Provincial Congress. His name was Isaac Sears. His identity was not, in itself, surprising. Almost any New Yorker, if told that kidnappers were after the Governor, would have guessed that Captain Sears—or "King" Sears, as his political enemies called him—was involved, for Sears was New York's foremost political agitator. As one of the earliest New York Sons of Liberty and a senior member of the New York City mob, Sears had organized or taken part in almost every demonstration, riot, and protest march for the past fifteen years. His longevity as a public figure was the key to understanding him in the summer of 1775. Sears was a man of action whose most active years were past. At forty-five, he was ambitious, healthy, and energetic, but many of the men who had admired him in his heyday—ten years earlier, during protests over the Stamp Act—now found him embarrassing. Sears's associates in the Provincial Congress, old radicals like McDougall, John Lamb (who was leaving the Provincial Congress to command an artillery battery), and John Morin Scott, hesitated to entrust him with any assignment that required more than muscle. It was like Sears to think of regaining some of his old prestige by a spectacular exploit like a kidnapping.

Unless one knew Sears well, he seemed plausible, self-assured, and even charming. He had been a sailor most of his life—hence his title, "Captain." At the age of twenty-two, he had commanded a sloop in the New York-to-Canada coastal trade, and he had been the skipper of a small privateer, the *Harlequin*, during the French and Indian War. He had made enough money at sea to settle down, open a shop, marry Sarah Drake, and have eleven children. His wife was the daughter of

Jasper Drake, whose alehouse, on the waterfront near the head of Beekman's Slip (close to what is now the intersection of Pearl and Fulton streets), was a favorite among sailors, boatmen, and dockworkers. Now, as ever, Sears could count on many of his father-in-law's customers to fall in at his command, and march or fight wherever he wanted them to. The waterfront in general, added to Drake's clientele in particular, provided Sears with a small mob who hated the British and admired the Captain in something like equal measure. It was, for a mob, singularly well behaved. It had set some fires and roughed up several Tories, and the noises it made were frightful, especially in the middle of the night; but the New York mob had never killed a soul, not even by accident. The sailors and stevedores hardly ever used firearms; their weapons were paving stones and wooden clubs. Its members thought of themselves as political agitators, not gangsters. Considering the informality of their organization, they were under good discipline, and although many New Yorkers were apprehensive about what the mob might do next, it had not yet done much.

Sears's standing with the New York mob had been anything but an asset when it came to the Provincial Congress elections. Among the former Liberty Boys who wanted a seat in Provincial Congress, only Sears had had a hard time winning one. He had finally made it, but not until the beginning of June, when, after a special election, Sears had replaced a conservative merchant, George Folliot. (Folliot had won one of the New York County seats, thought things over, and then had declined to serve.) Since then, Sears had been indefatigable. He had worked on four or five Provincial Congress subcommittees, had helped survey the city's wretched powder supply, and had bustled all over town on one official errand or another. He had ridden up to Wooster's headquarters in Connecticut to deliver New York's formal request for military assistance. (It was not generally known that Sears had written to Wooster earlier, predicting the invitation, and so enabled Wooster to get ready to march ahead of time.) On that trip, Sears, a talented storyteller, had shocked his Connecticut friends with lurid reports of the prevalence of Crown sympathizers on the New York scene, thus persuading many of Wooster's men that their most dangerous enemies in New York were likely to be New Yorkers, not the British. Sears had also ridden down to Philadelphia, hoping to get the Continental Congress to endorse his plan to kidnap Governor Tryon on the night of July 3, carry him off to Hartford, and hold him there as a hostage for the safety and well-being of New York City. Sears had not succeeded. Undaunted, he had hurried back to New York to tell Schuyler about the project. Schuyler had been horrified. Before leaving for Albany, Schuyler had told Sears about Washington's written order against any such action, and Schuyler himself had ordered Sears to abandon the idea.

Tryon's knowledge of what Sears had been thinking did nothing to lessen the strain in the tense and unequal relationship between the *Asia*, the *Kingfisher*, and New York City. On a word from her commander, Captain George Vandeput, the *Asia* could destroy New York City with a broadside or two, while the city's only effective weapon against the warships was the withholding of food and drink. The British officers and crews wanted fresh provisions—bread, butter, meat, and cheese—and quantities of rum, wine, beer, and ale. New York merchants and brewers, with the full approval of the Provincial Congress, were selling them everything they could pay for. Abraham Lott, a leading merchant, had been the official victualer for the King's ships in New York Harbor for some time, and he still was. Small boats, loaded with provisions, constantly made their way out to the warships. The possibility existed—not much had been said about it so far—that New York would order this traffic stopped.

During July, recruiting went a little faster. A full complement of officers had finally been cajoled into serving. Most of New York's young gentlemen were still dragging their feet, but her poor had been persuaded to enlist. McDougall's First New York Regiment was filling up. A disproportionate number of his soldiers came from the Out Ward, which covered everything north of the built-up area, including the slums near the slaughterhouses and the shipyards, in the vicinity of what is now Chinatown, and from the farms scattered throughout the rural parts of the island. In civilian life, some of the enlisted men had been skilled or semiskilled, and had worked as farmers, gardeners, butchers, ropemakers, cobblers, and carpenters, but the largest group, by far, was classified in the catchall category, "laborer." Almost none of them had lived on a frontier, and few were expert at hunting and camping. The only Indians most of them had seen were those who occasionally turned up in the city to shop. And since there was no plan to train these young men, apart from teaching them to march, it was not clear how good they would be as soldiers. Still, each man enlisted gave New York a full credit against the Continental quota. The squads of the First New York began drilling on the Commons in front of the Upper Barracks (the site is now occupied by the City Courts Building), where they were quartered.

Reports of recruiting progress were coming in from the three other New York regiments: Colonel James Holmes's Fourth, recruiting in Westchester, Queens, Kings, Richmond, and parts of Dutchess counties; Colonel James Clinton's Third, from the rest of Dutchess, Suffolk, Ulster, and Orange; and Colonel Gose Van Schaick's Second, which drew on all of the province's most northern districts, particularly Albany County. In view of all this encouraging news, it seemed unwise to provoke trouble with the warships and sensible to keep the provisioning arrangements as they were. Most of the Provincial Congress delegates, moreover, believed that the dispute with Great Britain had not gone beyond the possibility of peaceful, negotiated settlement. Shortly before Tryon's return, the Provincial Congress had begun work on a position paper that it sent to New York's delegates at the Continental Congress early in July. It was not a set of instructions but simply a statement of the hopes, if not the exact expectations, of the majority in the Provincial Congress and their notion of their constituents' ideas. The peace terms New York suggested took continued loyalty to the Crown so much for granted that the subject was not even mentioned—suggesting that Lord Dartmouth's definition of "rebellion" was somewhat too mechanical. The New Yorkers wanted the Coercive Acts, which Parliament had passed in 1774, after the Boston Tea Party, repealed. But the Provincial Congress was quite willing to reimburse Great Britain for the cost of governing New York, provided that the New York Assembly be allowed to decide what taxes were necessary to raise the sum. New York thought that an improved Assembly, with its members elected every three years instead of every seven, ought to make all the laws that pertained to New York's affairs—subject, of course, to the King's veto. That, along with a guarantee that Parliament would not compromise religious freedom, was the substance of all New York asked as the price of placing itself solidly within the British Empire for all time to come.

Meanwhile, hour by hour, every incident that might affect the undeclared truce between the town and the warships was upsetting. The hot summer weeks were filled with provocations and suspense. On July 12, for instance, while the Provincial Congress was still attempting to recover the military stores that had been stolen in June, the Turtle Bay storehouse was raided a second time. Armed men made off with the loot (mostly round shot, powder horns, and assorted crates and boxes) that the first band of robbers had left behind. Again, it was not clear who had done it. The thieves may have been Connecticut men—conceivably the same ones, repeating their earlier success. But other evidence suggested that this time they were New Yorkers. What made the second robbery more serious than the first was this: one of the *Asia*'s small boats was involved. Somehow or other, the raiders had managed to capture a British boat and drag it onto the shore. They "arrested" its crew and turned the sailors over to Wooster, along with the stolen goods. Then—almost as if the raiders meant to stretch Captain Vandeput's patience past the breaking point—they had burned the *Asia*'s boat. Despite this challenge, Captain Vandeput refrained from shooting. The following morning he wrote a stiff protest. The Provincial Congress again expressed surprise and disapproval, and ordered an investigation. Since Wooster had released the British crew before Vandeput's complaint arrived, some of the affair's potential seriousness was avoided. Yet one mishap led to another, and repercussions of the boat-burning incident troubled the city for weeks to come. The Provincial Congress' investigation, in which the city magistrates, Mayor Whitehead Hicks, and the Court of Aldermen all cooperated, was a failure. Depositions were taken, and several warrants were issued for suspects, but in the end the investigators were unable to determine who had committed the crimes. The Grand Jury, which was in session at the time, finally decided that the evidence collected was insufficient for proceedings against anyone. The best New York could do, by way of amends, was to offer to build the British a new boat.

There was more trouble about that. On the night of August 1, when the replacement boat was almost finished, "disorderly and evil-disposed persons" (as the Provincial Congress subsequently described them) made their way into the shipyard and sawed the new boat to pieces. Wooster's men could not have done it, because they had been called north and had started for Albany the week before. The *Asia* still did not fire, but the boat-sawing gave New York another chance to bungle an investigation. This time a seven-man subcommittee of the New York City Committee got nowhere. The Provincial Congress, promising an immediate replacement for the replacement, did strengthen the language with which it condemned the unidentified rascals ("insolent violators of the Association" and "factious offenders" who should be brought to "condign punishment"); yet, looking at the whole record, Vandeput must have thought that New York's lack of action spoke louder than words. In any case, Vandeput's official language remained temperate.

Next, the carpenters working on the second substitute boat walked off the job in mid-August, saying that they were afraid because certain New Yorkers, whom they did not wish to name, had threatened to beat them up unless they quit. To keep construction going, the Provincial Congress ordered Lasher's battalion to provide guards for the carpenters. Even with military protection, the work went slowly.

The Provincial Congress really meant to replace the *Asia*'s burned boat, and the indignation it repeatedly expressed was wholly genuine. Only its militant minority, the small bloc in which Sears's voice was loudest, thought that New York should risk tormenting the *Asia*. Yet, as the end of August approached, the Provincial Congress grew noticeably bolder. It took a surprisingly aggressive vote on August 22. The attendance that day was light—only twenty-eight delegates, representing six of the eleven counties, exactly a quorum. All the members were tired from overwork, and some men had been taking off an occasional afternoon or a day or two, and, for some reason, most of the absentees were conservatives. All the records for faithful attendance were held by belligerents. If a small house was a radical house on this account, it made no difference, for a legal quorum was a legal quorum, and whatever it decided was decided.

The debate concerned the fortification of the Highlands, the high ground on either side of a narrow stretch of the Hudson River between Peekskill and West Point, where the Americans hoped to emplace shore batteries. If passage up the Hudson to Albany could be denied the British Navy, the Highlands was the likely place to make the effort. The Continental Congress had assigned the whole project, including its design and construction, to New York. The Provincial Congress envisioned three new forts, added to the one that already existed at West Point. Its plans were grandiose, but except for a few barracks and some earthworks on the site of the fort opposite West Point, named Fort Constitution in honor of the British Constitution, which the New Yorkers considered they were upholding, next to nothing was finished. New York lacked everything the forts needed—particularly what they needed most, cannon.

Isaac Sears moved that the Provincial Congress empower the subcommittee in charge of the Highland forts to secure the necessary cannon and cannon stores. That seemed reasonable, and Sears's motion was passed unanimously. There followed a slight pause. Some members, wondering what Sears had in mind, asked for more debate. What exactly could the subcommittee do about securing nonexistent cannon? Isaac Low, a conservative delegate and a rich merchant who was distressed because he felt that the Association, which he had helped form, was heading toward a complete break with Great Britain, guessed the answer. Low put the question directly to Sears: Did the resolution just passed empower the Highlands subcommittee to remove the British cannon from the Grand Battery in front of Fort George? Sears admitted that this was what he was thinking of. It seemed fair, once the resolution's surprising intent had been disclosed, to take another vote. The Sears motion passed the second time: eighteen votes in favor, six opposed, and four abstentions.

Late the next night, Wednesday, August 23, several members of the Highlands subcommittee, with a work party of enthusiastic citizens and soldiers from Lasher's battalion and Captain John Lamb's artillery company, assembled near Fort George. They went to work. The soldiers formed a semicircle of musketmen facing toward the water—for any British objection would presumably come from that direction—while the rest of the men, using ropes, began dragging the cannon, which were mounted on carriages, off the ramparts and up Broadway to the Commons. There were twenty-one such guns in all, an assortment of twelve- and eighteen-pounders. Each was a struggle. They were naval guns, weighing a ton or more apiece, and their carriages had small wheels that were not designed for cross-country travel. Manhandling them up the hill between Bowling Green and Wall Street was especially hard. It would have been difficult to haul the guns quietly, but inasmuch as the job was officially authorized, no one was trying for stealth, and the work party made a lot of noise. All the men knew that Tryon and Vandeput were not likely to approve of what they were doing, but only a few—members of the perimeter guard—fully appreciated the situation's ticklishness: the British were watching. One of the *Asia*'s sloops, carrying a full complement of armed sailors, had been waiting just off the Battery, standing in close to the shore, to see what the Americans would do—for Tryon had learned about the plan and had told Vandeput what he knew.

Lasher's guards had spotted the British boat, lying quietly, with its sails down, the moment they had taken their posts, but the Highlands subcommittee members had decided to ignore the British as long as they merely watched. There seemed to be no reason to alarm the rest of the Americans by making a fuss about the sloop's presence. The guards' muskets were loaded, primed, and cocked, and they waited alertly for the British to make a move. For an hour or so, in which time ten or eleven of the big guns had been pulled out of position and hauled away, the British observers did nothing. Lieutenant Alexander Hamilton, a student who had left King's College to join the New York artillery, was in the guard detail. After a time, Hamilton decided that he would be of more use by helping haul the cannon. He turned his musket over to another soldier and went off to assist in dragging one of the guns up Broadway.

At about half past midnight, one of the British sailors in the stern of the sloop fired his musket. No one on shore knew if it was an aimed shot, an accident, or a signal to the *Asia*, a thousand yards or so away in the East River off Murray's Wharf at the foot of Wall Street, but Lasher's men answered with a volley. The sloop hurriedly raised sail, and as it pulled away, the British and Americans continued to shoot at each other. One of the British crew was fatally wounded. Even after the sloop was beyond musket range, and hitting anybody or being hit was most unlikely, the exchange of shots continued until, with an impressive boom, the *Asia* fired. One round of solid shot came first, and then, after an interval, several rounds of grapeshot. The lead sizzled harmlessly through the air over the work party's heads. No one had been hurt, but everything came to a standstill. The cannon-hauling stopped. Then the New Yorkers, who were strung out between the Battery and the Commons, gathered and conferred about what to do in the face of the *Asia*'s unmistakable warning. They decided to ignore it, and went back to working, faster than before.

There was no immediate response from Captain Vandeput, but since the *Asia*'s shots had awakened everyone who was not already awake, and since most of the city's residents had no idea what was happening or why, New York went into panic. The alarm drums began to beat. That was a new sound, terrifying in itself. Militiamen rushed through the darkness trying to find their battle stations which had just been assigned them. Many of the men assumed that a British invasion had started. Some house-holders ran into the streets, where they found that nobody knew anything. Others made for their cellars. Hundreds, thinking it was best to flee, headed for the New Jersey and Brooklyn ferries or north toward the suburban countryside, trying to take every-thing they owned with them, without knowing how much time they dared spend on moving valuables.

Just as the disorder reached its peak, at about three o'clock in the morning, the *Asia* fired again. This time she delivered a full thirty-two-gun broadside, an assortment of nine-, eighteen-, and twenty-four-pound shells. To those who lived near the east end of Wall Street, the ship seemed close enough to touch. The whole sky was lit up by the muzzle blasts, and New York shook with the reverberations. Nothing of the kind had ever hap-pened, and those who heard the broadside never forgot it. The blast was accompanied by the thumping and cracking of the shots that found targets.

The *Asia*'s terrible display was intended not as an attempt to destroy the city but as a further warning. Captain Vandeput, who had thought that his first few rounds had stopped the cannons' removal, was merely repeating the earlier admonition in a louder form. His gunners, consequently, were aiming for Fort George, not the city proper, and they were using solid lead, not firebombs. Their aim was good, though slightly low. Shells tore open the roof of Roger Morris' town house, and of Fraunces' Tavern, and severely damaged half a dozen smaller buildings on Whitehall Street—all short of Fort George, which was hardly hurt at all. Only three or four New Yorkers were wounded, one quite seriously. No one was killed. The *Asia*, having thus objected at the top of its voice, did not fire again. In the morning, when it was possible to examine the results, it seemed remarkable that a thirty-two-gun broadside could do so little damage.

Most of the refugees had not gone far, and as soon as they realized that they had no place to hide, or at least none that they could afford, they came filtering back to their jobs and homes, having been reminded, most unpleasantly, that New York's fate and their own were inseparable. They could no longer regard the bombardment of New York as a figment of alarmist propaganda, and that was a hard reality to face. Governor Tryon, too, was noticeably shaken by what had happened. He had been spending the night of the twenty-third with friends on Long Island, and the sound of the *Asia*'s guns had brought him rushing back to town. He had been especially shocked by the sight of refugees trying to reach Long Island. On Tryon's initiative, a strange conference was called on the morning of the twenty-fourth—a joint meeting of members of the Governor's Council, the Corporation of the City of New York, members of the Provincial Congress, and the New York City Committee. The meeting was strange because Tryon was not supposed to admit that these last two bodies existed. Tryon addressed the group in the Council Room at City Hall. His message was simple: Let everybody keep calm.

The Provincial Congress, by now slightly sheepish about its audacity, was almost overeager to cooperate. What had been done was undeniable, for there, on the Commons, stood eleven of the cannon, as conspicuous, in the main public square, as a herd of elephants. Tryon could not sanction the theft of Crown property any more than he could forget his demands that the *Asia*'s boat be replaced and that the matériel stolen from the King's warehouse be returned. On the other hand, moving the guns back to the Battery was as big a job as moving them to the Commons. Tryon's political judgment told him that the Provincial Congress would not be able to remount the guns on their old sites. The situation called for compromise, and one was found. Tryon said the King's cannon could stay where they were as long as they were moved no farther away from where they belonged. It was up to New York to match Tryon's concession. The Provincial Congress offered to provide Tryon himself with a military guard, but the Governor did not want a guard. There was another conciliatory gesture New York could make to prove its willingness to forgive having been fired on. It could and it did decide to let Mr. Lott go on supplying the *Asia* with fresh provisions.

After frantic activity, New York showed another symptom of shock: apathy. The moderates in the Provincial Congress were discouraged by the failure of their summer policy of accommodation with the warships, and doubtful that the new truce could last. The militants were anything but proud of having proved that Great Britain's local representatives would stand for only so much and no more. In retrospect, the gun-removal scheme looked foolhardy. Caution and aggressiveness were both, for the moment, in civic disrepute. That left the field to confusion.

There was a sudden flurry of newspaper advertisements for houses to rent on Long Island and in New Jersey, and rentals were brisk. Now those New Yorkers who moved out of town did so deliberately, concluding that the city and everyone in it were in danger. Moving to the country was expensive. An end to the troubles with Great Britain was nowhere in sight, and only the wealthy could afford to plan to stay away for an indefinite time—perhaps as long as a year. Leonard Lispenard, Jacobus Van Zandt, Samuel Verplanck, and Mayor Hicks were among those who managed to make out-of-town arrangements. Some rich New Yorkers left their wives, children, and household furniture safely in the country and then returned to New York or Philadelphia or wherever their affairs required them to be. Philip Livingston and James Duane, two of the New York delegates to the Continental Congress, closed not only their New York City town houses but nearby country retreats as well—Livingston his Brooklyn Heights place and Duane his house east of the Bowery Road, some two miles north of the city, which included land that is now Gramercy Square. That combination—a house in town and an accessible country retreat— was the ideal solution to the drawbacks of New York living. In summer, when the city was often extremely hot, and the streets, as usual, were jammed with traffic, a New Yorker who opened a window to cool off filled his house with noise and dirt. It cost a fortune to own two places and enough servants to maintain them—the 3,000 blacks in the city were nearly all slaves in domestic service—so most New Yorkers merely dreamed of the day when they might emulate the rich and summer out of town. Livingston and Duane feared that their suburban retreats were hardly any safer than their town houses. In both men's cases, the solution was easy. Since Duane's wife, Mary, belonged to the Livingston family—she was a niece of Philip—they both moved their families up the Hudson to houses on Livingston property, an immense spread of land on both sides of the river, which had been assembled a hundred years or so earlier by Robert R. Livingston, Philip's grandfather and Mary Duane's great-grandfather. Before the end of September, the cumulative effect of such removals was noticeable. Closed-up houses, with their doors and shutters boarded up, were scattered throughout the town, and gave a forlorn look to whole blocks of the more fashionable streets. In addition to the well-to-do who could take temporary refuge in the country, some New Yorkers decided to move away permanently, hoping that they could find jobs or make careers in some less beleaguered place. The city was also missing nearly a thousand of its young men, because various units, including the First New York, had sailed up the Hudson to join Schuyler's forces. The town seemed unnaturally quiet without them, and, almost overnight, it had become nearly impossible to hire a boy for an odd job. (Paradoxically, in the midst of the unskilled-labor shortage, a good many skilled workers were unemployed, particularly those in the shipbuilding trades.)

Brigadier General Richard Montgomery, who was a former British Army officer, a Livingston son-in-law, a delegate to the Provincial Congress, and a handsome thirty-seven-year-old of whom everyone expected great things, had gone north in mid-July. In contrast to Montgomery, most of the New Yorkers who had gone off to war did not look like soldiers at all, but like reluctant lambs. They had not worn decent civilian clothes, let alone uniforms. Because the troop movement had been executed in several sections, there had been no occasion for one stirring public sendoff. Schuyler had been desperate for men. A parade might have lifted the city's morale, whatever the recruits would have thought of it. Nothing of the sort had taken place.

Instead of leading his regiment to Albany, Colonel Mc-Dougall had entrusted the men to his second-in-command, Lieu-

tenant Colonel Rudolphus Ritzema. McDougall stayed behind
with a detachment of recruiters to finish the enlistment drive,
which still had a way to go. If he had left town, McDougall
thought, the New York quota might never be filled. Several of
his military colleagues thought McDougall was right to stay,
but his decision was being questioned just the same. Mc-
Dougall's critics said the average New Yorker could not understand McDougall's decision. After all the fervent recruiting
speeches the Colonel had made, it did seem odd that he could
let another officer march at the head of his First New York.

On September 2, the Provincial Congress decided to give its
members an official rest rather than to struggle, day after day, to
raise a quorum. It adjourned for a month. Before it stopped
work, the Congress set up an interim Committee of Safety and
gave it enough power to deal with almost any emergency. A
small group of men should have operated more efficiently than
the Provincial Congress as a whole, but because several counties
were not represented at all, and New York County had more
than a fair share of members—on some days, depending on who
attended, as much as one-third of the total vote—the Committee
of Safety lacked the Provincial Congress' moral authority, the
consensual quality that had enabled the upstart body to function
as well as it had. The Committee of Safety was well aware of its
limitations. New York City dominance made the Committee
somewhat more radical than the Congress, but all during September the belligerents behaved with circumspection. The little
new business considered was inconsequential. Was it time to
move the New York City records, including the city's invaluable
real-estate title files, to some safe country village like Yonkers or
White Plains? If the Committee of Safety initiated nothing of
importance, it at least made no serious blunders, and in that
sense its record was perfect. But even after the Provincial Con-

gress reconvened, in October, New York's listlessness persisted.

The city was unusually dull because there were no English imports—none of the goods that ordinarily made October the year's busiest shopping month. English merchandise arrived only twice a year (the other month was April) because the merchant ships in the English trade moved on schedule, almost together, taking six months for the round trip between New York and London, and spending about half that time loading and unloading. New York retailers all wanted to be the first to display the new English goods—each season, prices began high and gradually came down—and the competition among them had turned the Atlantic crossing into an informal, semiannual race. Shoppers from miles around, attracted by the thrill of seeing this entire fleet sail into New York Harbor within a few days, would pour into the city ahead of time and stay for a week or even two. October was therefore a boom period for businesses of all kinds, including hotels, restaurants, and taverns. In terms of cash volume, New York's peacetime trade with England was considerably smaller than its trade with the West Indies. But cargoes from the Caribbean—sugar, molasses, mules, cotton, and the like—were boring compared with those from England. In everything that had to do with style, including clothing, furniture, carriages, and books, New York depended heavily on London fashions. In October, one could discover what the best-dressed ladies would be wearing (at least until April), how the newest houses would be furnished, and which authors were likely to dominate polite conversation. In the fall of 1775, for the first time in years, all this excitement was missing.

While good Associators had to be proud that the Continental Association's ban on English imports was working so well, the marketplaces and auction rooms were empty. Stocks of imported staple necessities—pins and needles, for instance—were low.

Business was so bad that, on several days, the Coffee House, at the intersection of Wall and Queen (now Pearl) streets, did not bother to light candles; there were not enough patrons to pay the overhead. When the Coffee House was dark, New York had reached a nadir. It was not only a shop where businessmen, merchants, and politicians could drink coffee, but also a kind of public club besides, popular as an informal place to do business, pick up the latest gossip and news (the management subscribed to a wide selection of newspapers and magazines), and keep track of the mass of detailed domestic and foreign information upon which traders depended. On a normal business day, an empty seat at one of the Coffee House's long tables had been rare; to find them nearly all unoccupied was almost unbelievable.

Tryon took no pleasure in New York's depression. He shared it. His gout was slightly worse, and he was embarrassed by his position as Governor in name only. He still hoped to return to England, and although he had just received technical permission to do so, along with a major's commission in the King's First Regiment of Foot Guards, he knew that Dartmouth really wanted him to stay. Tryon had been granted only discretionary leave, and discretion told him that, wretched as he was, he should do his best to endure New York. He did not think that his odd, semipeaceful stalemate with the Provincial Congress could last. In mid-September, he had finally received Dartmouth's definition of a rebellious city, and if he had obeyed the letter of his instructions, he should have immediately ordered the *Asia* to bombard New York. Instead, he had made another attempt to explain his predicament to the rebels. Mayor Hicks, acting as Tryon's go-between, had delivered his message to the Committee of Safety: unless New York stopped stealing Crown property (not to mention building fortifications and recruiting soldiers), Tryon would have to order the *Asia* to fire.

The Committee of Safety had listened attentively. For the next three weeks New York had been fairly compliant in deed, if not in spirit. Then, on the afternoon of October 9, some of Lasher's men held a formal guard mount and a parade in front of the Lower Barracks, where the battalion was quartered. (The Lower Barracks, just south of Fort George, was the southernmost of the buildings behind the Battery ramparts; if it were still standing, it would block State Street and part of the automobile and truck approach to the South Ferry.) That evening, Tryon learned that thirty-odd cartloads of British Army hospital supplies, which had been stored in the garret of the Lower Barracks, were missing. The Governor immediately demanded their return.

In less than twenty-four hours, the Provincial Congress, sitting again, found and restored the goods. Tryon could hardly have been more surprised. The Congress had always before failed to recover the Crown's stolen property, and in this case Tryon's informants had provided him with several scraps of intelligence that he had interpreted, incorrectly, to mean that it would not even try. Tryon knew that, on the very morning of the day of the theft, the Provincial Congress had received a bag of mail from the Continental Congress, including secret orders to arrest anyone who "might endanger the safety of the Colonies if left at large." Tryon, not unreasonably, had assumed that the Continental Congress was thinking of Crown officers like himself. He had also been informed that the mail had contained extracts copied from letters written to the Continental Congress by correspondents in London. One of them said Tryon was expected to play an essential part in a British plan to seize the Hudson; another named Tryon as the plan's military architect, adding, as an aside, that kidnapping Tryon would be "a capital stroke." Putting all this together, Tryon had imagined that New York had concocted a plot. He thought the theft of the hospital supplies was a trick, a provocation ordered by the Provincial Congress to lead him into doing something rash that would justify his arrest. In his grumpy discouragement, moreover, Tryon had decided to give New York the excuse he thought it wanted. The uncharacteristically peremptory tone of his note about the hospital supplies was calculatingly offensive. Tryon expected that New York would order his arrest. He sent Captain Vandeput written orders to fire on the city as soon as he had been taken into custody.

Tryon's imagination had led him far from reality. New York had no such scheme in mind, Washington's prohibition against arresting the Governor remained in effect, and, only a few days earlier, Duane had explained carefully to the Continental Congress that New York did not want to take Tryon into custody. Furthermore, the Continental Congress' new arrest orders were not aimed at Crown officers, although such officers were not specifically exempted from arrest; the Continental Congress was concerned primarily about American non-Associators. The New York Provincial Congress had not ordered the theft of the hospital supplies. They had been stolen, no doubt, by New York Associators—with help, very likely, from some of Lasher's men—but there was no ulterior motive for the theft. The reason for the crime was simply that New York needed hospital supplies.

All summer long Tryon had been making the mistake of overestimating the Provincial Congress' ability to control affairs in the province and the city. His new error was in the opposite direction. Now he swung over to the fear that the New York mob was about to defy the restraints the Provincial Congress' moderation had imposed upon it, and run wild. Tryon brooded over this for several days. On October 12 he decided to leave the city. He sailed over to Governor's Island, where he spent the day. That night one of the *Asia*'s small boats took him to

Brooklyn, and Tryon went into something like hiding (except that the Provincial Congress knew where he was) at William Axtell's estate, near the village of Flatbush. From there, Tryon wrote Mayor Hicks a letter that perfectly reflected his confused emotions. He started by warning New York not to arrest him, lest the British warships demand his release with "their whole power." In the next passage he placed his fate in the city's hands. If the New Yorkers did not want him to stay, they had only to say so; he would move to the *Asia*, asking no more than a safe conduct for his servants and himself between his house and the ship.

In reply, New York did what it could to reassure the Governor. The City Committee, the magistrates, and the Corporation agreed that they wanted Tryon to stay in town. The City Committee offered Tryon a guard—provided that this "be consistent with the great principle of our safety and preservation." (The proviso was only a sop to the Continental Congress.) But Tryon, by this time suspicious of everybody, managed to find the *pro forma* qualification offensive. Although he calmed down enough to return from Flatbush, he stayed in New York only a few more days. On the nineteenth, he left the city and moved, with Attorney-General John Tabor Kempe and a few other Crown officers, not to the *Asia* but to a merchant ship, the *Earl of Halifax*. Then, eleven days later, Tryon and his party transferred to the *Duchess of Gordon*, another commercial vessel in the New York–London trade, owned by the New York firm of Murray, Sansom and Company. The *Duchess of Gordon* was considerably more comfortable than the *Asia*, where, as on any warship, passenger space was sacrificed to fire power. A merchant ship also had the advantage, compared to a warship, of letting Tryon pretend that his cabin was the floating equivalent of an office in town. While protected by the *Asia's* guns, he avoided the poor examples set by three of his colleagues, the governors

of Virginia, North Carolina, and South Carolina, who had all
taken refuge on British warships and were all engaged in semi-
private wars against the colonies they were supposed to be
administering. And then, in order to maintain any semblance of
political power in New York, Tryon needed to have visitors.
The Provincial Congress might have balked at giving permission to New Yorkers to go aboard the *Asia,* but it did not seem
to care how many people went out to the *Duchess of Gordon;* a
sentry merely made a note of who they were. The Governor's
Council began to meet regularly on the *Duchess of Gordon,* and
Tryon, with his aides, gave a number of small dinner parties for
those of his New York friends who were not afraid to have their
names recorded. The Governor's main worry, for the time
being, was that New York might stop selling him fresh food. In
that case, he wrote Dartmouth, his "bilious condition" might
become acute.

New York regretted Tryon's retreat, as it had proclaimed
it would, but another problem, which was growing in uncertainty and intensity, was taking up more and more time: What
should be done about internal enemies? The Continental Congress, in the secret orders that had unstrung the Governor's
nerves, had called for the arrest of men who, left free, might
endanger a colony's safety. New York, taking that power for
granted, had been locking up various non-Associators since June.
But the definition of "dangerous" was becoming increasingly
elusive—and that, precisely, was the difficulty. Since a majority
of New Yorkers still admitted to some degree of loyalty to
Great Britain, "dangerous" had to involve something worse
than that. How much worse? And then, supposing a man had
been proved very much worse, what were the limits on New
York's powers to punish him?

In the first weeks after Lexington and Concord, New York had answered the main question in precise military terms. An "internal enemy" had been an American who gave the British armed forces direct aid or comfort—a New Yorker who spied for the British, say, or shipped matériel to the King's forces at Boston. The Provincial Congress had caught a few such men, taken testimony, voted them guilty, and had fined and imprisoned them. But by November, while the concept of inimicality had certainly been extended, it was extremely hard to decide just where it had got to. Mere opinions were becoming dangerous. It was still permissible to say that one admired King George III personally, but a New Yorker who expressed admiration for his ministers or for British colonial policy was likely to have considerable explaining to do. If, in addition, he had failed to sign a formal oath of allegiance to the Continental Association, such a point of view might send a man to jail—although the chances were that it would not.

Jail space in the city was limited, and some outspoken non-Associators were free on that account alone. But the Provincial Congress realized that additional cells would have to be provided, because inimicality—whatever it was—could not be disregarded. In more cases than New York cared to admit, inimical opinions were the prelude to inimical acts. One investigation by a subcommittee of the Provincial Congress had revealed, for instance, that non-Associators on eastern Long Island, whose complaints against the Continental Congress and all its committees had seemed annoying rather than sinister, had actually assisted in a series of British raids on Fisher's, Gardiner's, Plum, and Block islands in August. The result was that the King's armed forces at Boston had enjoyed fresh supplies of mutton, beef, pork, poultry, bread, cheese, and potatoes.

This revelation and others suggested a careful check of New

York men to determine who was, and who was not, inimical. The Provincial Congress found itself with several long lists of names, each supposedly the master tally sheet of non-Associators—and every list inaccurate, incomplete, and out of date. The compilers had started with the register of voters and had subtracted the names of sworn Associators; the remaining names, for the time being, were suspects who needed further investigation. Clerical errors apart, this subtraction method had flaws. To begin with, the voting lists were limited to property owners, so only the names of well-to-do inimicals could be expected to show up. Then, New Yorkers had had almost too many chances to subscribe to the Association—although a surprisingly large number of men now claimed that they had never heard of it. Three or more versions of the oath, starting with one that dated back to the days of the First Continental Congress had been offered; and local committees had attempted to canvass the province house by house in order not to miss a single citizen. As a result, a good Associator might have refused the third version because he had already taken the first or the second; and some men who had sworn in 1774 had since changed their minds and might be getting credit, in 1775, that they no longer deserved. Moreover, some inimicals had sworn loyalty to the Association falsely, just to get rid of the canvasser.

The Provincial Congress, fully conscious of these and other faults in the lists, now felt the inventory had to be straightened out. It wanted to separate the accidental or indifferent non-Associators from those who were truly hostile to the American cause and capable of some dangerous act. It was trying to do so, a few non-Associators at a time, by asking them all what exactly their failure to subscribe was supposed to mean. One subcommittee of the Congress was carrying most of the work load. On busy days it was hearing as many as one hundred prima facie inimicals who had been invited, by mail, to appear. Many of the suspects were able to explain their failures convincingly. Representatives of a group of 312 Westchester residents, for instance, who had boasted about refusing to sign in a letter published in the New York City newspapers, claimed that they had been mixed up about what they were doing. One of them, Jeremiah Hunter, testified that he had allowed his signature to be used on the open letter only because he was for "liberty and peace." Whether that made him a Whig or a Tory, Hunter said, he didn't properly know.

Others, on being heard, admitted that they had refused to take the Association oath and said that they would not take it now. In such cases, the Provincial Congress as a whole voted on what to do with them. Most of the men who disapproved of the Association on principle were released on parole, provided that they would swear not to help the British forces and not to violate the Association's rules against trading with Great Britain. When the Provincial Congress doubted the value of a man's word, it required that he post a bond as security for his good behavior.

Nonsigners released on these terms were expected to suffer. Their names were published on handbills, which the Provincial Congress distributed widely, and listed in the New York newspapers. The publicity was supposed to lead to their ostracism by the community. In many cases it had. Two of the first men denounced in this way were the brothers William Ustick and Henry Ustick, who had been declared "enemies of liberty" back in April because they had sold the British Army spades, shovels, and pickaxes. The Usticks' retail business had fallen off, and they had been miserable ever since. In the routine city elections in September, Henry was not reelected Assessor of the North Ward.

As for those who would not sign and would not even promise to be good, they were sentenced to jail. The same fate, of course, awaited New Yorkers who were voted guilty of specific acts against the Association, especially recruiting for the British. The combination of inimicals waiting to be heard, men suspected of criminal acts, dangerous persons under confinement, and New York's usual lot of nonpolitical prisoners added up to many more than the city jail and the jail rooms at City Hall could hold. The Provincial Congress had been forced to use the guardhouses at the Upper and Lower Barracks as auxiliary jails, and even to lock up the overflow in the barracks' storerooms. When all those improvisations had proved inadequate, New York had taken the unusual step of shipping convicted New Yorkers off to Fairfield, Connecticut, for safekeeping in the county jail there, under the eye of the county sheriff, Thaddeus Burr.

The purpose of these continuous loyalty hearings was partly educational. The Provincial Congress wanted to show that, whether or not New Yorkers agreed with the Association, they had no choice about obeying its orders. As one case of disobedience after another was written into the record, the Provincial Congress felt compelled to become increasingly stern; and, as its sentences increased in severity, the crowding in the jails grew worse. Even so, the lesson did not seem to be getting across. If anything, the inimicals appeared to be growing more numerous. The Provincial Congress hoped that this was an illusion. Perhaps what looked like an increase in inimicals was just an increase in the attention being paid them.

A few New Yorkers were making fun in public of the Association, the Provincial Congress, the Continental Congress, and the whole protest movement. One such man, whose taunts were especially annoying and conspicuously well expressed, was the

Reverend Dr. Samuel Seabury, a Church of England clergyman and the rector of the West Chester Parish, which included everything (the Borough-Town of West Chester, East Chester Patent, and Pelham Manor) between the Bronx River and Long Island Sound, from Throg's Neck north to Scarsdale. Under the nom de plume "A Westchester Farmer," Seabury had written a series of sparkling anti-Association pamphlets, and these were being read and admired, as well as hated, throughout the colonies. "If I must be enslaved," Seabury wrote, "let it be by a King, at least, and not by a parcel of upstart, lawless committeemen. If I must be devoured, let it be by the jaws of a lion, and not gnawed to death by rats and vermin." Seabury spoke as convincingly as he wrote. He was an imposingly large man, forty-six years old, who possessed an aura of personal authority. His church, St. Peter's, was a modest wooden building (the present St. Peter's is Victorian stone, on the same site, just north of the intersection of Tremont and Westchester avenues in the Bronx), and it was lucky to draw as many as two hundred worshipers on an ordinary Sunday, but Seabury nevertheless had an influence over his entire neighborhood. He was the only clergyman for nine miles around, which meant that he buried and married not only his own parishioners but also many who were not Anglicans. In his youth, he had studied medicine at the University of Edinburgh, and so he was also one of West Chester's busiest doctors. As an anti-Association propagandist, Seabury criticized England's colonial policies almost as tellingly as he argued against the Association. That was deft. So were most of his specific assertions. He said, for instance, that the Association's nonimportation program would hurt Americans more than Englishmen. New York businessmen were already hurt by the boycott, and Seabury's prediction was bound to add to their worries. Seabury frightened farmers by telling them of the merchants, moneylenders, and profiteers in the city who, he said, were waiting, with vast cash reserves, to snap up farm properties at distress prices. He told New Yorkers—farmers and merchants alike—that Bostonians were making fools of them, growing rich and insolent on New York aid while New Yorkers suffered shortages and deprivations. Seabury argued that it was illegal for the Association to force its will on Americans who did not believe in it. By stressing the individual's liberty to dissent, he chose the most persuasive of premises for his attack on the loyalty investigation. "A most hateful inquisition," he called it. He despised the idea that any committee should inquire into the affairs, let alone the opinions, of British subjects. Seabury wrote as if he alone cared for English liberties. (In fact, the Provincial Congress was deeply upset that it had to invade men's privacy. It was trying, as far as it dared, to ask about public opinions without going into private affairs.)

New York had no positive proof that Seabury was "A Westchester Farmer," and he had refused to admit to the pseudonym. Still, as time passed, some of Seabury's arguments began to look academic. After Massachusetts had caught a full-fledged spy, Dr. Benjamin Church, who admitted having passed information, for pay, to General Thomas Gage, the Commander of the British forces in America, the loyalty-oath program seemed a trifle less harebrained than Seabury alleged. (On the other hand, Church had succeeded in his espionage because he had never appeared inimical in the slightest degree. Until his arrest, he had been a prominent Associator, enjoying the Massachusetts Provincial Congress' affection and respect.) Then Alexander Hamilton, before he left college for the artillery, felt he could debate "A Westchester Farmer, " and, writing as "The Friend of America," had turned out two excellent pamphlets answering the essayist's charges. Hamilton's literary style was not as colorful as Seabury's, but his logic was often better. (Unhappily, The Friend of America's replies aroused new interest in A Westchester Farmer's original statements, and increased the Farmer's already good sales.)

Seabury's arguments were mainly his own, but many Anglicans shared his views. Some saw the Association as just another Presbyterian plot. Others recognized that broader issues were involved, but would not listen to arguments because they believed what the Church of England taught—that loyalty to George III, along with obedience to British laws, were matters of religious duty, not subjects for debate. The Anglican ministers in the New York area worked closely together, and the Provincial Congress knew that Seabury in West Chester was in close touch with his colleagues in Manhattan, Queens, Brooklyn, Staten Island, and eastern New Jersey. (Dr. Charles Inglis, an assistant rector of Trinity Church in New York City, was temporarily in charge of Trinity parish during Dr. Samuel Auchmuty's absence. No man was more zealous than Inglis in spreading lack of faith in the Association.) The Provincial Congress appreciated all this, but could think of no acceptable way to fight the Anglican network. A formal attempt to silence Seabury or restrain Inglis seemed likely to do more harm than good. It might bear out Seabury's charge that the Association's methods were illegal, and even imply a lack of concern for religious liberty.

Seabury's publisher, James Rivington, was another outspoken scoffer, and nearly as annoying to the Provincial Congress as Seabury himself. Rivington's press was on the northwest corner of Queen and Wall streets, diagonally across from the Coffee House. Jemmy Rivington, in addition to being a printer and a bookseller (his store, the London Bookshop, occupied the ground floor of his print shop), owned and edited the city's leading newspaper, the *New-York Gazetteer: or Connecticut,*

New-Jersey, Hudson's River, and Quebec Weekly Advertiser.
Its page size was about that of a modern tabloid's, like nearly all
the fifty-odd American newspapers, and it appeared every
Thursday morning. Technically, the *Gazetteer* was far superior
to its New York competition—John Holt's *Journal,* Hugh
Gaine's *Mercury,* and John Anderson's *Constitutional Gazette,*
which had started publication in August. The *Gazetteer's* typog-
raphy was better, and it printed more news. Its foreign correspondence was particularly good. Anderson's paper was written
in a more sensational style, but as an editor Anderson was no
match for Rivington. The *Gazetteer* was livelier, funnier, and
much more enterprising than the other three. As a result, its
circulation—something more than thirty-five hundred—was the
largest in New York and among the largest in the country.

But the *Gazetteer's* editorial policy, from the beginning of the
troubles, had been distinctly anti-Association and pro-British.
While the paper had gone through a period of good behavior
early in the summer, as the fall wore on, it was sliding back
toward inimicality. Those Associators who knew Rivington best
were especially irritated with him because they thought that he
had no strong political convictions of his own, and that he was
printing what he thought the society leaders wanted to read in
order to enhance his own social standing, which otherwise depended upon his second wife's excellent family connections.
(She was Elizabeth, a daughter of the late Cornelius Van
Horne.)

Rivington got little or no credit for the *Gazetteer's* temporary
reform; it had been forced upon him. On the night of May 10,
Rivington had missed being mobbed by the narrowest of mar-
gins. That evening the waterfront strong-arm boys, with a host
of eager assistants, had stormed through the city hunting for the
men they called "The Odious Six": Colden, Cooper, James De

Lancey, John Watts, Henry White (a merchant and member of the Council), and Rivington. The phrase came from a Philadelphia handbill that had named New York's "worst Tories" and had explained how they had started the war. (It was said that the Six had led the British to believe that, in case of war, New York would defect from the Continental Association. This misinformation, in turn, had encouraged the British to march on Lexington and Concord prepared to shoot; and that had done it.) Luckily for the hunted men, the mob had been unable to find any of them. (Watts had sailed for London six days earlier.) Rivington had escaped—like Cooper he had been warned that he was in danger—to the *Kingfisher*, in the East River.

In one important respect, Rivington was not in the same class as the other five: he was not nearly so rich. Unlike Watts, Cooper, and, later, White, Rivington could not afford to retreat to England. He could not afford to ignore the bad publicity, as De Lancey and Colden were trying to do. Rivington's fortunes depended directly upon circulation, advertising, book sales, and printing jobs—in short, upon the good will of many New Yorkers. His one chance had been to beg New York's forgiveness, to convince the Provincial Congress not to take any official action against him. That was what he had done. Throughout the rest of May—while the *Gazetteer*, despite its editor's absence, appeared on Thursdays, as usual, but in a chastened frame of editorial mind—Rivington had conducted his own letter-writing defense from a cabin on the *Kingfisher*. He addressed the Provincial Congress, the Continental Congress, and his countless New York friends. Despite his political sins, Rivington was popular. While he was too fat to be called handsome, he was an impressive figure in an overblown style. He was a well-powdered model of gentlemanliness in his dress, even though he was engaged in nothing more genteel than keeping shop. He had been an amusing guest at hundreds of parties, collecting and dispensing anecdotes. He was an expert at all forms of gambling, and an enthusiastic drinking companion with a penchant for recitations, especially speeches from Shakespeare, which he delivered, when tipsy, in the florid declamatory style of the London theater. Before his success in New York, Rivington had been through two bankruptcies—one in England, which had been responsible for his emigrating, and a second in the colonies. Failure had improved his manner. At his boastful worst, when he tried to play the snob, he usually managed to soften the offense by making a self-deprecatory joke.

In his plea for forgiveness, Rivington denied everything and promised never to do it again. He said he had been giving space to both sides of the controversy because he was devoted to freedom of the press. He had pointed to pro-Association pieces the *Gazetteer* had carried. He reminded New York that he had published not only the best-selling arguments of "A Westchester Farmer" but also Hamilton's best-selling responses, and a good many other pro-Association pamphlets, too. But what had angered the Philadelphia handbill-writer, inflamed the New York mob, and had provoked a total of twenty-one local committees into passing anti-*Gazetteer* resolutions was something else—the stuff the paper had been printing as news: hundreds of snide items, some entirely false, others merely unnecessary, still others deliberately embarrassing to Associators. For example, the *Gazetteer* had usually reported the attendance at Association rallies as less than it had been. If the paper had had to admit that a big crowd had been present at a rally, then it had commented on the speakers' popularity among ignorant riffraff. The *Gazetteer* had made fun of all the leading Associators; if there was a man among them whom it had not actually libeled,

Rivington had at least invented some comic, derogatory phrase for him. These insulting descriptions appeared in news stories as if they were facts and matters of common knowledge in the bargain. (Rivington's favorite target, Sears, had been called "a political cracker," "a tool of the lowest order," and "the laughing stock of the whole town"; and, at every chance, the *Gazetteer* had called attention to Sears's large and prominent ears.) Even the *Gazetteer*'s society news was biased. An account of one fashionable White Plains wedding, for instance, had pointed out quite gratuitously that the distinguished guest list included "not a single Whig."

Associators in New Brunswick, New Jersey, had hanged Rivington in effigy (a deed done, according to the *Gazetteer*, by "some of the lower class of inhabitants"). The South Carolina Provincial Congress had banned his "scurrilous sheet." New York Associators had tried, with some success, to persuade Rivington's readers and his advertisers to boycott the paper. Although Rivington had been appointed Royal Printer for New York in April, at a hundred pounds a year, the compensation did not begin to make up for the business he was losing.

In desperation, Rivington had taken the Association oath and had prepared, for general distribution, a handbill in which he swore that he intended to keep it. On June 7, the Provincial Congress had voted to give Rivington another chance. One delegate, twenty-three-year-old Gouverneur Morris, of Westchester County, had explained that he had voted for Rivington out of pity. Morris had argued that since Rivington was no more than "indifferently wise," and had been led into his errors by his Tory friends, the Provincial Congress ought to show magnanimity.

Rivington's return to the evil journalistic ways he had forsworn was even more bold than his original errors. He could hardly hope to be given the benefit of the doubt on a second occasion, yet, by November, the *Gazetteer* was printing a suspiciously large number of discontented letters from readers who complained about the dreary nature of the times or who described, without complaining, the boldness of the inimicals in their neighborhoods. It was also running a peculiar series of parables, whose major theme was that tangling with John Bull was futile. The *Gazetteer* was back to underplaying good news —on those rare occasions when the Association had any—and exaggerating American reverses. In his November 16 issue, for instance, Rivington gave only a few lines to the splendid report that the Canadian town of St. Johns had capitulated to the advancing American Army, including New Yorkers under Montgomery's command. The story was easily worth several columns, which was how Holt's *Journal* had treated it.

By mid-November, the Provincial Congress was in adjournment again, and in no position to discuss the *Gazetteer*, Seabury's influence, or anything at all. It had called for new elections, hoping that within ten days all the counties could elect freshly approved sets of delegates. It hoped to forestall any criticism that its own authority had grown stale, and to get something like a vote of popular confidence for all it had been doing. The Congress had extended the franchise in an effort to enlarge its base of support: besides landowners, tenants who rented property worth eighty pounds or more had been qualified to vote.

These good ideas had not worked out. Instead of renewed approval, the Provincial Congress got a rebuff. In some towns, hardly any voters went to the polls, and even in New York City, the stronghold of Association support and enthusiasm, fewer than two hundred men voted. (A year earlier, the vote had exceeded one thousand.) Tryon, enchanted by a display of apathy exceeding his hopes, wrote Dartmouth that it looked as if Westchester, Dutchess, Kings, Queens, and Richmond were now predominantly pro-British, and that he suspected the political tide was running in the King's favor in several other counties, too. New York County's twenty-one-man delegation, in the midst of the failures, was strengthened. Fourteen old delegates were reelected, but the seven new men were better, on the whole, than the delegates they replaced—a list that included John De Lancey (one of James De Lancey's nephews), Isaac Low, Abraham Walton, and Leonard Lispenard, General Washington's erstwhile host. None of the seven men replaced had been attending sessions regularly, if at all. The delegation's political complexion was not changed—it was pro-Association moderate, as before—but the county could now expect more of its men to be on hand to help with the Congress' work. However, when the new Provincial Congress attempted to convene on November 14, New Yorkers saw that this slight improvement might be wiped out by the losses elsewhere. A quorum—a majority of the counties—could not be raised. Some county delegations had not yet been elected. Some of the elected delegations were not in town. Under its own rules, the Provincial Congress could not conduct any business, and there was no telling when the missing delegations might turn up, since there was no way of predicting what the negligent counties would do. The old Congress, through a dreadful oversight, had forgotten to appoint an interim Committee of Safety, and the powers granted to the September Committee of Safety had expired. In this technical impasse, New York Province had no functioning government.

Those delegates who were on hand were powerless to do more than meet daily at City Hall, call the roll, record the lack of a quorum, open the official mail and—since they were not even empowered to write letters promising that an answer would come later—arrange it in neat piles for the future Congress' future attention. A week went by. There was still no quorum on Tuesday, November 21, and no sign that the delegations required would arrive soon.

At this critical moment on the morning of the twenty-first, Isaac Sears was riding south from New Haven, along the Post Road, leading nearly a hundred mounted men whom he had recruited in Connecticut to raid New York. Sears had told his followers they were going to disarm "all" the inimicals in Westchester County, including Dr. Seabury, but since that might have taken months, Sears's intentions may always have been less ambitious. In any case, he had invented the mission for himself. He did not have the approval of Connecticut or New York, and the Westchester County Committee—the proper agency to do whatever needed doing about Westchester inimicals—had not even heard of Sears's scheme. Sears had just been reelected to the New York Provincial Congress, and he should have been waiting for a quorum with the other New York County delegates. It was peculiar, to say the least, that a New York congressman should be invading New York at the head of a column of Connecticut citizens. But Sears had been born in Connecticut, and had moved his family to New Haven not long after the *Asia* shelled New York City. Rumor had it that he was planning to make Connecticut his home again. In that case, of course, he should not have run again in the New York elections.

Sears was not much interested in such fussy formalities. As the commander of a pickup cavalry troop, with no superiors to report to, he was in his element and confident that true Associators everywhere would applaud his acts. Sears had recruited his first sixteen troopers at New Haven, where he had mapped out his expedition. The rest had fallen in as the column moved toward New York. The men had been waiting near the Post Road for Sears to come by, which showed considerable preparation. On Wednesday, November 22, Sears crossed the border. A detachment left the main body and rode to Mamaroneck, which was notorious as a center of inimical opinion. The raiders' task was to capture and destroy a small sloop there. According to gossip, Captain Vandeput had bought the boat and was keeping it ready against the day when the Provincial Congress would stop supplying His Majesty's ships, and the British would have to smuggle fresh food. Though Sears's men arrived in broad daylight, they took Mamaroneck by surprise. They quickly found the sloop and burned it. The job was done before the town realized what was happening, and no one tried to interfere.

Meanwhile, Sears's main column rode through Scarsdale Manor into East Chester Patent, headed for the town of East Chester. Sears had apparently stopped thinking about disarming Tories en masse; in East Chester, he and his men went directly to the home of Judge Jonathan Fowler, who sat on the bench of the Inferior Court of Common Pleas at White Plains. As a man appointed by the Crown, Fowler, like most New York judges, supported the Royal Government. His professional standing made him one of East Chester's leading citizens, but his rank as an inimical hardly seemed to warrant the priority Sears was allotting him. The Judge's most daring anti-Association gesture had been to sign Westchester's April protest, along with three hundred and eleven of his neighbors. He had almost immediately apologized in writing for his mistake, explaining that he had not taken enough time to consider what signing meant. Sears may have had some other information against Fowler, but Fowler appeared to be anything but guilty: he was at home, off guard, and astonished at being arrested—or, as a judge might describe it, kidnapped. Fowler gave up without a struggle. Sears's men confiscated his weapons—a sword, a musket, and some pistols. Then, leaving Fowler in his house for the time being, with a guard to watch him, the raiders headed south toward the town of West Chester, where Seabury lived.

Like East Chester, West Chester was full of non-Associators. Dr. Seabury, who preached in both villages, dividing his time between them as fairly as possible, would have been proud to take full credit for their political backwardness. He could hardly do so, however, because so much of the rest of Westchester County, including sections where Seabury rarely visited, showed the same lack of enthusiasm for the Association. Most Westchester County residents were farmers. More than half of them were tenants on one of the six manors—Van Cortlandt, Philipse, Fordham, Scarsdale, Pelham, and Morrisania—which, together, made up more than half the county's total acreage. Tenants also farmed in the patents, East Chester, Harrison, Rye, North Castle, and Bedford, and in the Borough-Town of West Chester. Tenants' rights and duties varied from place to place, and, until just now, they had not been allowed to vote, but their lot in general was far from feudal. A tenant's obligations to the lord of the manor usually boiled down to little more than a modest real-estate tax. The tenant usually had the security of a long written lease, up to and including "in perpetuity." His rent was often low, and in some cases it was merely a token rent; his land, in general, was fairly productive. All things considered, the majority of Westchester farmers were doing well, and even the most diligent local Associators, like Gilbert Drake, chairman of the County Committee, lacked revolutionary zeal.

Seabury lived in the St. Peter's parsonage, a small house as unpretentious as the church itself, but he was not home when

Sears's troops arrived. Seabury's wife, with several of the six children, met the raiding party at the door. The Connecticut men demanded to know where Seabury was. Neither Mrs. Seabury nor the children would tell. A few of the troopers pushed their way into the house and searched for Seabury, ripping furniture apart, cursing, and stamping up and down stairs. Mrs. Seabury and the children were terrified. One of the men brandished a bayonet and threatened to stab one of the Seabury girls if she did not talk. He lifted off her cap with the tip of his weapon and cut the kerchief she wore at her neck. She did not say a word. Finally, while some of Sears's men stayed to hunt through Seabury's papers for documentary proof that Seabury was "A Westchester Farmer," most of the others began to search the neighborhood.

Seabury was not hard to find. He was just a few doors down the road, teaching school. In addition to his work as a clergyman, physician, and pamphleteer, Seabury was, by economic necessity, a part-time farmer and a part-time schoolmaster. He kept pigs and cows, and grew hay and corn as cash crops; and he ran a small school for boys. His pupils—he had ten of them— were boarded in private West Chester homes, and classes were held in a large private house, not far from the church.

In a few minutes, the raiders found him. They took him back to his house, made him saddle one of his horses, and rode away with him as their prisoner. They also took with them—a feature of the kidnapping that rather lowered its high political tone— three dollars and some loose change, Seabury's new beaver hat, a silver-handled whip, and two silver spoons.

Sears's men had one more stop to make in West Chester. The third victim on their list was the mayor, Nathaniel Underhill. Like Fowler and Seabury, Underhill had signed the Westchester protest. He had not recanted, and he may have been slightly more steadfast a Tory than Fowler. Even so, apart from his office, he seemed to be an obscure candidate for kidnapping. Like the others, Underhill was astonished when the Connecticut men appeared, and he surrendered quietly. Underhill and Seabury were ridden north, under guard, to East Chester. There the party picked up Fowler and Fowler's guard, and the combined group went on to the first town across the Connecticut border, Horse Neck, now Greenwich.

Sears himself, with the rest of the raiders—seventy-five or eighty men—camped for the night at West Chester. Early the next morning, November 23, they rode west, following the Post Road, which meandered across Fordham Manor to the King's Bridge. There, by prearrangement, they met a party of New Yorkers who had ridden out of the city, starting before daybreak, to escort Sears into the city. The escort was larger than Sears's column—a hundred or perhaps a hundred and twenty-five New Yorkers in all, including two City Committee members, John Woodward and Samuel Broome, together with many of the men in Sears's tried-and-true band, Liberty Boys, members of the New York mob, and patrons of his father-in-law's saloon. The party rode down the Post Road, until it entered the Bowery Road (close to the present intersection of Fifth Avenue and Twenty-third Street), and then down the Bowery Road into the city proper and along Queen Street—the direct route to Rivington's shop. When the men reached the *Gazetteer*'s office, they found that Rivington was not there. The Connecticut men then produced a number of cloth sacks from their saddlebags. While some spent the next hour or two wrecking Rivington's establishment, others filled their sacks with his precious imported type. Since there were only one or two small type foundries in America—and none capable of producing fonts in a class with Rivington's imported equipment—the type was irreplaceable. Sears's men smashed Rivington's presses and spilled his files. They worked in a systematic manner, making no effort to conceal what they were doing and seemingly certain that no one in New York would try to stop them. They drew quite an audience. A wooden platform, called the Coffee House Bridge, which was used as an open-air marketplace, especially for auctions, ran down the middle of Wall Street for one block, from Queen Street to Dock Street (now Water Street), and as Sears's men broke up the shop, a crowd of spectators formed. Most of them seemed to enjoy the spectacle. The New Yorkers cheered from time to time. If there were any cries of protest, they were drowned out by shouts of approval. No one lifted a finger to save Rivington's property. By one o'clock, the *Gazetteer* had been put out of business.

One of the raiders wrote out a comic document to leave amid the wreckage—a bill, addressed to Governor Dunmore of Virginia, for the value of Rivington's type. (The joke assumed a keen interest in current events on its audience's part. Three weeks earlier, as careful readers of the New York newspapers might know, Dunmore's soldiers had raided the Norfolk office of a pro-Association newspaper, the *Virginia Gazette*—not to be confused with a couple of other newspapers with the same name that were published in Williamsburg—edited by John Hunter Holt—not to be confused with his uncle, John Holt, the publisher of the *New-York Journal*. With the *Gazette*'s equipment, Dunmore had started to print an anti-Association paper on his warship-sanctuary. And so, with far-fetched logic, as a type-stealer Dunmore deserved to pay for Rivington's misfortune.)

No one could deny that Sears, in the matter of jokes about his big ears, had more than evened the score with Rivington, but if Sears had also expected that his raid would help move New York from apathy to militancy, he was mistaken. That same afternoon, as the Connecticut party rode home, the City Committee—the closest approximation to a New York governing body—discussed what had happened. Some members may have approved of Sears's treatment of Seabury, Fowler, Underhill, and Rivington, but most of the City Committee was outraged. It looked on the raid not as a demonstration on behalf of the Association's ideals but as an unprovoked attack by Connecticut on New York. Lancaster Burling, who was among the furious, introduced a motion that Sears, Woodward, and Broome (all Committee members) be ordered to appear to answer the charge that the raid had been a "hostile act" against New York and, therefore, "a breach of the Association"—as serious an accusation as the City Committee could make. John Broome, Samuel Broome's brother, was the chairman of the session. Burling's motion put him in an embarrassing position. There was some thought that Broome ought to turn his gavel over to another member. Broome did not offer to do so, and the point was not pressed. The extraordinary number of delegates who wanted to speak on the motion solved Broome's family problem. Before they had all had their say, it was time to adjourn, and overnight Burling either changed his mind or had it changed for him. When the City Committee reconvened, at any rate, he withdrew his original motion in favor of a substitute, which was quickly passed. No action was to be taken against any individual. The City Committee merely voted to ask the Provincial Congress, when it reconvened, to "devise some expedient" to prevent anything like the Sears raid from happening again.

The moral passions Sears had succeeded in arousing on both sides of several issues slowly petered out, if only for lack of a clear-cut denouement. Rivington's stolen type had disappeared. Sears and his men, discovering that their lead-filled sacks were terribly heavy, had apparently thrown them away; at least they no longer had them when they crossed the Connecticut border. At Horse Neck, Sears's troopers picked up Seabury, Fowler, and Underhill, and took them to New Haven, but within the week Fowler and Underhill were released. Both men swore that they were "heartily sorry" and promised never again to oppose in any sense the measures of the Continental Congress. (Fowler's recantation was merely a repetition of the statement he had made in New York months earlier.) And, judging by his cooperativeness, Underhill was anything but a hardened inimical.

Seabury's case was quite different. He refused to recant the past or to make promises about the future. His stubborn attitude more or less forced his captors to keep him under arrest at Mrs. Lyman's boardinghouse, where he was guarded by five Connecticut soldiers. There were four charges against Seabury. He admitted that he was guilty of the first: he had signed the Westchester protest. He admitted the second: St. Peter's had not been open on Thursday, July 20, a day that the Continental Congress had set aside for humiliation, fasting, and prayer on behalf of the Continental cause; but, as Seabury pointed out, this failure had already been investigated by the New York Provincial Congress, and the complaint, which Sears had brought, had been dismissed. (Seabury had explained that he had never heard about the fast day, unofficially, officially, or in any way whatever.) As for the third charge—that he had conspired to kidnap Sears and take him aboard a British warship—Seabury called it preposterous. His most interesting defense concerned the fourth allegation—that he had written pamphlets and newspaper articles "against the liberties of America." He had done nothing of the sort, Seabury said. As usual, he would neither admit nor deny having written the Westchester Farmer essays. His point was that nothing he admitted having written was against American liberties. Seabury remarked further that if there was an example of liberties infringed, it was carrying citizens from one colony to another at the point of a bayonet.

Connecticut's patriots had never before dealt with a foe of Seabury's caliber. He was perhaps more dangerous as a prisoner than he had been as a free man, but the raiders, having taken him, could not let him go without an excuse. Seabury's friends and admirers in New Haven were treating him like a visiting celebrity, asking for permission (which was refused) to call on him at Mrs. Lyman's. He got an invitation, which he could not accept, to preach at the Reverend Bela Hubbard's church. All in all, Connecticut may have felt some measure of relief when, on December 12, the New York Provincial Congress (which at last had a quorum on December 6) wrote Governor Trumbull a formal complaint about the Sears raid. New York assumed, correctly, that Connecticut had not authorized the invasion. Still, New York asked for Rivington's type, or compensation for it, and for Trumbull's "friendly interposition" for Seabury's release, "considering his ecclesiastical character, which, perhaps is venerated by many friends to liberty, the severity that had been used towards him may be subject to misconstructions prejudicial to the common cause." Trumbull resisted any temptation to reply that Seabury had been kidnapped by a member of New York Provincial Congress; in fact, he did not answer New York's letter at all for more than six months. But, on December 23, without any public explanation, the guards at Mrs. Lyman's were withdrawn. Seabury understood that he was free to go home. He went. Despite the spirit with which he had defended himself, Seabury was downcast. Apart from the chance that Sears's example might inspire other self-appointed guardians of the Association's interests to think of ways of making his life miserable, Seabury realized that his pupils' parents, in view of what had happened, were likely to feel that his school was unsafe and withdraw their boys. His loss, Seabury calculated, might come to as much as one hundred pounds a year.

Rivington was more disheartened than Seabury. He could not afford to buy new type of any kind or repair his presses, and, by force of circumstance, the *Gazetteer* was suspended. Two New York newspapers promptly leaped to life. Hugh Gaine started one, the *Universal Register,* thus becoming the first New York publisher of two newspapers. Sam Loudon, a ship chandler turned bookseller, started the other. The first issue of his *New-York Packet* appeared on January 4. Loudon had a reputation as a shrewd business opportunist; he had previously bought, at a bargain, a part interest in a printing shop, and was trying to improve its business. Both papers obviously hoped to capture the *Gazetteer*'s former readers, but editorially they were both unmistakably pro-Association, with no nonsense about giving space to the British point of view. New Yorkers who had appreciated the *Gazetteer* were left with a poor choice; they had to pick among five second-rate papers all trying to outdo one another in lackluster fidelity to the American cause. As for Rivington, he, with half a dozen other men who were discouraged about New York, sailed for London on January 10. The New York papers almost entirely ignored his departure. So many other, more urgent matters had arisen that the newspapers were crowded for space; still, if Rivington had been running a paper he would undoubtedly have found room for some comment on the event. All the notice he got, however, was his name on the list of the *Samson*'s cabin passengers, down in the perfunctory shipping news.

II. December, 1775, to February, 1776

☆

IN December of 1775, before New York City had stopped talking about the Sears raid, another topic arose—a report that
British forces at Boston were about to leave for New York. The
rumor had been repeated at intervals since the beginning of the
summer, and each time the British move sounded a little more
likely. In December, the alarm once again seemed urgent. The
open questions were: When would the British come? In what
strength? And why?

New York City had been the headquarters of the British
Army in North America until the British Army went to Boston,
in 1774, leaving only a garrison force of token strength behind, and perhaps the British intended to make it their headquarters again. In that case, surely, the British Army would
have asked the British Navy not to burn New York or knock
down useful buildings. Yet there was another possibility—that
the British might be coming to wipe out New York City as they
had recently wiped out Falmouth, Massachusetts (now Falmouth, Maine, a part of greater Portland), on October 18. The
British had felt—with some justification—that Falmouth had
been too enthusiastic in contributing to the infant and informal
American Navy, a flotilla of fishing boats, some as big as whalers,
that was interfering with British supplies bound for Boston. To
punish Falmouth, a British naval squadron had bombarded the

place and set fire to most of the buildings. No one had been hurt, because the British commander, conducting an experiment in limited frightfulness, had given the inhabitants a warning, and then had allowed them time to flee before he opened fire. Even so, the physical destruction of an entire town had horrified all America and had reminded every American seaport of its vulnerability to British naval power. New York, at least as frightened as any of the others, feared that the New York Provincial Congress knew for certain that New York was the next target, but was withholding the information. The Provincial Congress knew nothing about it, and made the mistake of saying so. The disclaimer inspired the gossips to improve their story: the Congress had taken to lying, they said, to avert mass panic.

The British were in fact considering shelling Portsmouth, New Hampshire. (Portsmouth had contributed about as much as Falmouth to the American fleet.) When Portsmouth heard rumors that it was to be shelled, the town appealed to General Washington for soldiers, or gunpowder, or both. Washington had nothing to spare. His army was spread in a thin semicircle around Boston, and he was still short of gunpowder. He did what he could: he detached one of his best generals, John Sullivan, to act as technical adviser on Portsmouth's defense, and he gave Sullivan a few infantrymen as an escort. Sullivan knew he could not keep the British warships from demolishing the place if they felt so inclined, but, just to raise Portsmouth's spirits, he marched his tiny company up one street and down the next. In the course of his visit, Sullivan discovered that Portsmouth was full of outspoken Tories. They laughed at Sullivan's mission and openly proclaimed their contempt for the Continental Association, the Continental Congress, and the Continental Army. Sullivan was shocked. His orders gave him no authority over these civilians, and though he was tempted to lock them up immediately, he wrote instead to Washington and requested permission to take action against what he called "the infernal crew."

The Commander-in-Chief had been so busy with other difficulties that he had not been giving much thought to inimicality, and he had no answer for the difficult question Sullivan's letter posed: What could the Continental Army do when it found a sizable part of an American community in sympathy with the enemy? Washington instructed Sullivan to arrest "those Crown officers" who had been "acting as enemies of their country"— meaning the United Colonies. But Crown officers were only a small part of the crew that had upset Sullivan, and the Continental Congress had already told the provincial assemblies to arrest *all* dangerous persons, Crown officers or not, and, if needs be, to arrest them on mere suspicion. The limit on what the Army could or could not do was as unclear as before. In the middle of November, Washington had sent Governor Trumbull of Connecticut an edited copy of his instructions to Sullivan, thinking, in innocent good faith, that they might serve Connecticut as a model. The General had also urged Connecticut to pay serious attention to inimicality. Connecticut was well ahead of all the other provinces, and of Washington himself, in thinking about, and acting against, inimical Americans. By mid-December, after several months of study, the Connecticut legislature had passed a comprehensive set of anti-inimical laws, the first systematic attempt by any province to deal with clear-cut acts against the Association. Secret sympathies did not come within the scope of the laws, but Connecticut defined specific crimes, such as spying or recruiting for the British, and prescribed for the guilty punishments up to and including forfeiture of a man's entire property and imprisonment for three years.

One New Yorker commented that a province with nothing

better than New Haven for a seaport could risk defying British seapower. Still, jokes could not conceal the contrast between Connecticut's pace-setting efforts and New York's indecisiveness, especially when New York seemed to have many more inimicals than her neighbor. Since the city's own Continental regiment was away fighting in Canada, leaving nothing on hand except the militia battalions, the inimicality problem looked, especially to out-of-province patriots, as if it might be more than New York could manage by herself. The New York Provincial Congress agreed that New York would need military help. However, the New Yorkers were deeply concerned with an associated question that had not been resolved in the nine months or so since the beginning of the war: Who would have the final authority over troops from outside New York once they had set foot on New York soil? The New York Provincial Congress felt strongly that it, or any other host province, should have this ultimate power, and New York worried because the principle had not been spelled out in unmistakable form. From December 6, when the legislators reconvened, until adjournment on the twenty-second, the Provincial Congress was unable to forget, dismiss, or table the question; the discussion rambled along, taking time that might have been spent on other affairs, and, during the distraction, most of the inimicals in and around the city remained free to commit whatever evils they intended. If other provinces regarded New York's preoccupation with this legal technicality as pettifogging, the New Yorkers, for their part, could not understand why the other congresses and assemblies were not equally jealous of their provincial rights.

New York saw the matter as anything but academic. The Provincial Congress was looking ahead to at least two military visits that would raise the issue. Governor Trumbull had promised New York that if the British came he would send Connecticut soldiers to help the city defend itself. The commitment was generous, yet a knot of skeptical New York delegates felt alarm instead of gratitude. While the command question remained unclear, they felt, New York's sovereignty might be jeopardized. Then, in the second place, there was the impending arrival of New Jersey's Colonel Lord Stirling (his Christian name was not "Lord" but Alexander, and although a claim he had made to a Scottish earldom had been rejected by the House of Lords, Americans used the title out of politeness). Lord Stirling, with six companies of New Jersey men, most of them from around New Brunswick, was about to cross the Hudson to help New York garrison Fort Constitution, the strongpoint under construction on the east side of the river about opposite West Point. Stirling's men were to reinforce the New York troops already there, and the Colonel would be entering New York on orders from the Continental Congress, to which New York had appealed for this military aid. The Provincial Congress wished it could be made clear—before the New Jersey men arrived —that, in the last analysis, New York had the right to give Stirling orders. New York hoped, to be sure, that the New Jersey expedition would proceed smoothly. If there were no arguments, and therefore no test questions, the definition of the principle could take a little longer. But one point of friction had developed while Stirling's men were still on the New Jersey side of the Hudson. It was just a supply problem, but it hinted of possible trouble ahead. Only half of Stirling's 540 men had muskets, and the Colonel thought New York should supply the rest. New York thought not. As Brigadier General Nathaniel Woodhull, a prosperous Suffolk County farmer who had succeeded Peter Van Brugh Livingston as President of the Provincial Congress, wrote Stirling, New York felt that arming New Jersey soldiers was clearly a New Jersey responsibility—or, if New Jersey could not afford the expense, a Continental responsibility. In any case, Woodhull explained, New York did not have the money to pay for 270 muskets, if, indeed, it could find that many guns for sale. To prove New York's good faith, Woodhull promised that the Provincial Congress would look for muskets, but he doubted that it could find more than a hundred, no matter how much New Jersey was willing to pay. Stirling had replied that he was shocked to find New York, the beneficiary of New Jersey's prospective assistance, balking at his reasonable request. The disagreement was small, but it was not a happy beginning to New York's dealings with Stirling. And while the argument over muskets was going on, Stirling ran into another disappointment. The construction work at Fort Constitution, he learned, was so far behind schedule that only one of its three barracks was ready, and it was fully occupied by the New Yorkers there. Stirling did not want his men to spend the worst of the winter months in tents. The Provincial Congress had no immediate answer to Stirling's worry about that prospect, and it hardly had the heart to mention that even tentage was as scarce as muskets.

Stirling's dissatisfaction with the state of the Fort Constitution project was trivial compared to New York's. The Provincial Congress had just come to the realization that the entire installation was in the wrong place. It was just as well that construction had lagged. If the fort, on a swampy island south of what is now the town of Cold Spring, had been completed, it would have been worthless. The river there was unusually wide, and yet the fort was only a few feet above the water level; the guns would not have the advantage of an elevated site, and the British ships should not have serious difficulty in keeping out of range. Moreover, since the fort was at the bottom of a natural bowl, surrounded on three sides by high ground, its interior would be open to field-artillery fire from the ridges above. Most of the blame for Fort Constitution's terrible location belonged to Barnard Romans, a free-lance fortifications "expert" who knew next to nothing about the subject of his supposed expertise. Romans was a talented artist and engraver who, among other works, had produced a stirring picture of the Battle of Bunker's Hill. He had impressed the Continental and the Provincial Congresses by drawing beautiful plans for Fort Constitution, renderings so attractive that no one had questioned their military validity. Romans had no sinister motive. He had been looking for a job, and he had selected the idiotic site because he had not the faintest idea where to put a fort. Long after it had hired him, the Provincial Congress examined Romans' qualifications carefully and found that the best job he had ever held was His Majesty's Botanist for one of the Floridas.

Besides adopting Romans' plans for the fort, the Provincial Congress had employed him to oversee the construction—more authority, as it turned out, than Romans could handle. The first inkling of difficulty was a report that the laborers at Fort Constitution were drinking. A subcommittee of the Provincial Congress had gone up to investigate, and had found that indeed the workmen were appallingly drunk. The investigators had also seen, by the bye, the error in the fort's location. Now, in December—and with full awareness that the British might not allow the Fort Constitution project any more time—the Provincial Congress was trying to get out of its obligations to Romans and to find someone qualified to do the job. It had almost, but not quite, decided to give up on Fort Constitution and to divert the entire effort to another site, the crest of Popolop's Hill, on the west bank of the river, five or six miles downstream. The ground was high, the Hudson was narrow at that point, and American gunners shooting from above might be able to give passing British ships quite a hard time. (Popolop's Hill today helps support the western end of the Bear Mountain Bridge.) Meanwhile, the Provincial Congress had banned liquor salesmen from the Fort Constitution area—all but two or three who were approved by the troop commander, Colonel Isaac Nicholl. The construction workers were much less drunk than they had been, and they were working more efficiently, though on the wrong fort.

These discouragements did not subtract from New York's concern about the question of troop command. If anything, the Provincial Congress' interest in that subject increased as one thing after another appeared to be working out badly; and now it seemed likely that Stirling, already angry at New York's reluctance to buy muskets for his men, would be even angrier when he set eyes on Fort Constitution. About the middle of December, the Provincial Congress hit upon a clever idea. If the Continental Congress could be persuaded to pass a general resolution affirming the supremacy of provincial authority, the Provincial Congress thought, the issue would be raised to a level so high that no particular military man—not Stirling, not the commander of the Connecticut reinforcements, not anyone else —could take affront. On December 22, the Provincial Congress instructed the New York delegation in Philadelphia to introduce motions to that effect. On January 2, 1776, to New York's satisfaction and relief, the two New York resolutions were adopted.

The Continental Congress declared, first, that Continental troops moving on request into any province were to be subject to the host province's control. The second resolution said that no province was to be given armed help in dealing with its internal enemies until it had asked for such assistance. That was the product of New York's fear that one of its eager neighbors— Connecticut, in particular—might want to help with New York's inimicality difficulties in some violent, irregular manner or without waiting for an invitation.

The Provincial Congress' latest hearings on inimicality had been anything but pleasant. They had revealed that Queens County (which then included what are now Queens and Nassau counties as well as Floyd's Neck, today part of Suffolk County) contained an extraordinary number of non-Associators—perhaps as many per square mile as any other county in America, with the possible exception of Richmond County (Staten Island). The Queens situation was so bad that on December 6—the day the new Provincial Congress, with no help from Queens, had scraped together a legal quorum—Queens had decided, by the overwhelming majority of 788 to 221, that it did not choose to send a delegation, and therefore had no reason to elect one. Queens had declared, by more than three to one, for disassociation from the Association. Richmond County had done no better, perhaps worse. Richmond had not bothered to vote at all, which explained why a Richmond delegation had not shown up. Although the Provincial Congress had scolded Richmond by letter, there had been no immediate sign that the county felt any contrition. While the Richmond voters were ignoring the subject, the 788 disenchanted Queens men prepared an impassioned broadside to explain exactly how they felt. Their manifesto wavered between self-pity and belligerence. It warned that Queens men would rather fight than submit to being arrested or disarmed. It also confirmed a heinous accusation that several persons, testifying before the Provincial Congress, had brought against Queens—namely, that some of the Queens inimicals had been getting guns and ammunition from the British. The manifesto said: ". . . impelled by the most powerful arguments of self-defense, we have at last been driven to procure a supply of those means for protecting ourselves, of which we have been, till now, almost totally destitute; but we solemnly declare that we procured them for the sole purpose of defending ourselves from insults and injuries."

"Those means" of protection, which the Queens men delicately avoided naming, were evidently weapons. The British warships in the harbor were the only possible source for guns. As the Provincial Congress had explained to Stirling, New York's survey of available weapons had been quite careful, and after the Queens manifesto, as before it, there were just a few guns, exorbitantly priced, in the hands of dealers.

No matter what the provocation, the Provincial Congress disliked the idea of New York's using force against her own sons. Besides, the Congress feared that if shooting were required to bring inimicals into line, the captains of the warships, hearing musket fire from the land, would fire on the city. The Provincial Congress' actions, therefore, were peaceable and cautious. The Congress began by ordering the twenty-six men it considered ringleaders in Queens—there were some in each of the county's five townships: Jamaica, Newton, Flushing, Hempstead, and Oyster Bay—to appear and explain what they thought they were doing. The chances that these men would answer their summonses seemed slight, but, to improve the odds, the hearings were not scheduled until December 20. This gave the delinquents at least five or six days to prepare their answers or, if they wished, to reconsider and reform.

In the interim, the Provincial Congress heard from Staten Island. There, in response to the scolding, the voters, on December 15, had at least held an election. But, like Queens, Richmond had decided not to send a delegation to the Provincial Congress. Staten Island had reported this result, by letter, in a remarkably casual way, explaining that a majority of Richmond County voters opposed further participation in the Association because, in their opinion, hopes for a reconciliation with Great Britain had vanished. That did not mean that Staten Island was getting ready to fight Great Britain all by herself; it meant that—no matter what the rest of New York decided—if the Association could not patch things up, Staten Island was ready to accept whatever terms King George might be willing to grant it.

On December 20, to no one's surprise, the Queens ringleaders failed to appear. The Provincial Congress then did what it had dreaded doing: it declared that both Queens and Richmond, having "broken the Association," were "in open contempt"—the most serious judgment the Provincial Congress could make against a county. The names of all the Queens and Richmond men who had voted nay were to be printed in the newspapers and distributed on handbills as "delinquents against the common cause." Even as it ordered the sentence, the Congress was well aware that in some Queens neighborhoods, and on Staten Island, too, publication of one's name as a delinquent might be looked on not as a stigma but as an honor. Then another difficulty arose: the Provincial Congress did not have a list of the Richmond County naysayers, and therefore could not publish their names. New York wrote and asked Staten Island for the list, but the men who had the voting records, all of them now delinquents, did not feel like sending it.

Having done this much, the Provincial Congress wrote the Continental Congress and explained why New York had not done more: it feared that British warships might fire on the city again. (The *Asia* continued to lie off the foot of Wall Street. It had been joined by the *Phoenix*, a forty-gun frigate, which was anchored off Burling's Slip, a little farther north, at about the point where the Brooklyn Bridge now crosses the East River.) Even if the ships did not fire, they might stop all outgoing shipping—and that, the Provincial Congress reminded the Continental Congress, would ruin a secret Continental trading venture which was being discussed as little as possible. Three New York merchants, John Van Derbilt, Jacobus Van Zandt, and Comfort Sands, acting as agents for the Continental Congress, and with 5,000 pounds of the Continental's money to spend, were nosing quietly around New York looking for a pair of ships to charter. The scheme was to load wheat, sneak out of the harbor past the British, go to Europe, preferably to France, sell the wheat, and invest the proceeds in gunpowder—or, if the equivalent in gunpowder was unobtainable, in saltpeter, muskets, Russia drilling, raven's-duck, Osnaburg, cheap linens, coarse-thread hose, or shirting for uniforms, in that order of preference.

The Provincial Congress did not say in so many words that New York wanted Continental soldiers to help control Queens and Richmond, yet that was what it did want. Asking for armed help in dealing with internal enemies without seeming to ask for it was a refinement beyond the concept of the second of the two New York resolutions on out-of-province troops, which was then about to come to a vote in the Continental Congress. Nevertheless, New York hoped that the Continental Congress would understand the unspoken invitation and send some soldiers, and thus allow the colony to appear passive and innocent in the eyes of Governor Tryon and the warships' captains. (New York's slyness was unnecessary. Tryon knew the city and the province; he was no fool; and his intelligence sources were much too good to be confused by a piffling deception of this sort. New York's safety was not to be achieved by the Provincial Congress' circumspection; it depended on Tryon's reluctance to burn the city.) For all the ambiguity, the Continental Congress did understand New York's letter, and immediately appointed a three-man subcommittee—which included one New Yorker,

John Jay—to investigate. The Congress heard the subcommittee's report on January 3, and then ordered Colonel Nathaniel Heard, of Woodbridge, New Jersey, to march to Queens as soon as he could get five hundred New Jersey men ready. There was no reason that Queens should have had priority over Richmond, but there was no reason why it should not, either. Heard was to disarm all the 788 men who had signed the Queens manifesto and to arrest the 26 "principal men" who had failed to answer their summonses. The Colonel was given $500 as an advance against expenses, and the Continental Congress set about arranging with Pennsylvania to provide him with 200 pounds of gunpowder. With the troops promised from Connecticut in case of invasion, and Stirling's companies destined for Fort Constitution, Heard's column became the third planned intrusion upon New York soil by out-of-province soldiers.

At General Washington's headquarters in Cambridge, a fourth intrusion onto New York soil was being considered. Isaac Sears, fresh from what he considered his Westchester County and New York City victories, had arrived in Cambridge at the end of December, accompanied by several of his Connecticut friends, all zealous patriots. They had horrified Washington and his headquarters staff with their reports on Long Island inimicality, and, to hear Sears tell it, the pro-British attitude of the New York Provincial Congress was a disgrace and at least as dangerous as the overt disloyalty of the King's armed friends in Queens. Sears and his friends had an advantage over many persons who were trying to persuade the Commander-in-Chief to believe this or that on various subjects: Washington's sober good judgment did not operate in its usual way when New York was discussed. He regarded New York City as a queer and special case, he could believe almost anything about the town

and its environs, and so he thought that Sears's description
might be correct. Washington did understand that the proximity
of the British warships inhibited the New York Provincial
Congress, and he was fully aware of all of New York's contributions to the cause, beginning with gunpowder supplies sent to
Boston in June. Nevertheless, the General thought there were
far too many New Yorkers who still believed that conciliation
with Great Britain was desirable. Washington felt that he himself had been slow to see the impossibility of a settlement—he
had believed that the British might offer acceptable terms even
after the fighting at Bunker's Hill. Now, however, he suspected
the good faith of New Yorkers who still felt as he himself had
felt as late as October. (It had been the reports of Dartmouth's
instructions to Gage, authorizing the use of Indians in the war
against the colonies as part of a new intensification of the British
war effort, that had changed Washington's mind.)

Washington was quite unfair. Numbers of New Yorkers who
were not inimical, delinquent, stupid, or King's agents imagined
that a peaceful solution might be negotiated. Even those New
Yorkers who felt that the United Colonies would have to win
the war in order to get proper treatment were not persuaded
that the American victory should lead to a separation from
Great Britain—and, in fact, "separation" was a word that one
did not use in public in New York. In Cambridge, by contrast,
the men on Washington's staff, the visitors to headquarters, and
the members of the Massachusetts Provincial Congress, among
others, talked about separation all the time, though not all of
them favored it. In the New York Provincial Congress, nobody
brought up long-range war aims because such a debate, besides
upsetting nearly everybody, would sidetrack the house from
immediate practical problems. Another word New Yorkers sel-
dom used was "Tory" to describe non-Associators, inimicals,

British sympathizers, or what have you. As a loose term of vilification, it was popular in New England. Some New Yorkers felt that New Englanders had already worked it to death, but, apart from that, the objection to "Tory" was that the word failed to distinguish between those Americans who supported King George, generally considered a good man, and those who supported his ministers, generally considered wicked. (It had been some time, admittedly, since the good King had done anything to live up to his New York reputation.) In any case, New Yorkers disliked the imprecision of "Tory," and they did not ordinarily call Associators "Whigs," either.

On one point, Washington agreed with New York: the city was as defenseless as it thought. Furthermore, the General's intelligence indicated that the city was a probable British objective. But Washington was not able to send men to New York. The Continental Army was smaller at the beginning of 1776 than it had been in October, when Washington had been unable to assist Portsmouth, because slightly more than half the soldiers had left in December on the expiration of their enlistments. Most of Washington's New England men had resisted all efforts to persuade them to stay longer, and had gone home. Washington was not certain that a new half army—ten thousand men were needed—could be recruited. He wondered whether new men could take their places in the front lines under the eyes of the British without bringing on a British attack. The Continental Army was still short of gunpowder. The American war effort depended as much on Washington's ability to bluff as on his army's ability to fight, and the strain was as much as the General could bear. Nevertheless, Washington knew that he could not afford to ignore New York's vulnerable condition. He was convinced that British strategy envisioned cutting New England off from the rest of the American colonies by gaining control of New York Harbor (and, incidentally, of the city), the Hudson, Lake George, Lake Champlain, the Richelieu River, and the St. Lawrence. Washington had high hopes that the American expedition to Canada, which had so far gone well, might forestall the British plan in the north. How to defend in the south and keep the lower Hudson under American control was the unsolved puzzle.

Washington's military expert, Charles Lee, claimed to have the answer. Perhaps Washington's desperation made him less critical than usual, for he had begun to have some doubts about Lee's judgment. (At the time the Continental Congress selected the general officers, Washington had had almost no doubts.) Lee's experience—he was a veteran of thirty years' military service, most of it in the British Army—was his strong credit. He had actually been a general in the Polish Army. And, since June, Lee had been of considerable help to Washington. But Lee had been a disappointment, too. His military education had been good, and he was unusually intelligent. At the same time, Lee's personality was impossible. He was arrogant, rude, and so unstable that his associates could never be sure, from one moment to the next, whether Lee would be up in the clouds or down in the dumps. It was distressing to Washington, furthermore, to find out that he could not rely on Lee to instruct him about subjects like the administration of a whole army. Despite Lee's having been a general, he had never commanded anything as large as a regiment. The Polish rank of "general," it now appeared, had been a courtesy rank that went with Lee's post as military aide to King Stanislaus Augustus Poniatowski, and it had involved no command duties whatever. Lee's combat experience in America during the French and Indian War, and in Portugal fighting the Spaniards in 1762, was no more than Washington's. Still, when Lee felt like it, he could be persuasive. Early in January, he felt like it, because he was eager for a separate command of his own, even a small one. He concocted an expedition down to New York to rout the Queens Tories and to prepare the city to defend itself against a British assault, and described his idea to Washington in a letter dated January 5. Instead of asking Washington for soldiers, Lee offered to recruit his own as he marched south, for Sears and his friends had persuaded Lee that Connecticut was full of men who would quickly volunteer for a mission of that sort. Anticipating Washington's immediate reaction, Lee pointed out that if the Commander-in-Chief waited too long the element of surprise would be lost, and admonished, "The salvation of the whole depends on your striking, at certain crises, vigorous strokes without previously communicating your intentions."

Washington found Lee's proposal tempting. One of the factors lending plausibility to Lee's scheme was the success of Lee's expedition, not long before, to Rhode Island. At the invitation of Governor Nicholas Cooke, Lee had gone to Newport to advise the city on its coastal defenses. Like General Sullivan at Portsmouth, Lee had been shocked to find Newport teeming with Tories, but Lee, instead of asking for further instructions, had invented his own way of dealing with them. He had arrested eight of the most prominent and had offered them a version he had written of the standard oath of allegiance to the Continental Association. Lee's oath was most demanding. Besides all the usual promises—obeying the Continental Congress, honoring the embargoes on imports and exports, and so forth—it asked a man to swear that he would take up arms in America's defense, if he was needed. Lee, in his capacity as a Continental Army officer, had administered the oath—and so had intruded the military into a sphere that had previously been reserved to civilian authorities. However, five of the eight Newport Tories had taken Lee's oath, a set of mind changes so abrupt that their friends and neighbors could scarcely believe the news. The three who refused had been clapped into the Newport jail. The Rhode Island legislature, almost as pleased with Lee's achievement as was Lee himself, had voted Lee special thanks, and its members had raised money to buy him a handsome present. Amid the jubilation, almost everybody overlooked the fact that Newport remained as vulnerable to a seaborne attack as it had been before Lee's visit.

All this had impressed Washington, and so did Lee's argument for speed. Still, the Commander-in-Chief wished he knew what the Continental Congress would think of the idea. By luck, Washington's good friend John Adams, a Massachusetts delegate to the Continental Congress, happened to be in Cambridge. Washington greatly respected Adams, and so sent him a note to get an advisory opinion. Would he be exceeding his authority, Washington asked, by ordering an occupation of New York without specific prior permission from Philadelphia? Since Adams had been away from Philadelphia, he was no more aware than Washington and Lee that the Continental Congress had ordered Colonel Heard to march on Queens. Adams' prompt reply to Washington's note was all for Lee's plan. "Your commission constitutes you commander of all the forces . . . and you are vested with full power and authority to act as you shall think for the good of the service," Adams said. New York City, Adams thought, "as a kind of key to the whole continent," was certainly within the geographical limits of Washington's authority. Adams' unequivocal approval was enough for Washington. The General wrote Governor Trumbull, explaining Lee's mission and requesting Connecticut's cooperation. Washington became almost as enthusiastic as Lee about Lee's project. He particularly liked the fact that the plan would not cost much, for, Washington assumed, the Connecticut volunteers would surely donate their time; and on that account, in writing Trumbull, Washington added a phrase saying that "the public"—meaning the Continental Congress—would be willing to pay for the "marching expenses" of the expedition. It seemed fair, if Connecticut's young men were willing to make such a contribution and run some risks, for the government to pay for their food and ammunition.

Washington handed Lee his written orders on January 8. Lee was to proceed to New York, starting as soon as he could and recruiting volunteers along the way, to put the city "into the best posture of defense which the season and circumstances will admit of." Three days later, Lee left Cambridge with a small party of aides and escorts. He was having trouble—gout, his doctors said—with one leg, but the pain did not affect his spirits. He was brimming with self-assurance, completely confident that, starting with nothing, he would be able to borrow everything he needed before he reached Queens. Lee's euphoria depended on ignorance compounded with misunderstanding; he had still not learned about Colonel Heard's expedition, and, furthermore, Washington and Lee, for all their consultations, were not entirely agreed about Lee's main purpose. Washington was thinking in essentially military terms—Lee was to arrange matters to keep the lower Hudson out of British hands. Washington's interest in the inimicals in Queens stemmed from his concern with that strategy. Manhattan, as he saw it, was essential to holding the river, and control of Queens was essential to the defense of Manhattan. Lee, on the other hand, was concentrating on the delightful prospect of running down Tories and forcing them to take his loyalty oath. He did understand that he was also supposed to improve New York City's defenses, and he took it for granted that he could do so, if only because any action would constitute an improvement. But Lee was not greatly interested in a New York City defense scheme, and he had not seriously studied the complexities of defending the island.

Even though Lee had cleverly played on Washington's interest in the bargain aspect of the expedition, he soon forgot about it. And Isaac Sears, who delivered Washington's letter to Trumbull and was acting as Lee's advance man, had evidently missed the point about Washington's interest in thrift. At any rate, when Trumbull began to turn out soldiers for Lee, hoping to have the nucleus of a small army ready by the time Lee himself reached New Haven, the Governor offered recruits full pay at the Continental Army rate, plus a food allowance as a bonus. It was surprising that Trumbull, who knew that Lee's mission was partly a duplicate of Heard's, showed no concern about the redundancy. In fact, Trumbull had ordered Colonel David Waterbury, of Stamford, and his regiment to march with Lee, even though the Continental Congress itself had originally considered and abandoned a similar idea. Trumbull felt, apparently, that the Continental Congress had erred, and that the task really demanded the dash and determination that only Connecticut men could provide.

New York City, meanwhile, was unaware of the help that Sears, Lee, Washington, and Trumbull were planning to give it. December and January brought wholly absorbing bad news, piece by piece. Judge Robert R. Livingston, the father of Robert R. Livingston, the Continental Congress delegate, died on December 9. His son was stricken with grief, and the whole province mourned with him. In January, a report arrived from Virginia to the effect that Norfolk had been bombarded by the British warship *Liverpool* on New Year's Day, while Lord Dunmore, the Virginia Governor, aboard his ship, the *Dun-*

more, had watched. The fire damage had been appalling. After the shelling, landing parties had gone ashore and set fire to nearly all the buildings that were not already aflame. (The full story, when it came out later, was even worse. Norfolk's militiamen, instead of fighting the fires, had looted houses and stores and were to blame for a large part of the total property loss.) The ominous possible parallel to New York was all too evident. Then, the Committee of Safety discovered that all three of New York City's militia battalions—Colonel John Lasher's, Colonel William Heyer's, and Colonel Abraham P. Lott's (not to be confused with Abraham Lott, the agent-victualer, his older, richer relative)—were in bad shape. To begin with, the soldiers were not properly armed or equipped. Militiamen were supposed to bring or buy their own muskets and provide themselves with ammunition—at least as many lead balls as the particular weapon could fire with a half-pound of gunpowder. But scores of the militiamen had no weapons at all, let alone powder and shot. The standard excuse—of some merit, admittedly—was that they could not find a gun for sale for less than the preposterously high price of four pounds. The musket shortage was partly artificial, and a British plot. Tryon, with the other royal governors, was hiring—or bribing—American gunsmiths to go to England for the duration of the conflict on terms so generous they were hard to resist. Tryon had persuaded three of New York's best craftsmen—John Woods, Thomas Allen, and William Tunx—to work for high wages in one of the royal armories. Each man had been given fifty guineas for passage and expenses—far more than the trip would actually cost. Tryon reported to Lord Dartmouth, optimistically, that the departure of these three New Yorkers, added to the successes the other governors had had, left America with only one first-class gunsmith. Although Tryon did not name him, he doubtless was thinking of Gilbert Forbes, whose place of business, the Sign of the Sportsman, was at 18 Broadway, not far north of Bowling Green. Tryon was wrong. There were many other first-class gunsmiths in America, including some, especially in eastern Pennsylvania, at least as good as Gilbert Forbes. Even so, the production of American guns was certain to remain small for a long time, and New York City did have only a few men besides Forbes who were capable of more than simple gun repairs.

The three militia colonels testified that a large number of the young men on their rolls, especially those who were well-to-do, did not want to serve. They were not turning out, which meant that a few men, most of them comparatively poor, were carrying a disproportionate share of each regiment's duties. Some of the companies were politically confused, perhaps actually pro-British. One company, for instance, had elected as its captain a man named Benjamin James, who had sometimes talked like an inimical. Like all militia captains, James was supposed to take the Association oath as a matter of routine on receiving his commission, and when he had refused, everybody realized that he meant what he had been saying. The tradition of political noninterference in militia elections was strong, and the Committee of Safety believed in it, but the James case seemed to warrant an exception. New York had ordered a new company election, taking it for granted that the militiamen did not want a confirmed inimical for their captain. The men voted again, and James won the second election. No one on the Committee was quite certain whether the vote was for James, the man, or against interference, or in favor of inimicality. There was also a rumor, never substantiated, that sixteen of Captain William Remsen's men were thinking of deserting to join the enemy's forces as soon as the British appeared. In the light of these scandals, the Committee of Safety decided that militia elections would have to be suspended for the time being—even at the cost of making militia service less popular than ever. In order to appoint militia officers, the Committee of Safety needed permission from the Continental Congress. The New Yorkers hated to write to Philadelphia and admit that they doubted the loyalty of freely elected militia officers, so the letter simply said, "We apprehend, for reasons too tedious to mention, great danger for want of a proper arrangement . . . for the appointment of officers," and so on. Apparently the reasons were not too tedious to have been talked about in Philadelphia. The Continental Congress immediately gave New York the authority it wanted.

About the same time, New York sustained a financial disappointment: the Continental Congress refused to lend the province 112,500 Continental dollars—the equivalent, perhaps, of 32,000 pounds. New York wanted the loan for immediate expenses connected with its war effort, and the rebuff meant that the province would have to issue 112,500 dollars of its own bills, backed by future tax collections anticipated all the way to March, 1778. The city's businessmen regarded such currency as a first step on the way to financial chaos, and New York had hoped that the Continent would grasp what New York saw so clearly: that one improvised currency—the Continental Congress' own Continental dollars—was plenty. Confusion about the exchange value of the Continental dollar was already great. Three and a half dollars were supposed to be worth one pound sterling, but British pounds were almost unobtainable at any price, as was true of all British money. Since there was no formal American money market, one man's guess about the real rate of exchange was as good as another's. New York had hoped that the Congress would make Continental dollars a national currency by lending them to all the provinces and arranging for ultimate repayment by each colony; and that some solid backing for the Continental money would be provided, apart from the Congress' assurance that the dollars would ultimately be redeemable in gold or sterling. Otherwise, as was happening, New York thought every colony would resort to the printing press and, like New York, issue bills of its own devising. The New Yorkers expected that some of the other provinces would not be sufficiently conscientious about backing their scrip. New York itself was far from proud of tax anticipation as a basis of finance, but it was something.

The New Yorkers' interest in sound money was shared by only a few of the delegates in Philadelphia. There were no bankers in the Continental Congress, because there were no American banks. The functions of banking, so far as they were carried out at all, were mostly incorporated in the subtle contracts that merchants, especially importers and exporters like those in New York, made constantly (in normal times) and then remade, discounted, and rediscounted. To those who earned their livelihood in other ways, like farming, finance was as incomprehensible as it was uninteresting. In rejecting New York's request for the loan, the Continental Congress showed how little it understood what the New York delegation had tried to explain. No reflection on New York's credit was intended, it said, but if the Continent agreed to lend New York money, it might have to do as much for all the other provinces.

Money troubles began, to no one's surprise, as soon as the first New York dollars were issued, not long after the loan was refused. The militiamen were paid, and most of them preferred the new currency to not being paid at all, but the paper bills horrified New Yorkers who had money out on loan. They were counting on repayment, with interest, in English pounds, and they did not regard New York dollars as an adequate substitute. A number of lenders agreed among themselves to accept only

English money, which led, as they might have guessed, to debate in the Provincial Congress on a proposed debt moratorium. Action on the suggestion was postponed—the money-lenders, though few in number, were remarkably influential.

John Jay had a suggestion for helping the New York currency. Jay, a thirty-year-old lawyer, a King's College graduate, and the brand-new husband of William Livingston's daughter, Sarah, had a lively imagination. As a member of the New York delegation in Philadelphia, he had tried to explain the virtues of sound money to his colleagues from the other provinces; since he had not won that argument, he was ready to try another tack. If New York could actually collect the taxes it was anticipating, Jay argued, the New York dollars might maintain a good deal of their declared value. Jay said New York should accept goods, instead of sterling, in payment of taxes. He suggested that the Provincial Congress make a list of all the things its war effort needed most—saltpeter, yarns, and some manufactured articles, to begin with—and announce a tax-barter plan, which would not only provide something of substance behind the New York money, but would also provide New Yorkers with an incentive to start making things instead of sitting around complaining about shortages. Manufacturing establishments might start up, Jay added, and they could provide jobs for the unemployed, whose numbers had steadily increased during New York's shut-down as a port. But Jay's scheme was too daring for the moderate men who dominated the Provincial Congress; the majority thought it would be wiser to go slowly, and to give the New York dollars a trial. The printing and engraving of the paper was of a high quality. Perhaps the money would be popular just because it was handsome.

Money was only one of the things on Jay's mind. He and his friend Alexander Hamilton, with some others, had discovered

that Governor Tryon, his Council, and his friends were planning
to hold new elections for the New York Assembly. Hamilton
had noticed that on January 2, instead of proroguing the Assembly, and thus continuing its technical life in adjournment, as
Tryon had been doing at the correct intervals since June, the
Governor had dissolved it. Dissolution, Hamilton reminded
Jay, was the legal prelude to new elections. The procedure had
almost been forgotten because the last Assembly elections, for
seven-year terms, had been held in 1769. Hamilton's suspicions
were correct. The scheduled year to elect a new Assembly had
come, and Tryon planned to hold elections and convene the
traditional colonial legislature on February 14. The Governor
hoped that by making as little as possible of the election, and by
keeping the vote small, New York's conservative voters would
be able to fill the Assembly with Crown supporters. Then, as a
kind of mirror-image of the Provincial Congress, and by taking
contrary action whenever the Provincial Congress passed a resolution, the Assembly might add considerable confusion to the
already confused New York scene.

Jay and Hamilton, fearing that Tryon's attempt to ruin the
Provincial Congress' hard-won authority might be treated
almost as a joke, decided to meet Tryon head on. If they could
publicize the Assembly elections and turn out a big New York
vote, they thought they could elect a considerable number of pro-
Association men to the Assembly, perhaps enough to dominate
the debates. At Jay's urging, the Committee of Safety quickly
printed a circular for distribution to all the county committees
explaining Tryon's scheme and urging the Associators to take
the Assembly elections with great seriousness. The local committees were asked to put up their very best pro-Association candidates and to work hard for their election. And, with that in
mind, the New York County Committee met on January 17 at

Mrs. Vandewater's Tavern, just east of the Commons, and nominated an extremely strong New York County ticket: Jay himself, Philip Livingston, John Alsop, and Colonel Alexander McDougall. All the candidates were proven vote-getters. Jay, Livingston, and Alsop were already delegates to the Continental Congress and the Provincial Congress. And in the New York Assembly elections they could be expected, as moderates, to attract quite a few borderline votes from Tryon's nominees without losing the radicals' support; the radicals would have no place else to go. McDougall was considerably more radical than the three others, and although some New Yorkers still thought he should have gone to Canada, his prestige as a leader was expected to stand him in good stead with middle-of-the-road voters. He was the ranking soldier in town, and a man with a reputation for getting things done.

In the midst of these political maneuvers, New York heard a report of such gravity that no one could think of anything else. The report said that the American Army in Canada, made up to a large extent of New Yorkers, had suffered a terrible defeat. Sam Smith, a postrider, who came into New York on January 16, brought the first account of the tragedy. Smith had been in Poughkeepsie, where he had spoken to Sergeant Edward Antil, who was on his way from Quebec, where the disaster had occurred, to Philadelphia, to report to the Continental Congress and try to get some help for the battered survivors of General Montgomery's force. As Smith repeated what Antil had told him, Montgomery had attacked Quebec on the last day of December. The British, commanded by Sir Guy Carleton, had not only beaten off the American attack, but had inflicted heavy losses on the Americans. Montgomery was dead, hit by a burst of musket and cannon fire. (Antil had seen him fall.) Montgomery's two aides, Captain John Macpherson and Captain

Jacob Cheesman (who had commanded the 5th Company of New York City's own First New York, and whose family owned a shipyard on the East River), were both dead. Colonel Benedict Arnold, who had struggled through the forests with his New England forces to meet Montgomery at Quebec, had been badly wounded in the assault. Colonel John Lamb's artillery, a New York City outfit, had suffered many casualties, and Lamb himself, along with Lieutenant John McDougall, Colonel McDougall's oldest son, had been taken prisoner. (A younger McDougall boy, Ranald, had been captured five weeks earlier at St. Johns.) These details were all Smith had, and they were not only bad but stunning, since previous reports of Montgomery's campaign had all been excellent. As Montgomery's column had advanced from Ticonderoga to Montreal and then beyond, his rapid pace alone had suggested a string of marvelous victories. Two of the New York newspapers on the presses when Smith rode in contained grotesquely cheerful stories still to be published: both Loudon's *Packet,* dated January 18, and Gaine's *Mercury,* in its January 22 issue, printed excerpts from a bold letter that Montgomery had written Carleton on December 6 from just outside Quebec's walls—an attempt to frighten the British into surrendering. If the earlier dispatches from Canada had been more candid, or more complete, New Yorkers might have understood that Carleton's weaknesses, rather than Montgomery's strengths, had explained the speed of the initial American advance. Furthermore, before the attack, after the Americans had reached the fortress city of Quebec, Carleton's army had gained in strength while Montgomery's and Arnold's weaknesses had grown. There had been no miraculous improvement in the capabilities of Montgomery's troops. The New York City men, for instance, who had looked woebegone as they embarked in September, still looked woebegone as they marched from Montreal to Quebec in December. Montgomery, in a private letter, described them as "the sweepings of the . . . streets"—a harsh truth.

Montgomery had been beset by countless other troubles: savage rivalries among units from different provinces, wrangling among his subordinate officers, and an almost total breakdown of his supply system. He had not had the equipment his men needed. He had not had the money for their pay. In December, Montgomery had found himself, like Washington, pleading with his soldiers to stay. In this respect, at least, the New Yorkers had given him a happy surprise, for they were almost the only ones who agreed to do so. Arnold's column had been reduced to six hundred of his original eleven hundred New Englanders by the hardships of the march from Newburyport, Massachusetts. During the last leg of Montgomery's approach, from Montreal to Quebec, his strength had fallen to fewer than four hundred men—the other two thousand were sick or had walked away from the war and gone home. With a few exceptions, the men Montgomery had led in the assault were the loyal "sweepings" who belonged to the First New York and to Lamb's artillery. New York City had no way of knowing how many men were dead or wounded or taken prisoner. Families and friends of the men in the expedition—except those who had already had tragic news—would have to wait in dreadful suspense for an indefinite period of time. There were no official casualty lists; there was no system for notifying next of kin, nor even any regular postal system between Canada and New York.

The idea that Montgomery was dead was unthinkable. New York had needed its own military hero, and had fixed on Montgomery as the man. People who had never laid eyes on him felt his death as a personal loss. Montgomery's brief career in America—he had arrived only in 1772—had been so promising

that its sudden end seemed a betrayal. When Montgomery had
come to New York, he had intended to put military life behind
him. His sixteen years' service as a career officer in the British
Army—he had entered it, at twenty, after his graduation from
Trinity College, Dublin—had ended in a disappointment, and
he had sold his captaincy in the 17th Regiment of Foot because
he had failed to get a majority, even though he had raised the
money to pay for it, and his record, he felt, should have entitled
him to a preference. He had come to New York and had bought
a farm just off the Post Road not far north of the King's Bridge.
(Some of Montgomery's sixty-five acres now lie beneath the
waters of the Jerome Park Reservoir.) He had lived there only
until July, 1773, when he had married Janet Livingston, Judge
Robert R. Livingston's oldest daughter, and the young people
moved to a much larger farm at Rhinebeck, in Dutchess County,
close to Judge Livingston's magnificent estate, Clermont. But
this prosperous marriage was only one of the reasons that New
Yorkers had assumed Montgomery would, in due course, become one of the province's leading figures. Montgomery had
been a most attractive man, remarkably good-looking, intelligent
and charming. He had been elected a Dutchess County delegate
to the Provincial Congress, and had served for two months.
That had been long enough to persuade Montgomery that, little
as he liked soldiering, he preferred it to politics and long-
winded speeches; at his first opportunity, he had joined the New
York forces.

The city was still dazed by the news from Quebec—and
dreading the further reports to come—when, as it awoke on the
morning of January 18, it learned that during the night almost
all its cannon had been spiked. The city had collected about
three hundred guns and had moved them with great labor to

three gun parks in Westchester—one at the King's Bridge and the others two miles east of there, near the Bronx River—where they were thought to be safe. Most of the pieces were small and in need of some repair. Many had been the private property of New York shipowners, and had last seen service on privateering cruises during the French and Indian War. Still, they were nearly all the artillery New York had—or had had, for, apparently, they were ruined.

Who could have done it? The British—perhaps a party of sailors or marines off the warships—were immediate suspects. Could it have been the work of New York inimicals? Whoever had done the deed had put a complete stop to the city's rough defense plan, which envisioned using some of the guns, after repairs, to keep the British from approaching Manhattan from the north by way of the two side-by-side bridges across the Harlem River—the Philipse family's privately owned King's Bridge, which had given the neighborhood its name, and the comparatively new Free Bridge a few hundred yards distant. (The Free Bridge, built in 1759, by public subscription, was the only other bridge across the Harlem River's whole length. The Free Bridge had been designed to break the Philipses' long-standing toll-collecting monopoly, and it had done so. By 1776, both bridges were toll-free. The Philipse family, despite its loss of income, seemed to be managing extremely well.) Exactly where the other guns were to go was not decided. Some of them, undoubtedly, were needed at the southern end of the island, perhaps in batteries at the ends of the many city streets that ran to the waterfront. That question now seemed academic, however; on first inspection, it looked as if the spikers had destroyed every gun worth destroying.

The Committee of Safety, with hardly a clue to start on, began to investigate immediately. No valuable evidence had been left at the scenes of the crime. From the bridges, going north and east, the Post Road zigzagged up a steep ascent, meandered across the rolling high ground, and then dropped down again into the Bronx River's pretty valley. Some of the spiked cannon were parked on the Williams farm on the east bank. (The Post Road crossed the river on what was known as Williams's Bridge.) Other guns were on the Valentine farm, on the west bank. (Isaac Valentine's house, now called the Varian Homestead, still stands; it is near Bainbridge Avenue and 208th Street at the edge of the Williamsbridge playground and it is now a museum of Bronx history.) Inspection of these and of the guns near the King's Bridge showed only that the saboteurs had known what they were about and had planned their project in advance. In addition to driving rocks into the muzzles of some—no great technological feat—they had spiked a good many with pronged steel plugs, which were not only more effective, but must have been custom-made for the purpose. Then, some of the cannons' touchholes, through which the fuse reached the powder charge, had been ruined with expert sledgehammer blows. Beyond these two deductions—which eliminated the possibility that the gun-spiking had been a spur-of-the-moment prank—the investigators were stumped. No one, it seemed, had seen or heard anything at any of the three parks. The City Watch, which served New York as a volunteer night guard, had been responsible for the guns' safety but knew nothing because its sentries had not been posted; and now that it was too late, everyone recalled that William Leary, the Town Major, had just testified that the City Watch was not to be trusted. Two days earlier, before the Committee of Safety, Leary had predicted some kind of disaster unless more, and better, men quickly volunteered for City Watch service. Most of the men had been coming from the independent militia battalions, but one City Watch officer, confirming Leary's criticism, had told the Committee of Safety that on a recent occasion some of his watchmen had looked like such ruffians that he had not dared tell them the night's countersign. "I did not think it prudent," he said.

Heard's men began arriving in the city January 18, the morning after the gun spiking. As his column was finally put together, it contained nearly six hundred New Jersey minutemen, half of them Stirling's detachment, led by Major William De Hart. They landed at the Whitehall Slip, and the British warships nearby—the *Asia*, the *Phoenix*, and a new arrival, the *Viper*, fired, but only a formal salute of blanks in honor of Queen Charlotte's thirty-second birthday. Loudon's *Packet* had warned the city that this might happen, so no one was frightened. The next day, January 19, when the New Jersey troops were all ashore, the whole force headed up the Bowery, along the Post Road, and east to Horn's Hook, on the East River. (Horn's Hook, its projecting shoreline concealed by the East River Drive, is now part of Carl Schurz Park.) With flags flying and drums beating out the cadence, the march looked and sounded like a New Jersey parade, but the British warships took no notice of the movement and did nothing to interfere with it. From Horn's Hook, Heard led his men, by ferry, over to Hallett's Point. (Hallett's Point, in Astoria, is now part of the site of a large housing development, the Astoria Houses.) While the march to Queens was going on, the Committee of Safety made a gesture of good will toward Tryon and the three-ship fleet. William Allen, the shoemaker, was given a pass to visit the warships, as he had been requested to do, and teach the British sailors and marines how to make shoes.

Heard advanced in an orderly manner, relying on a copy of the December 6 voting record for the names of the inimicals he was to seek, and establishing collection points first in one village and then the next, leaving a small detachment of soldiers in each. His men fanned out from these local headquarters to search for the delinquents, starting by calling at their homes. Nothing could have been simpler. Most of the men were farmers, and most of them were at work on their farms. Considering the defiant tone of their manifesto, they seemed, on the whole, curiously affable. Heard had a bargain to offer: if, on arrest, a Queens delinquent would turn in his weapons and sign the standard Association loyalty oath, he would be released immediately and allowed to go on about his business. Every one of the 788 who could be found accepted these terms, and without any violence. This was true even in Hempstead, supposedly the most inimical town in the county. The Hempstead men came into the collection point by themselves carrying their weapons with them, before the soldiers had time to make any arrests. They waited patiently in line to give their names and addresses to Heard's men, who ticketed each gun in order to know, later, who had turned in what. After seeing Hempstead's tractability, Heard decided his force was twice as big as necessary. He sent De Hart and Stirling's three hundred men back to New Jersey.

Within two days, Heard's men had collected more than three hundred delinquents' guns. Within two weeks, they had disarmed most of the 788. They were holding nineteen of the twenty-six ringleaders. (Heard was not allowed to offer them any bargain release.) Heard's tally was not quite perfect, partly because the voting record contained a number of errors. And seven of the most dangerous twenty-six could not be found at all. Still, in Heard's judgment, Queens had been brought under control, so he wrote to the Continental Congress and asked for further orders.

One of the faults with Heard's list of Queens inimicals was

that it was out of date. The records had not been corrected to take account of changes since December 6. For instance, Captain Jacob Mott of Cow Neck (now Manhasset) was still listed as a delinquent, although he had gone to great trouble to secure his restoration. Mott did not deny that he had voted the wrong way on December 6, but, he had explained later, he had not, at that time, given enough thought to the "ill consequence" of not sending a Queens delegation to the new Provincial Congress. By January, Mott had said, he had realized that the elections were "highly necessary for the preservation of American liberty." Benjamin Sands, chairman of the Association's Cow Neck Committee, had certified that Mott really had had a complete change of heart. The New York Committee of Safety was satisfied, and had restored him. It had given Mott a signed certificate of restoration to display in case anyone doubted him. Shortly after Mott returned to Cow Neck with this certificate, Heard's men arrested him. Since Heard knew nothing about certificates of restoration, and assumed his list was accurate, he did not see how he could turn Mott loose. And, when Heard asked the Committee of Safety what to do, the Committee failed Mott miserably. It confirmed his statement that he had been restored, but added that Heard ought not to release Mott unless Heard felt sure that Mott had not misbehaved in the time since his restoration— a matter of less than one week. Heard had no idea what Mott had been doing in the past several days, and no time to find out. So he kept Mott under arrest, waiting until some responsible higher authority could decide the case.

A few other names appeared on Heard's list through accident or misunderstanding. One was Joseph French, of Jamaica, who had been listed among the twenty-six inimical ringleaders in Queens. French had been summoned to testify with the others but had not answered his summons. He had not voted in favor of a new election on December 6, even though he had been a member of the Provincial Congress during the previous session, but he had not voted against it, either—at least that was his story—because he had been sick in bed throughout the month and had not voted at all. French's friends and associates realized that French might very well have voted no if he had been well enough to go to the polls, but that could not be proved. Heard's list also erred in the other direction—it was short a few names, no doubt, just because the men had not declared themselves on December 6. Furthermore, the seven missing men of the infamous twenty-six could hardly be forgotten about just because no one knew how to find them. Captain Richard Hewlett, of Rockaway, was in that category, along with his friends Jacob Norstrant, Isaac Denton, Jr., and John Smith. Finding these men was, in fact, a major concern, for if the Provincial Congress had been correctly informed, these four had several cannon, small arms, and a substantial amount of ammunition, all from the *Asia,* hidden in the marshy lands along Long Island's southern shore—a landscape pierced by countless inlets, streams, and creeks, and so wild in its desolation that it could easily conceal several regiments. The suspicion arose that Heard's fine effort had disarmed only the willing, and had let the determined men get away. One of Heard's soldiers wrote his family in New Jersey how easy the mission had been. But he added that inimicality in Queens had not been exaggerated. The Queens inimicals, he said, had been expecting war with Connecticut, and considered that yielding peaceably to New Jersey was a way out.

When Heard's request for further orders reached the Continental Congress, no one in Philadelphia knew what to say. Heard, for his part, did not know how to dispose of his nineteen prisoners, including Mott. For want of a better idea, he decided to take them to Philadelphia. They were as cooperative a lot of dangerous men as any guard could ask. Before they started on the trip, on February 3, Heard made them all promise not to escape, and they were as good as their word. The group arrived intact on February 6, but the Continental Congress, not at all sure who the nineteen were, or what, exactly, they were supposed to have done, and having no prison facilities, was sorry to see them. After a few days, the Congress decided that the pertinent records, with the evidence against the Queens men, must be in the files of the New York Provincial Congress. It ordered Heard to take his captives, including Mott, to New York City, leave them there under whatever detention arrangements seemed suitable, find out the exact charges against them, and report back to Philadelphia.

Heard got the nineteen to New York with as little trouble as he had had in bringing them to Philadelphia. On February 10, to his relief, the Committee of Safety agreed to take responsibility for the Queens men and their cases. Mott was even more relieved than Heard because, in view of his special history, the Committee of Safety let him go home right away on his "promise parole"—meaning that he swore to appear before the Committee of Safety or the Provincial Congress if either should ask him.

As for the others, the Committee of Safety ordered them to rent a house in the city, at their own expense, and to stay in it, under a guard that Colonel Lasher was to furnish, but that they were to pay for, until the Provincial Congress reassembled. The Committee felt that the disposition of the eighteen was something the full Provincial Congress had better decide—particularly since the Continental Congress, whose officer had made the arrests, was involved, however reluctantly. The Provincial Congress should be functioning again soon. By the tenth of February, the new session was ten days late, but only a few men short of a quorum. (The shortage showed how Queens and Richmond, by dragging their feet, could keep the Provincial Congress from getting to work.) Meanwhile, the eighteen men could do nothing except wait. Their crime had been opposing a new session. Now they found themselves wishing that the new session would begin with a minimum of delay, so the Provincial Congress could act on their cases.

Colonel Heard deserved praise for his quiet success in Queens, and, under other circumstances, New York undoubtedly would have given it to him. But the city was distracted by General Lee, who in mid-January was assembling his expeditionary force near Stamford. Lee himself had arrived there not long after the first of his troops. Almost immediately—at about the time Heard was starting to make arrests—Lee had been forced to go to bed with an attack of gout. His pain was intense, and he could scarcely move his legs. Lee's presence so near the city worried New Yorkers, especially since his men, who were busy drilling, were clearly preparing for military action. Some New Yorkers said that Lee's illness was a fraud, although no one could explain what advantage he might be gaining by malingering. Others held that he intended to annoy the British warships and goad them into firing again—and so destroy New York by proxy. A third theory—which did not exclude the second—was that Lee had his own private list of New York "Tories," an index with more names than any other list so far, and that he meant to hunt them down. This last rumor seemed believable, not to mention horrifying, because a number of New Yorkers, through private letters, had been informed that Lee, recruiting in Connecticut, had told potential volunteers about the delights of "catching and swearing" the King's friends, almost as if it were a new field sport. Isaac Sears, whom Lee had made adjutant of the expedition, with the rank of lieutenant colonel— a splendid start for a civilian without any previous army experience—had been particularly graphic about the New York "conspirators" and the dangers they posed.

Neither Lee nor anyone else in his command could have told New York their plans, for they had none. Lee had learned of the New York resolutions on troops from outside the province and wondered, in view of the Continental Congress' action, whether he could enter New York without a formal invitation. Whatever he was about to do, Lee's recruiting campaign had made his purposes sound too exciting. Some of his recruits were certain to be disappointed. One improvised twenty-four-man cavalry troop, for instance, which called itself "the Gentlemen Horse Volunteers of Hartford," believed that it was going to help Lee burn New York City to the ground, and its members were looking forward to that appealing enterprise. Lee had not exactly promised them they would have the chance to burn the city, but when he had spoken at a rally at Hartford he had asked for help in suppressing "a dangerous conspiracy" in New York, without describing the conspiracy or naming any of the conspirators. Just at that time, as luck had had it, Hartford was buzzing with a rumor that the New York Provincial Congress, despite all its declarations of loyalty to the Association, was actually pro-British, and that the Congress itself had been caught in the act of supplying the British armed forces at Boston. What other conspiracy, the Hartford gentlemen had thought, could Lee be talking about? None other. Burning the city seemed a minimal punishment. Having convinced themselves, and eager to help, the Hartford men had signed up. Most of them were middle-aged, well-to-do farmers and squires, who had outfitted themselves at their own expense and had

provided their own mounts—ordinary saddle horses without
cavalry training. The Hartford Volunteers had all arranged
their private affairs so they could be absent from Hartford for
two or three weeks, and they had agreed among themselves that
Colonel Thomas Seymour, the Connecticut Attorney-General,
should command the troop. Lee had seemed delighted to have
some cavalry along, and the outfit had ridden south with conspicuous élan. If the Horse Volunteers were weak in military
prowess, they were marvelously strong on rank. Besides
Seymour, there was another colonel as well as six captains and
one lieutenant—nine officers commanding fifteen enlisted men.
That was a trifle unusual, but any cavalry unit was a rarity
among the American forces, and impressive for that reason
alone.

Lee had not asked New York's permission to enter the
province—he had neglected to correspond with New York at all.
The Committee of Safety had also had no word from Washington about Lee's plans, despite the Commander-in-Chief's usual
diligence in keeping everyone informed. An outright violation
of the January 2 resolutions would not have been more disturbing than the doubts these silences raised.

While New York worried, Lee struggled with his gout, and
his foot soldiers practiced close-order marching. Their total
number was about twelve hundred—considerably fewer than the
ten thousand Lee had boasted he would raise. And the majority,
after all, were not exactly volunteers, but Connecticut militiamen. Most of the men who did not belong to Waterbury's
regiment belonged to Colonel Andrew Ward's. It was Trumbull's instructions to join Lee, not Lee's or Sears's inspirational
oratory, that had brought them out.

Waterbury, the ranking commander during Lee's illness, was
doing an excellent job of getting the men ready for action,

despite his handicap of not knowing what sort of action was contemplated. He was fitting the minority of new men into old companies, trying to give each soldier a sense of belonging to a unit he could recognize on the field, and practicing the fundamentals of drilling and shooting that ought to be useful under almost any circumstances. Waterbury was hoping for a Continental appointment and, perhaps, a promotion to general officer —both, in his opinion, long overdue. He had left the Canadian expedition after commanding a Connecticut regiment at St. Johns and Montreal because he felt his services had not received adequate recognition. His new burst of activity, combined with his renewed ambitions, put him in a good temper.

After a week, the New York Committee of Safety was unable to stand the suspense, and on January 21 it wrote Lee, asking for some official word about his plans. The Committee explained that it was taking the liberty of inquiring because it was concerned for those New York City residents who were frightened by rumors that Lee was thinking of entering New York Province with a considerable body of men for "active service" in the city. Of course, the Committee continued, it knew that such apprehensions were foolish, for if Lee were actually preparing to enter New York on active service, his entrance would have been preceded by "some intimations to us on the subject from the Continental Congress, General Washington, or yourself." Then the Committee listed the reasons that Lee ought to stay where he was. First, the expense to those New York families who were already fleeing the town in fright, and the shortage of places for New Yorkers to go. There was the danger that "hundreds" might perish, given the terrible weather, for lack of shelter. Furthermore, the Committee reminded Lee, New York had less than three tons of gunpowder on hand, and the city had practically no fortifications. (No mention was made of the fact that the city's cannon had been spiked.) The Committee suggested that hostilities with the British men-of-war be put off until March at the earliest. Finally, the Committee asked that if Lee really meant to enter New York with a large body of troops, would he wait where he was long enough to explain his reasons for doing so?

Inconsistent as the letter was in its requests, it did make one point plain—that the Committee feared the mere sight of a large-scale troop movement into the city would be enough to touch off another naval bombardment. The most interesting omission was the lack of a reference to the January 2 resolutions. The Committee had not forgotten about them. It was restraining itself because some of its members believed that Lee must be acting with General Washington's complete backing. New York was really asking for information, moreover—although it knew more than it pretended—and there was no sense in opening the discussion with Lee as if New York were in the last stages of a dispute with him.

Lee understood that the January 2 resolutions had damaged, if not destroyed, the validity of his old orders. He had received no new instructions from Cambridge. All he could do now was scheme to restore status to his project. From his sickbed, he dispatched a set of four remarkably clever letters. The first was addressed to John Hancock, as President of the Continental Congress. Lee described his plans for New York in detail and with enthusiasm. First, he told Hancock, he was going to disarm all the "manifestly disaffected" New Yorkers, require them to deposit, as security for their future good behavior, a sum equal to at least half their total worth, and force them to take "the strongest possible" loyalty oath. Lee added that he realized the oath device left something to be desired; a disaffected person might swear falsely, no matter what the penalties. Still, Lee declared, he could separate the "desperate fanatics" (those who refused to take the oath) from the "reclaimable" citizens (those who agreed to take the oath), although that seemed to ignore his own insight that the boldest inimicals might acquire a sheen of reclaimability by swearing falsely. Not a moment could be lost, Lee went on, because the British were going to attack New York right away. He not only had a deserter's word for it, but all his other intelligence confirmed his prediction. Then, in a generous spirit, Lee said that the New Yorkers probably did not know the British attack was imminent, so their complacency might be excused as ignorance. However, Lee continued, he was marching at once, taking only "one division" of his force with him—just enough men to "secure the city" against the enemy's immediate designs. He closed the letter by saying that he hoped, when he got to the city, he would find awaiting him a letter from the Continental Congress that would give him the authority to be there.

Some of Lee's mistakes in that letter may have been honest. The General may have believed that he could identify New York's manifestly disaffected persons. But he did not know—not for certain, at any rate—that the British were going to attack New York immediately. He had talked to one British deserter, who, like most deserters, had known next to nothing. Otherwise, Lee's information about the British intentions was no better than the Continental Congress' or New York City's. Optimism is a military virtue, but Lee was misleading Hancock by saying that just one of his divisions (Lee meant something like one-half of his total force, not a military unit of a particular size) could protect New York against a British attack—as if his intelligence also included the size of the British attacking force. Lee's use of the word "secure" implied some scheme for coping with the British warships in New York harbor. He had none.

Lee's second letter was to Robert Morris, of Philadelphia. Morris—no relation to the New York Morrises of Morrisania—was Lee's friend and admirer, an ardent Associator, and an important member of the Pennsylvania Assembly's Council of Safety. He was a merchant trader and a financial expert, and for some time he had been helping Lee manage his private business affairs. (Morris had Lee's power of attorney, and with it he had just arranged the purchase of an estate for Lee in the Shenandoah Valley.) Most of Lee's letter was devoted to a harangue—the last thing Morris needed—against Pennsylvania's cautious attitude toward independence. Lee's first few sentences were interesting because they showed that he was aware of the poppycock in his letter to Hancock: ". . . I have written a long and indeed presumptuous letter to the Congress. I beg you will be one of my advocates if it is taken in this light—nothing but zeal should have forc'd me upon it but their complacency to the Provincial Congress will I am afraid be in the end fatal—New York will be one day or the other the Ministry's. . . ."

Later the same day, January 23, Lee got around to answering the New York Committee of Safety. This third letter was addressed to Peter Van Brugh Livingston, who was presiding over the Committee of Safety. It was polite and, on its surface, conciliatory, but it was anything but reassuring. Lee apologized for not having told New York that he was marching to the city. His excuse was that he had thought the Continental Congress had done so. (He managed to imply that he had got his orders from Philadelphia.) Lee denied—something the Committee had not even brought up in its letter—that his business "was to commence active hostilities against the men of war in your harbor." General Washington's only motive for detaching him, Lee explained, was to prevent the British from taking up military posts in New York City or from lodging themselves on

Long Island. (That read as if Lee had up-to-date orders from Cambridge.) He said that, in "compliance with" New York's request, he was bringing only a minimum force with him—"just strong enough to secure it against any designs of the enemy"— and leaving "the main body" on the western frontiers of Connecticut. Lee, contradicting himself immediately, admitted that there were "some subordinate purposes" in his mind, but added that they were "much more proper to communicate by word of mouth than by writing." (If he meant Tory-hunting, he had just written Hancock all his plans.) And, as for the danger of reaction by the British warships, Lee insisted that the British did not want to destroy New York City: "The seaport towns are the only holds they have in America; they are considered as the pledges of servitude; the menacing destruction to them may indeed be of admirable use, but the real destruction of them must extinguish all hopes of success."

It was not a bad argument, but it had already been refuted by the destruction of Falmouth and Norfolk.

On the following day, January 24, Lee wrote the fourth letter in the set, a report to General Washington in which he enclosed copies of everything, except his letter to Morris, along with the Committee of Safety's letter to Lee. He remarked "that this last breathed the very essence of the spirit of procrastination . . . It is woefully hysterical."

Lee's report to Washington implied, as had his letter to Hancock, that he was as good as on his way. Only in writing to Washington did Lee mention the January 2 resolutions:

. . . I conclude I shall receive the orders of the General Congress [Continental Congress] before, or immediately on my arrival, otherwise I should not venture to march into the Province, as by the late resolve every detachment of the Continental troops is to be under the direction of the Provincial Congress in which they are—a resolve,

I must say, with submission to their wisdom, fraught with difficulties and evils—it is impossible, having two sovereigns, that any business should be carried on.

Most of Lee's men, at the time he wrote Washington, were still drilling at Stamford. Colonel Waterbury, with a few aides, was riding toward New York City, but the "first division" was not following, and Ward's regiment was about to be dismissed. The only troop movement involved a company or so of Waterbury's regiment, an advance guard, which was illegally crossing the New York border. It was not headed for the city, or even Manhattan Island, but only for Rye Neck. This violation of the January 2 resolves was deliberate and complete, but Lee's intruders were few in number, and the distance between Stamford and Rye was a mere ten or twelve miles. Lee thought that a modest infraction of the rules, if unchallenged, might set a precedent for a major transgression later on.

No one challenged Lee's advance guard. However, the General did not have to continue with his sneak invasion, because his first letter, to Hancock, worked perfectly. It was read out loud to the Continental Congress on January 26, and the delegates discussed a suitable response. They imagined, from the text, that Lee was already encamped on Manhattan Island, and that the violation of the January 2 resolves was, therefore, an accomplished fact. (So it was, but the movement had gone only as far as Rye Neck.) Most of the men in Philadelphia, like the members of the New York Committee of Safety, thought that Lee was acting under General Washington's specific, direct orders. That made them reluctant to rebuke Lee, lest a scolding addressed to him might seem to be a scolding meant for the Commander-in-Chief. And yet it was not like Washington to have ordered Lee to violate the Continental Congress' rules. Some of the delegates felt that when all the facts were known, a satisfactory answer to the puzzle would undoubtedly appear. No one even imagined the truth: that Washington, distracted by more serious concerns, had been paying almost no attention to the Lee expedition; that he was even more vague about the details than he had been earlier; and that, insofar as he had any opinion at all, he thought that Lee might well forget about his project. A long letter from Washington to Lee, sent on January 23 (crossing Lee's letter to Washington of the twenty-fourth), had said: ". . . As Congress seem to have altered their views in this instance [about landing the two Connecticut regiments on Long Island to support Heard], and the men which went with you to Connecticut are upon a very different footing from what I expected, it might be right to give Congress the earliest notice of your proceeding, and to disband your troops as soon as you think circumstances will admit of it."

After a loud, short debate, the Continental Congress reached a decision. Given its misconceptions, it acted sensibly. It appointed a special committee of three men to go to New York, see what was what, and do what it could to repair the damage that had been done to local pride and interprovincial relations. Colonel Benjamin Harrison, of Virginia, Thomas Lynch III, of South Carolina, and Andrew Allen, of Pennsylvania, were the men named. They were to leave as soon as possible and to meet with Lee and the New York Committee of Safety in New York City.

Lee received Hancock's letter containing this news on January 29. It was just what he wanted, and he was delighted. He took the designation of the meeting place as a Continental order to move from Stamford to New York. It was a sufficiently broad authorization, in Lee's opinion, to warrant his bringing his "first division" along with him. Lee had a copy of Hancock's letter made for General Washington to see—thinking, correctly, that it would be enough to change Washington's mind about disbanding Lee's troops.

The special committee's membership was much to Lee's liking. Lee knew that Harrison and Lynch, both good friends of General Washington, favored aggressive prosecution of the war, and he believed they would both despise New York's conduct as much as Lee did. It did not much matter, therefore, that Allen, a Philadelphian and the son of Pennsylvania's Chief Justice, was in favor of conciliation. Allen was bound to be outvoted by his fellow committee members.

Just as Lee's letter-writing plan was succeeding, and his expedition seemed to have acquired new life, his gout took a turn for the worse. He was in too much pain to ride a horse from Stamford to New York City. He had been worried about the ordeal even before his relapse, and his aides had tried to rig up a horse-drawn sleigh, but a premature thaw had melted the snow on the Post Road, and the ground, usually frozen solid in January, was on the point of turning to mud. The sleigh idea had been abandoned. Lee wanted to get to New York immediately, but his gout kept him in bed. He could, however, move his advance guard forward from Rye Neck to New Rochelle and then fill in the Rye Neck position with some of his other companies. By January 31, Lee had squeezed all but a few of Waterbury's men onto the soil of New York Province.

The New York Committee of Safety made no comment. It had reconciled itself to the inevitability of Lee's march into New York and had decided, therefore, that a "welcome" for the General would be "politic." It ordered Captain Leary's company of light horse to get ready to ride out to meet Lee and escort him into town whenever the General approached.

Harrison, Lynch, and Allen arrived in New York on January 30, and were astonished to learn that Lee was still in Connecticut. John Morin Scott and Colonel McDougall, representing the Committee of Safety, called on the three congressmen right away. The Committee of Safety wanted to assist in any way it could, and it would have been happy to set forth New York's side of the story before Lee got a word in. Harrison, Lynch, and Allen rejected the offer. It would be best, they said, for them to find out exactly when Lee would be available for a joint conference. The Committee of Safety need not get in touch with them; they would inform the Committee. Four days passed before Lee was well enough to make the trip to the city, and even then, on Sunday, February 4, he had to be carried most of the way on a stretcher. The day was gray and drizzly. Captain Leary's light horse, and a small reception committee of a few prominent citizens, met Lee at the King's Bridge and escorted him to Mrs. de la Montaigne's Inn, which overlooked the Commons from the west, and which was to serve as Lee's temporary headquarters. (The site is now 253 Broadway.) Though the official welcome was correct, the crowds of New Yorkers along the last few blocks of the route, the Bowery Road, were thin and anything but ecstatic.

Two weeks had passed since Lee's warning that the British attack on New York would come immediately. It looked as if the General's prediction was better than the intelligence on which it had been based, for the word from Washington's headquarters in Cambridge was that the British general Sir Henry Clinton had sailed from Boston on January 22 in the twenty-four-gun frigate *Mercury*. Washington was not sure, but headquarters thought Clinton might have as many as five or six hundred soldiers in his fleet. In any case, New York was to keep alert. On February 4, while Lee was getting settled at Mrs. de la Montaigne's, the New York lookouts at New Dorp, Staten Island, and Sandy Hook, New Jersey, spotted the *Mercury* and

one transport ship approaching New York Harbor. The watch-
man at a telescope on the roof of No. 1 Broadway got the visual
signal from the relay station on Staten Island's highest ground,
the hill behind the bluffs at the northern end of the island, now
part of St. George.

The news started another panic. By the time it was dark, New
York City was in turmoil, more agitated than at any time since
the night of August 23, when the *Asia* had fired on the city
to scold New York for stealing the British cannon from
Fort George. Men who had stayed on through all the earlier
alarms now lost their nerve. Clinton's arrival, combined with
anxiety about Lee's intentions, was more than they could bear.
They hurried to get out of town, along with men and women
who had fled before, or several times before, and had returned.
The result, as one letter writer later described it, was "a convul-
sion." The Sunday-night jam of wagons and carts heading for
the docks caused a greater traffic tieup than anyone could recall
—which was bad indeed, for New York suffered from chronic
traffic troubles, and neither Broadway nor Broad Street, the
widest of the city's thoroughfares, was big enough to accommodate the peaks of ordinary business-day demands. New
Yorkers lucky enough to find wagons got their possessions as far
as the waterfront, but only a few boats and boatmen were available at night. Piles of luggage, mixed with small pieces of
valuable furniture, were simply dumped on the wharves by
carters, who then tried to go back for second loads. Their way
back was blocked by streams of wagons coming toward them in
the narrow streets, especially on the East Side. By three o'clock
Monday morning, no vehicle of any size could move in any
direction.

Daylight was a comfort, and, to the city's surprise, there had
been no shooting or British action of any kind. Around noon,

Mayor Whitehead Hicks came back from the lower harbor in a small boat bearing incredibly good news. He had spoken to Clinton on board the *Mercury* and—if Clinton could be believed—there were no plans to attack New York City, at least not right away. Clinton did not have an army with him, only a few soldiers on board the accompanying transport. Clinton had said that he was simply sailing past the city on his way south and thought that he would visit his old friend, Governor Tryon. The Committee of Safety wanted to believe Hicks's report, but, nevertheless, it ordered the lookouts to remain vigilant. Clinton's assurances might be a ruse, and the horizon might be filled any minute with additional British ships.

As the hours passed and no more British ships appeared, New York gradually calmed down. Clinton's presence was both fascinating and galling. The General apparently had no fear at all for his personal safety, and, if Hicks's impression had been correct, Clinton was astonished to hear that he should not try to land on Manhattan Island, as he had planned to do. Small boats began to ply between the *Mercury* and the other British vessels as if New York Harbor were a British lake, and Clinton sailed over to pay his respects to Tryon. The Committee of Safety, unusually rattled, failed to prohibit traffic between the shore and Clinton's ship; and, before many hours had passed, numbers of New Yorkers—all of them men who were not worried about their political reputations—went down the bay by boat to talk to Clinton about one matter or another. The General, in his late thirties, was a good-looking man. He had a full, round face and large eyes set unusually far apart beneath thick black eyebrows. Clinton took himself with great seriousness, but on most subjects other than himself he had a fairly good sense of humor. He was an ardent violinist, and he was sensitive, intelligent, and—even with his good friends—somewhat aloof.

General Lee, meanwhile, acted as if Clinton and the *Mercury* did not exist. He went ahead with his own business, talking to individuals and to small groups of callers as fast as they could be ushered in and out of his temporary headquarters. Yet he was not ignoring the possibility of a British attack. If an attack came, Lee would command the city's defense, and he immediately raised his estimate of the men he might need from six hundred to five thousand. Lee ordered Waterbury to bring down the balance of "first division" from Westchester to Manhattan. He also called for his "second division," essentially Ward's regiment, which had just been dismissed. It was to reassemble, once again, and to march to the city on the double. Lee appealed to Lord Stirling, who was still at Elizabethtown, to pull together the balance of his regiment from New Brunswick and Amboy (now Perth Amboy) and move it across the Hudson as quickly as possible. Lee asked Colonel Samuel Drake, commander of the Westchester County Minutemen, to send down as many of his reservists as were available. And, on the assumption that these calls for help would actually produce the five thousand men he wanted, Lee asked the Committee of Safety to arrange for barracks room in town for that number. It was a staggering request. No count of the total number of beds in New York City was available, but at the last census, in 1771, the total number of inhabitants in the county had been 21,863—18,726 whites and 3,137 blacks. The increase in five years had added perhaps three thousand persons, but when one subtracted the number who lived north of the city limits, the town's normal accommodations did not add up to space for many more than twenty thousand. Yet, instead of saying that New York City could not possibly squeeze in five thousand extra men, McDougall and Scott told Lee that the Committee would do its best to comply. New York's prompt, cheerful acceptance of the next-to-impossible order not only surprised Lee but impressed him greatly.

In his hunt for additional troops, Lee gave no thought to the

Gentlemen Horse Volunteers of Hartford. They had been summarily dismissed, under confusing and unhappy circumstances. When, on February 1, the Volunteers, preceding Lee himself in the march on New York, clattered up to the King's Bridge, they had been met by Colonel Waterbury, who told Colonel Seymour that General Lee would not be needing the troop; the Hartford men could consider themselves dismissed and go home. Waterbury had no explanation. He was only doing, he said, what Lee had ordered him to do.

The Hartford Volunteers found it exceedingly difficult to disregard an order from Waterbury, the expedition's temporary, or acting, commander in New York. Yet, early that same morning, before the company had left Stamford, Seymour had spoken to Lee and received a definite impression—something not always easy to get in dealings with the mercurial General—that Lee was well pleased with the Hartford troop. For that reason, Seymour was positive that Waterbury was making a mistake. The Gentlemen Horse Volunteers conferred among themselves. Though they agreed with Seymour that Waterbury was in error, the troopers' feelings were hurt, and on the ground that Waterbury had to be obeyed, even when he was wrong, sixteen of the twenty-four men decided to do as they had been told. They wheeled about and set out for Hartford in a mood of self-righteous disappointment.

That left only eight horsemen, including Colonel Seymour. If they could no longer call themselves a troop, they remained Connecticut citizens, and, as a small group of individuals, there was nothing to prevent them from riding on into New York City; furthermore, Seymour, after the shock of having heard that the Gentlemen Horse troop was not wanted, had persuaded himself that the New York City conspirators might somehow have been responsible for his outfit's dismissal. He was confident that when Lee himself reached New York, the General would correct the error. Thus Seymour argued himself into thinking that it was his patriotic duty to disregard Waterbury's recommendation to go home. The least the eight Hartford men could do, Seymour felt, was to proceed to New York City and see, with their own eyes, just how terrible the place was.

So Seymour and his seven associates rode into town and waited, with everyone else, for Lee to make his appearance. The delay sobered them. By Monday morning, February 5, the Hartford men, though at least as fascinated as ever by the New York "conspiracy," had seen with their own eyes that New York was not what everybody in Hartford said. At last, moreover, they learned that, instead of setting fire to the city, Lee's expedition was supposed to protect it. But staying with Lee to help fight Clinton, if that proved necessary, did not interest them. At ten o'clock on the morning of the fifth, when three of the diehard eight, including Colonel Seymour, presented themselves at Mrs. de la Montaigne's, all they wanted was a confirmation of their dismissal—not that Waterbury had left any doubt about it—and the expense money they had been promised, according to their recollections.

General Lee was too busy to see them. They talked instead to William Palfrey, one of Lee's aides, and to Lieutenant Colonel Sears. The conversations were pleasant enough, and, by implication, Palfrey and Sears confirmed the dismissal: they wished Seymour and his friends "a pleasant ride" home. This, as Seymour wrote later, "we took for a formal dismission."

Seven of the eight, led by Colonel Seymour, soon started back for Hartford. The eighth, Captain Hugh Ledlie, stayed behind, hoping that eventually he would be able to see Lee and secure the General's signature on the expense sheets, a matter (including an estimate for the cost of the return trip) of 100 pounds 6 shillings, New York currency. On Thursday, February 8, one of Lee's aides told Ledlie that the General was still too busy to see him, and handed Ledlie a pair of letters. The first, addressed to Ledlie himself, turned down the request for expense money. It said that the General had understood that the Hartford Volunteers were to pay all their own expenses, except for rations, which they had already received from the Continental commissary. (This was true only of the trip down.) The second letter, addressed to the company as a whole, was, and remains, an oddity. It said,

Sɪʀ,

The Hartford Company of Volunteers were dismiss'd through a blunder. It was my intention to keep 'em. However, as it is too late to undo what has been done, it only remains that I should express the high sense I have of their zeal, activity, and spirit. I return them, therefore, with my sincerest thanks, and formally dismiss 'em for the present from any obligation of duty.

CHARLES LEE
Major General

On the whole, Lee's first week in New York was a success. From his hotel sickroom, he contrived to outshine his assorted rivals—Clinton, the British warships, the Continental Congressmen, and the Committee of Safety. For the few whose spirits were dashed, like the Hartford Volunteers, there were hundreds who responded to the General's leadership, and were inspired toward something like his own audacity. He had snapped New York out of its post-Canada shock, and he even created the happy and false impression that New York City was militarily defensible. In the process, the General and New York were both surprising each other. Lee had been unaware that New York's leaders were capable of anything as adroit as blocking Tryon's plan to pack the new Assembly. (Jay's stratagem had worked.

On February 1, at the open-air election meeting on the Commons, the New York County voters, in an unmistakable voice vote, had chosen the whole anti-Tryon slate of Jay, McDougall, Philip Livingston, and John Alsop.) New York City, for its part, had not expected that Lee would be capable of putting aside his obsession with swearing Tories in order to concentrate on fortifying the city. He could, and he did, and though no one in New York knew enough to appreciate his skill, his professional assessment of the area, considered as a number of battlefields, was masterly. Lee realized that the warships' guns made a degree of caution reasonable—although he himself continued to doubt that their captains would shoot unless the provocations were exceptional. But what pleased him most was the Committee of Safety's enthusiasm for going right ahead with fortifications. Lee had imagined that the New Yorkers were imagining that the warships would not tolerate such an effort.

Lee and the Committee of Safety agreed, right away, that little or nothing could be done to protect New York against a bombardment by British ships, but they did think, together, that Lee's five-thousand-man army—if it could ever be assembled—might be able to give a good account of itself, if it had good positions to defend. As Lee explained it to the New Yorkers, the key to the defense of their city was the high ground directly across the East River, Brooklyn Heights. There Lee planned a strong fortified camp for some three thousand men. He also sketched plans for gun positions at Horn's Hook and Hallett's Point. (The guns were to protect the ferry-crossing site, but, as it happened, the river there was so narrow that shore-based artillery might make the captain of a warship think twice before sailing past.) All this, combined with extensive minor entrenchments, barricades, and field fortifications, and in addition to the work that remained to be done at the Highlands, would require tens of thousands of hours of manual labor. To Lee's surprise, the Committee of Safety agreed that work should start immediately. When Lee wrote Washington on February 9, he described the New Yorkers as "men whose zeal and alacrity seem most fervent."

Whether the British would allow the Americans time to complete Lee's schemes—the Brooklyn Heights fortifications alone would take at least a month—was beyond knowing. At least Clinton had not lied in saying that he had no plans for an immediate attack on New York, but he had not told the whole truth, either. Clinton did have several nonsocial reasons for stopping at New York that he had not fully explained, although he was candid to the point of recklessness in telling what he meant to do in the South. He was on his way to attack North Carolina. Clinton believed that a powerful expeditionary force— six regiments of eight hundred men apiece, and ten men-of-war accompanying the transports—had sailed from Ireland and would soon be approaching Cape Fear. He expected to join his army and lead it ashore, and he hoped that he would promptly be joined by thousands of back-country North Carolinians who would help him restore the colony to British control. Clinton had wanted to talk to Tryon about that. He had hoped the former Governor of North Carolina could assure him—as Tryon now had done—that pro-British sentiment was really strong among the North Carolina Highlanders, families that had mostly come from Scotland. (A lot of bad news had not yet reached Clinton. The powerful expeditionary force, led by General Lord Cornwallis and Admiral Peter Parker, was still in the harbor at Cork. Delays of one kind or another had put it some two months behind schedule. On the other hand, the North Carolina Highlanders, in response to orders from Governor

Josiah Martin, Tryon's successor, had already risen. The High-landers were assembling near Cross Creek [Fayetteville today]. But there were only fifteen hundred of them—far fewer than Clinton was hoping for—and they were no match for the com-bined strength of the First, Second, and Fourth North Carolina Regiments, which were moving into position to put down the premature rebellion against the rebellion.)

Then, too, while Clinton had no immediate thought of attack-ing New York City, he thought that such an attack might well be his next assignment, after he had completed his Southern campaign; and so he was on a reconnaissance for future refer-ence. A question in his mind was whether a landing on Long Island, with Brooklyn Heights as its objective, would be a better approach to the city than a landing at the northern end of Manhattan, somewhere near King's Bridge. Clinton remem-bered the landscape from his boyhood. He had lived in New York for six years, during his father's ten-year term as Royal Governor. But his memories needed brushing up. He was sorry he could not walk over all the ground, but his observations were encouraging. Either one of the approaches, in Clinton's estimate, should do nicely. He thought that New York City was a marvelously easy military prize.

Clinton's third reason for stopping at New York was fanciful and secret: he dreamed of making himself famous by negotiat-ing a peace—in which case New York might not have to be captured at all. Clinton had no authority to work for peace, and no real plan in mind, but he was putting unrealistic hopes in a meeting he had scheduled with another self-appointed peace agent, a Scot who had been living in America, sometimes in New York and sometimes in New Jersey, for eight years, and who called himself Lord Drummond. (Drummond claimed the Earldom of Perth, as had his father before him. The last earl in the direct line of descent had died, an attainted Jacobite in France, and Drummond was indeed next in line in a younger branch of the family.) Drummond, who was in his early thirties, had been working on his conciliation scheme for a year and a half. Considering the lack of means at his disposal, his achievements had been considerable: a number of distinguished men, Clinton included, thought that Drummond might have a clue to a resolution of the troubles by negotiation. Independence-minded Americans, later on, suggested that Drummond's dabbling in conciliation was self-serving—an attempt to ingratiate himself with the Ministry and so improve his chances of getting his right to the title recognized and the Perth properties restored, but they had no proof of that. Whatever Drummond's motives, he said he knew for certain what would be acceptable peace terms: Each of the American colonies would agree to contribute a specific sum to the common defense; each colony would raise its contribution by internal taxation as it saw fit; and, in response, Great Britain would then waive Parliament's right to tax America. Drummond was working to persuade the Continental Congress to send an American peace commission to London to work out the details of such a bargain.

Since George III was as interested in raising money as in defending principles, Drummond's formula was not entirely ridiculous—and it was not original, either, since many other men had made similar suggestions. (For instance, the Drummond plan was close to the Provincial Congress' position paper as of midsummer, 1775, written to inform the delegates in Philadelphia about New York's thinking.) Drummond interested men who listened to his story, because he insisted that the North Ministry (secretly) and a substantial section of the Continental Congress (even more secretly) were already prepared to negotiate peace along the lines he suggested. Drummond said he had found out about the British position on a trip he had made to London in February, 1775, and he claimed to have a memorandum from Lord North describing acceptable terms in detail and including, among several British offers, the idea of scattering the British Army throughout the colonies instead of keeping it concentrated at New York, Boston, or anywhere else. The thought of lots of little British garrisons, each helpless by itself and each, therefore, a hostage for the Ministry's good intentions, would appeal to any American. Then, during August, Drummond had been in Boston, on the British side of the lines. He had talked to Major General James Robertson, one of General William Howe's staff officers. Robertson, as Drummond told it, had encouraged Drummond to keep on with his conciliation mission, and, in general, had reflected General Howe's well-known optimism about negotiations. From Boston, Drummond had traveled to New York City and, looking for someone to help him with his work, had approached his friend, Andrew Elliott. Elliott was the Crown's Customs Collector for the Port of New York—though of course, since the Association had imposed an embargo on trade, he had had no customs to collect—and his brother, Sir Gilbert, had a place in the North Ministry. While waiting for his situation to clarify, Elliott had been living quietly in his mansion, off the Bowery Road. He was well-to-do and well liked, and the many New Yorkers who counted him as their friend did not expect him to pretend enthusiasm for the American cause. All the Crown officers who had decided to stay in town—the remaining members of the Governor's Council, the judges, the mayor, the scores of others who worked part- or full-time for the British government—were, like Elliott, accorded a certain polite immunity from harassment; the difficulties of their positions were understood; they were given credit for staying at their posts instead of fleeing the country; they were allowed to come and go as they chose; and they were reasonably safe—so far, at least—from arrest or mistreatment of any sort. But the other side of the tacit arrangement was that none of them should act against or do harm to the Association. Even that *quid pro quo* was interpreted liberally. Elliott, for instance, was allowed to visit Tryon on the *Duchess of Gordon* whenever he cared to, although the Provincial Congress took it for granted that Elliott and most of Tryon's other visitors were presenting the Governor with as much political and military intelligence as they possessed. By and large, British jobholders in Elliott's class were treated so leniently by New York that those who had fled—mostly to Shelburne, Nova Scotia, or to St. Johns, or Fredericton, New Brunswick, in order to save the expense of traveling all the way to England—seemed to have been too fearful of the dangers of staying in the city.

When Drummond looked up Elliott, however, Elliott's status as an inactive bystander quickly came to an end. Drummond asked Elliott to travel with him to Philadelphia and to help sound out Continental Congress delegates in a search for support for the peace plan. Elliott had agreed to do it. Drummond and Elliott had been in Philadelphia only a few days when they were arrested on the orders of the Continental Congress. By January, 1776, the majority of the Congress had come to regard further talk about reconciliation as a minor form of comfort to the enemy, and, therefore, a crime. But instead of locking up the two men, the Congress had released them on their own paroles. Drummond and Elliott had sworn not to have further "dealings" on public affairs with anyone in Philadelphia. They had not kept their oaths. They continued to talk to delegates, and among the many who were willing to risk meeting with Drummond and Elliott were Jay, Duane, and most of the other New York delegates. The members of the

New York delegation did not agree perfectly with one another about much, if anything, but they did share a sense of uneasiness about the speed with which events were moving, and they all felt that the time for separation had not yet come. They were agreed that the Continental Congress should proceed slowly, although they differed, measure by measure, about what that meant. The New Yorkers were in the minority as far as reconciliation was concerned: they still thought there might be some substance to the rumors that Great Britain was interested in the subject. The Continental Congress had constantly heard, from one source after another, that royal peace commissioners were to be sent to America. While that persistent prediction was more than matched by indications that the British were primarily interested in intensifying the war, the New Yorkers felt that the Congress should wait longer—they could not say exactly how much longer—before it did anything to rule out the possibility of a negotiation.

One of Drummond's effective devices for impressing the men he and Elliott spoke with was to let them hold the memorandum from Lord North in their own hands. They were not allowed to have it for a long time, or study it carefully, but they could examine it and make a few notes on what it said. The memorandum looked authentic. (Some men wondered, however, whether Drummond's hocus-pocus with the paper indicated that it was a forgery.) Then, in arguing for his plan, Drummond made good use of reasonable understatement. He admitted that he might be wrong. Perhaps he had misunderstood the sentiments of the men he had spoken to in London. He did not think he had, but wouldn't a peace commission be an excellent way of checking up on the possibility that he was correct? The New Yorkers in Philadelphia feared that Drummond might be leading them into a snare, but they were too interested—and too hopeful—to answer Drummond's appeals for support with a flat no. Besides the New Yorkers, William Livingston, of New Jersey, Jay's father-in-law, thought there might be some merit in the Drummond-Elliott arguments. Andrew Allen was almost more optimistic about the plan than Drummond—or, at least, than Drummond wanted to appear. And Thomas Lynch, despite his reputation for belligerence, also took Drummond's story seriously. Lynch had a number of doubts, but he did think that Drummond's description of North's state of mind might be accurate. On that account, after Lynch was chosen to go to New York City to try to smooth over the differences between Lee and the province, he had decided to confer with Governor Tryon, if a chance arose, to see what the Governor and the King's other agents on the *Duchess of Gordon* thought of Drummond's story. He kept this idea secret from everyone except Drummond, Elliott, and Allen. Lynch had promised, more or less, that if the British in New York could to some extent confirm what Drummond was saying, he would do what he could, on his return to Philadelphia, to advance Drummond's peace plan.

Harrison, the third member of the committee, would have been appalled by Lynch's intentions—exactly why he had not been told about them. Harrison was at least as certain as, say, Washington, that good Americans should forget about conciliation. Beyond that, the irregularity of Lynch's scheme made it preposterous—a Continental Congress delegate was not supposed to have an unauthorized chat with a royal governor. Yet Harrison saw nothing suspicious in the fact that Drummond and Elliott accompanied the Congress committee on the journey to New York. Even General Lee, a man who was quick to question odd coincidences, suspected nothing.

But Lynch, who was anything but foolish, grew uneasy about

the undertaking, and so, in the end, the odd scheme on which
Drummond and Elliott had spent their energies did not progress much further. Lynch did go to some trouble checking the
several New York references Drummond had offered him.
Some New Yorkers thought well of the young man—for instance, William Smith, Jr., of the Governor's Council, Chief
Justice of New York since 1763, and the author of the outstand-
ing history of New York Province, told Lynch that Drummond
was a man "of faith and honesty" who had shown "more
prudence than is common to people of his years." On the whole,
however, Lynch's misgivings were increased by the answers he
got. He feared that Drummond, innocently or not, might be
helping an unscrupulous British trick, and that if an American
peace commission were dispatched, the British might capture the
commissioners on their way to London and hang them as rebels.
Drummond tried to allay this anxiety. He claimed that the
British—specifically General Robertson in Boston—would be
happy to provide safe-conduct passes with blank name spaces to
be filled in after the Continental Congress had chosen commissioners. Furthermore, Drummond said, he himself was perfectly
willing to serve as one of the commissioners. His offer was
calculated to show that he thought the danger of being hanged
was slight. Even so, Lynch felt more and more uneasy about the
whole idea and about his own role in the scheme, and when he
saw New York City panic at Clinton's arrival, Lynch decided
that the time was unpropitious for a secret meeting with Tryon,
and did nothing to arrange one. Drummond, thinking that safe
conduct was all that worried Lynch, wrote Robertson a request
for blank passports and handed the letter to Lynch for forwarding to General Washington. It was Drummond's sad misunderstanding that Washington was secretly sympathetic to conciliation; and, Drummond imagined, Washington would be happy

to send someone through the lines to deliver the note to
Robertson. Lynch did what Drummond asked: he forwarded
Drummond's letter to Cambridge headquarters.

Then Drummond, accompanied by Elliott but not by Lynch,
kept his appointment with Clinton. He went down to the
Mercury on the morning of February 5. Tryon was also present.
Drummond did nearly all the talking. Despite Drummond's
many past successes at persuasion, and despite Clinton's high
hopes for the conversation, the meeting was a fiasco. Clinton
quickly admitted that he had no authority to negotiate anything,
and that admission seemed to throw Drummond off stride. For
whatever reason, Drummond's usually engaging manner struck
Clinton as merely peculiar, and Drummond's questions as impu-
dent. Clinton got the impression, which was entirely inaccurate,
that Drummond was trying to persuade him not to invade the
Carolinas. Clinton suspected some sort of American trickery, and
from that point on he revealed nothing more about his dream of
arranging a peace. Drummond did not even get a chance to
describe the good work he and Elliott had done in Philadelphia
or to mention Lynch's interest in the Drummond plan. The
conversation slackened and then broke off, with each man be-
wildered by the other man's unaccountable behavior.

From that moment, the scheme was dead. Clinton was not
going to help Drummond, and Lynch was going no farther with
the intrigue—and without Lynch or someone equally influential
to sponsor the project in Philadelphia, it had no chance. But the
enterprise was hopeless, anyhow, because in London, Lord
George Germain, who had replaced Lord Dartmouth, on November 10, as Secretary of State for the Colonies, had greatly
increased the vigor of the war effort and was immersed in the
logistical details of mounting the heaviest imaginable military
blow against the rebellion. Germain would have had nothing to

discuss with American peace commissioners. The only peace Germain had in mind would follow the colonies' surrender. Furthermore, though New York had not yet received the news, Parliament had passed the Prohibitory Act on November 21 and the King had signed it on December 23—and the new law was more drastic than any of the measures passed earlier. The Act prohibited all trade with the colonies, and all trade among the colonies, and thus entailed a naval blockade that would complete Great Britain's acts of war against America.

It was perfectly true that, in the midst of preparations for a larger war, London was full of talk about a "peace commission," but the word "peace" was being used more nearly in Germain's sense than in Drummond's. Lord North had agreed, some time earlier, that the British should make one last "serious peace effort," as the Opposition had been demanding ever since the Battle of Bunker's Hill, and, with North's support, a resolution to that effect had been passed by Parliament. North was still trying to decide who the peace commissioner, or commissioners, should be. Germain was one possibility. Another was Admiral Richard Lord Howe, North's choice to command the fleet—and Howe said he would not accept the command unless an assignment as peace commissioner went with it. His brother, General Howe, was a third possibility; and General Howe would surely make trouble if he were not named because, through a misunderstanding, he believed that he already had been. There were surely going to be British commissioners—or, at least, one commissioner—but London's most generous concept of terms had nothing to do with "peace" as Americans used the word.

North himself was less vindictive toward the rebels than many of his colleagues, but he still had no thought of letting his commissioners deal directly with the rebellion itself—by which he meant the Continental Congress. He did think that some sort of administrative machinery to deal with American grievances might be established—a liberal sentiment by comparison with the belief that the colonies' grievances should be ignored. However, North did not intend to compromise Parliament's legislative supremacy one bit, and he felt that it extended over all matters, including taxation. In short, North wanted only to give the colonies one last chance to submit, one by one, before more blood was shed. After they had yielded, North felt, the British should be generous about granting pardons and restorations. Germain, for one, took an even simpler position: that the colonies should be forced to surrender unconditionally, and the sooner the better, by an overwhelming application of British military power. Whereas North had some slight misgivings about waging war on Americans, Germain had none. And, on the whole, Germain's certitude was more representative of the government's mood than North's doubts. If Drummond's scheme had succeeded, and if an American peace commission had arrived in London, its members might have escaped hanging, but they would not have found much to discuss with anyone in office.

As for Drummond's letter to Robertson, Washington took the liberty of reading it, and instead of forwarding it through the British lines, he sent it on to Philadelphia. He thought the Continental Congress should know about it. Washington also wrote, at considerable length, about how he would deal with a British peace commission if one should arrive:

I would not be deceived by artful declarations, nor specious pretences; nor would I be amused by unmeaning propositions; but in open, undisguised, and manly terms proclaim our wrongs and our resolution to be redressed. I would tell them that we have borne much, that we had long and ardently sought for reconciliation upon honourable terms, that all our attempts after peace had proved abortive, and had been grossly misrepresented, that we had done everything which could be expected from the best of subjects, that the spirit of freedom beat too high in us to submit to slavery, and that, if nothing else could satisfy a tyrant and his diabolical ministry, we are determined to shake off all connections with a state so unjust and unnatural. This I would tell them, not under covert, but in words as clear as the sun in its meridian brightness.

When the Continental Congress read what Drummond had written to Robertson it was irritated, again, by what Drummond had been trying to do, but it took no further action against him. Lynch's last-minute caution saved him embarrassment; he was not greatly blamed for having played a part—on the record, only a small one—and he emerged from the affair with his good reputation undamaged.

While Drummond's peacemaking scheme was dissolving, Lynch and the special committee, by being in New York, had at least been of great help to General Lee. In effect, the Continental Congress committee assumed final command authority over Lee's uninvited visiting troops. While that compromise improvisation made no particular legal sense, it was a way of easing New York's concern about the issue. No test question arose, because Lee ordered nothing that New York objected to. No one in New York entirely understood the trickery Lee had employed in getting into town, but as long as there was no great disagreement between the General and the Provincial Congress, New York had no inclination to look back and quibble over Lee's past border violations. At the same time, the Continental Congress committee, as Lee explained in a letter to Washington, had saved Lee from appearing to be "a most ridiculous figure"—a disciplinarian who had to answer to the delinquents. Harrison, Lynch, and Allen conferred with the Committee of Safety almost every day, sometimes more than once. Lee was usually present, too. And these meetings, constantly stressing the military urgency of New York's situation, not only worked against all demoralizing influences, but encouraged the New Yorkers to believe what Lee wanted them to—that hard work and firm resolution would enable the town to save itself. Only one member of the Committee of Safety—Comfort Sands, the merchant—remained skeptical of Lee's intentions and expected that the General would bring disaster upon the city. The other members of the Committee in attendance—usually Joseph Hallett, acting as chairman in the place of Peter Van Brugh Livingston, who was sick, Colonel Abraham Brasher, Samuel Brewster (Ulster County), Jeremiah Clarke (Orange), Colonel Mc-Dougall, Henry Othoudt (Peter R. Livingston's alternate, representing Albany County), John Morin Scott, Thomas Tredwell (Suffolk), and Colonel Pierre Van Cortlandt (Westchester)—were impressed by Lee's polite seriousness. Their reaction was to grow bolder in their dealings with the warships. When the purser of Clinton's ship, the *Mercury,* asked Abraham Lott, as agent-victualer for His Majesty's ships, to sell him a three months' supply of provisions, for instance, the Committee of Safety told Lott not to—even though, with the *Mercury's* twenty-four guns added to the combined fire power of the *Asia* and the *Phoenix,* the request might have become a demand. (But Lott continued to supply the other British ships, greatly to Lee's annoyance.)

Lord Stirling arrived in town on February 9 with about five hundred men, instead of the thousand that had been expected, and settled them into the Lower Barracks, next to Fort George. Stirling himself moved into his own handsome Broad Street town house, which was spacious enough so that in the past Tryon had occasionally rented it as the Governor's mansion. Stirling's men, added to Waterbury's regiment, raised Lee's total strength to more than a thousand, not counting the New York and West-chester companies. The city had never seen quite so many men in uniform (such as the uniforms were) before, and the proportion of military costumes to civilian dress was more noticeable because so many civilian New Yorkers were away from home, for one reason or another. Still, the number of soldiers, even when Ward's men arrived, would not be half as many as Lee thought he needed. The Committee of Safety asked Dutchess County to send down Colonel Jacobus Swartwout's Minutemen as soon as possible, and it authorized Lee to borrow troops from any place that would lend them. (The Committee's vote gave Lee a little extra authority for a request he had already made: Would the Continental Congress, if possible, send up a battalion of the Philadelphia Associators?) A few weeks earlier, New York had written Lee that the presence of an unusual number of soldiers in town might in itself provoke the warships. But now, with the city's streets filled with armed men, the Committee of Safety kept asking for more.

Apart from manpower, the city had been doing what it could to meet the other requirements for its defense. Before Lee's arrival, it had collected a fair supply of entrenching tools—spades, shovels, pickaxes. The repair work on the spiked cannon had been going better than expected, though few of the pieces were serviceable. New York still had almost no powder, although the Continental Congress had promised to send an emergency supply. The city did have a considerable stock of cannon shells of various sizes in the storehouse at Turtle Bay (borrowed from the Crown after the two robberies had all but emptied the place of the King's matériel). But Lee's defense plan called for a very large number of artillery positions. Besides those at Horn's Hook, Hallett's Point, and Brooklyn Heights (where a battery was to be emplaced on the high ground at what is now the foot of Clark Street, looking over the Brooklyn-Queens Expressway), Captain Stephen Badlam, Lee's artillery adviser, wanted to put guns at Coenties Slip, a block or so east of Fraunces' Tavern; and at the intersection of Catherine and Cherry streets (on the north side of what is now the site of the Alfred E. Smith Houses); and on Rutgers' first hill (not far from what is now the intersection of Rutgers and Cherry streets, but was then the open ground of Mr. Rutgers' huge estate), with the idea of making the mouth of the East River uncomfortable for British warships. All of this demanded more equipment than New York possessed, and, as a further embarrassment, the city had promised to send Colonel Henry Knox, the Continental artillery commander at Cambridge, several guns and several hundred shells—as Knox, with increasing impatience, kept reminding it.

New York was still honoring its agreement with Tryon to keep its hands off the remaining guns on the Battery—the ten pieces left behind on the night of August 23. Tryon had just reminded New York of that understanding. In answer to a question that the Committee of Safety raised about the security of the New York public records, Tryon had sent word that they would be perfectly safe where they were, in City Hall, looked after by Samuel Bayard, Jr., Deputy Secretary of the Province, unless New York was thinking of removing the Battery guns or engaging in hostilities against the British warships. But, as General Lee insisted repeatedly, he was certain that the warships would not fire again. He dismissed Tryon's, and all British, threats as "idle gasconades," and he thought the guns should be seized at once, along with some British artillery stores in the sheds near the Lower Barracks. Lee did not wait for the Committee of Safety to approve what he had in mind or warn it that he was going ahead with or without approval. Early on the morning of Sunday, February 11, a party of Stirling's and Waterbury's men began moving the rest of His Majesty's property—from the Battery to the Commons. Manhandling the big cannon up the Broadway hill from Bowling Green to Wall Street was, as before, a back-breaking effort. It took a long time. Lee's soldiers could have managed it by themselves, but they were grateful that a large group of enthusiastic civilians joined in to help, making "an astonishing uproar and shouting," according to William Smith, Jr., who disapproved of the whole enterprise. The Committee of Safety met at ten o'clock and noted for the record that the gun removals were none of its doing, but did not attempt to stop the work. The Committee did not even complain to Lee that he was taking too big a chance with New York's fate. It simply voted to move the public records immediately, with Bayard accompanying them, to the splendid estate of his uncle, Nicholas Bayard, in the Out Ward, about one mile north of the Commons. (The mansion, surrounded by a large formal garden, stood where Lafayette and Broome streets now intersect.) A detachment from Lasher's battalion was to guard the files and their custodian around the clock. (The Committee of Safety was not aware—Tryon had not mentioned it, and the committeemen had not thought to put the question—that the records being treated so solicitously were incomplete: the Governor had combed through the files and had taken with him to the *Duchess of Gordon* as many of the official papers as he had thought he might need.) The British sailors, like everyone in the vicinity, heard the commotion in the streets, and to get a better view of what was happening, the *Phoenix* sent a reconnaissance party in a tender around the tip of the island about noon. The officer in charge of the small boat, shouting through a speaking trumpet, reported back to his ship that "three thousand" men and boys were removing the cannon.

The British warships did not fire. Tryon, whose information had been better than the Committee of Safety's, had been warned a day earlier by one of his councillors, William Axtell, that Lee was thinking of removing the guns. The Governor had decided to ignore it. But New York knew nothing about Tryon's decision. Moving the guns took all day, and the suspense mounted hour by hour. For the second Sunday in a row, New Yorkers, fearing the worst, scrambled to get out of the range of the warships' guns. Some of those who owned carts or managed to rent them headed north on the Greenwich or Bowery roads with their most valuable possessions. Others, as before, tried to engage a boat to take them and their things away. But still others stayed, and Lee was greatly pleased with the "zeal and pleasure" shown by the soldiers' volunteer assistants. By dark, the guns were parked on the Commons, directly across Broadway from Mrs. de la Montaigne's, and Lee could see them from his windows. The British did not even send a letter of protest. Captain Hyde Parker, Jr., of the *Phoenix*, explained his restraint a few days afterward. Lee and his New England men, Parker said, had come to New York for the purpose of goading the warships into action, and he had no intention of giving Lee that satisfaction.

By calling Tryon's bluff and inspiring New Yorkers to help him do it, Lee had scored a little victory. For a few hours, it looked like a big one. The British warships all weighed anchor and left their positions near the Battery—but, with the exception of Clinton's *Mercury*, which was bound for Cape Fear, they were not going far. The *Asia* repositioned herself between Governor's Island and Bedloe's Island (now Liberty Island, and the site of the Statue of Liberty), with the *Duchess of Gordon* close beside her. The *Phoenix* sailed through the Narrows, but anchored just a few miles below the entrance to the harbor, not far from

Amboy. These shifts had no political significance; the ships' captains were only seeking protection from the battering of ice floes in the East River, and the terms of the confrontation between the warships and the city remained the same. After the showdown, as before it, Tryon's close political associates—Cadwallader Colden, the Lieutenant Governor; Mayor Hicks; Councillors Daniel Horsmanden, Oliver De Lancey, Charles Apthorpe, Hugh Wallace, William Axtell, John Harris Cruger, and William Smith, Jr.—and Tryon's doctor, Hugh Middleton, were still allowed to use their standing passes from the Provincial Congress and visit the *Duchess of Gordon* whenever they chose, and other friends of Tryon's had only to ask for a special pass to get one. The provisioning arrangements were reaffirmed the next day, Monday the twelfth, after some of Lee's sentinels at the wharves had interfered with one shipment. The Committee of Safety asked General Lee to straighten out the soldiers' confusion, and to repeat his consent to the ships' supply. He did both.

Lee's consent did not include his approval. He regarded the provisioning as wrong, and he intended to stop it as soon as he could, but he saw that the New York Provincial Congress, when it reconvened on February 12, was not yet ready to take the step. Cutting Tryon off, he realized, was a symbol of a finality that New York dreaded at least as much as it feared violent British retaliation. Besides, the Congress was overwhelmed with work on urgent old business. There was a six-week accumulation of unanswered mail—all the letters the Committee of Safety had held over because it lacked authority to deal with the problems they raised. Then, the New York County delegation was seriously below strength, with a number of its members absent for one reason or another. (Peter Van Brugh Livingston was still not well. Lieutenant Colonel Sears, who probably should not have been reelected, because he was now a Connecticut man both in point of residence and allegiance, was on military duty on Long Island. Gabriel Ludlow, Benjamin Kissam, and Theodorus Van Wyck were also among the five others who were missing, and their explanations were missing as well.) No alternates for the seven absent men had been chosen, so the Provincial Congress ordered a new election to fill their places.

A third urgent matter was more ridiculous than dangerous: Tryon wanted the Assembly to reconvene in the Assembly chamber in City Hall—the room the Provincial Congress had preempted. The Assembly was scheduled to meet on Wednesday, February 14. Two legislatures could not occupy a single room, but from the Provincial Congress' point of view, having to meet elsewhere would not be the worst of the nuisance. Since fifteen of the newly elected assemblymen were also Provincial Congress delegates—Jay's slate of Associators—someone would have to decide, if the sessions were concurrent, where each man was needed most: in the Assembly, ready to frustrate Tryon, or in the Congress, to assist with the business of running the province. The solution, once it was thought of, seemed obvious. New York City's Common Council meeting room, in the wing of City Hall opposite the Assembly chambers, was large enough to seat the Provincial Congress. It was not more than a hundred feet from the Assembly room, and connected with it by an open covered walk. Early on the morning of the fourteenth, the Provincial Congress asked Mayor Hicks, who had just been appointed by Tryon to a judgeship, and who was on the point of resigning the mayor's office, for permission to sit in the Common Council chambers. Permission was granted. The Congress rose and walked down the arcade to the other room. A few hours later, when the Assembly reconvened in its own room, no more than thirty assemblymen were present for the roll call, half of them Jay's men. Had it been necessary, the fifteen Associators could have run back and forth and played their parts in both rooms, but it was not necessary. Tryon's supporters knew that they had been outmaneuvered. The Assembly met only to adjourn, and before the day was done, Tryon, from his cabin on the *Duchess of Gordon,* prorogued the Assembly for a month.

A fourth immediate problem concerned Richmond County, where the County Committee, which had all but vanished in December, had recently come to life. Richmond had managed to elect two willing delegates—its full quota—to the Provincial Congress. Furthermore, the two men, Adrian Bancker and Richard Lawrence, who happened to be near neighbors on the splendid road along the bluffs overlooking the Kills (the equivalent of what is now Richmond Terrace), were eager to present themselves, have their credentials accepted, and take part in the forthcoming sessions. The difficulty was that Richmond was still proscribed, and a county "in open contempt" could hardly send delegates to the legislature that had proscribed it. Besides, if Richmond County deserved to be restored—which was doubtful—the Provincial Congress did not know how to go about it; there was no customary procedure for de-proscription, since the question had never arisen. Some members of the Provincial Congress had had the foresight to see that it might arise, and had asked the Continental Congress' opinion. On February 8, the Continental Congress had laid down a rule—delegates could not be seated until a majority of the county's "inhabitants" (the Continental Congress doubtless had meant "qualified voters") had subscribed to the Association. That requirement may have seemed elementary in Philadelphia, but it was a standard far too high for Staten Island. New York realized, too late, that it would have been wiser to invent its own formula. Most of the delegates were looking for an excuse to let

Lawrence and Bancker sit. When Lawrence and Bancker heard the decision, they claimed indignantly that "seven-eighths" of the Staten Islanders had subscribed to the Association long before. In that case, the Provincial Congress answered, it should be easy for Lawrence and Bancker to provide proof that a mere majority had done so. Lawrence and Bancker's applications had to be put aside, because the ratio of subscribers to nonsubscribers on Staten Island was, in fact, unknown.

In the midst of this argument, an unlucky military errand seemed to confirm Staten Island's impression that the rest of New York Province wanted to humiliate it. When Clinton's *Mercury* weighed anchor, the Provincial Congress suspected that the General might stop at Staten Island as he sailed out of the harbor and steal some of the Richmond County cattle, to take the place of the provisions New York had refused to sell him. New York asked New Jersey for help. New Jersey responded with admirable speed, which partly accounted for New York's failure to tell Staten Island what was coming. On February 17, Colonel Heard, who had returned to Elizabethtown after the Committee of Safety had taken his Queens prisoners off his hands, took seven hundred men, by ferry, to the northwest corner of the island. They marched briskly toward the key road intersections. Heard's only instructions were to guard the cattle, but the Staten Islanders, taken by surprise, leaped to the conclusion that Heard was going to do to Staten Island what he had done to Queens—that he was about to disarm and arrest the Richmond County inimicals. Before he had even completed his deployment, Heard learned that the *Mercury* and its accompanying transport had sailed past Staten Island without stopping. The hypothetical threat was gone. The cattle were safe.

Heard immediately wrote to the New York Provincial Congress—his orders were to take orders from New York—explaining that Clinton was gone and asking for new instructions. That night, and all the next day, February 18, while Heard and his regiment were waiting for an answer, they could not help hearing Staten Islanders talking with shocking freedom against the Association, cursing the Continental Congress and all its committees, and boasting that they had bootlegged supplies to the British warships. The Colonel was appalled. He had no authority to act, but the inimicality was so flagrant that, on his own initiative, he arrested four of the most outspoken Staten Islanders—Richard Conner, Isaac Decker, Minah Burger, and Abraham Harris—and had them taken under guard to Elizabethtown. New Jersey had no right to imprison New York inimicals, and on precisely that account, Robert Ogden, chairman of the Elizabethtown Committee, was disturbed to receive the four men. Furthermore, Ogden was not sure what charges, if any, were to be brought against them. He locked up the Staten Islanders, nonetheless, and assumed that someone would eventually explain to him what the affair was all about.

Heard's spur-of-the-moment arrests convinced Staten Island that there had been some substance to its reflexive fears of out-of-province invasions and Tory hunts. Although Heard's regiment withdrew on February 19, and no further arrests were made, Staten Island's sense of grievance lasted. (A month later, Conner, Decker, Burger, and Harris, who had been returned to Richmond County by the Elizabethtown Committee, came to trial. The witnesses who were expected to testify against them—their friends and neighbors, for the most part—pretended to know nothing. The cases collapsed, and the four men were freed.)

General Lee bided his time while the Provincial Congress argued and acted on this multitude of matters, confident that before long he could engineer a break between New York and

Governor Tryon. As part of that effort, Lee had been working to stir up New York's indignation over the five, or perhaps six, Americans who were being held prisoner on the *Asia*. One of them, Lieutenant Edward Tylee, of Wooster's Regiment, had been in confinement for five months, ever since he had been taken off the Amboy–New York ferry on September 25, 1775. Lee wanted Tylee, in particular, returned. And, since the British had refused to discuss the prisoners at all, Lee had retaliated by arresting Francis Stephens, Storekeeper of His Majesty's Ordnance, in order to have a prisoner to exchange for Lieutenant Tylee. Stephens' arrest was at least as provocative as the guns' removal. The man had done nothing except try, with conspicuous lack of success, to guard the Turtle Bay and Battery storehouses—but then, Tylee had not done anything, either, except ride the ferry. Lee had written Captain Vandeput of the *Asia*, and had proposed an exchange of Stephens for Tylee, but Vandeput had ignored the offer. However, if the Provincial Congress felt any profound concern about Tylee and the others, it was concealing it; and it had not thought, in any case, of stopping the constant shipments of provisions to the *Asia* from Murray, Sansom and Company, Joseph Bogart's butcher shop, Henry White's general store, Lispenard's brewery, and the Wallace brothers' (Hugh and Alexander) wine shop, which was sending out sherry by the 126-gallon cask, or pipe.

Digging was on everybody's mind. By the last week in February, some signs of progress on the fortifications were visible, especially at Horn's Hook, where Colonel Drake's Westchester Minutemen were working. The star-shaped gun position there was to be surrounded by entrenchments and breastworks. Jacob Walton's lovely lawn had to be sacrificed, and the Waltons had to move out of their mansion so the building could be turned into barracks. (The Walton house was close to the present-day site of the Gracie Mansion, which was built in 1799.)

Yet the work as a whole, Horn's Hook included, was already behind schedule. The ground had frozen again, after the thaw. The diggers were compelled to chop away, and it was evident that Lee's citywide fortifications plan, which the General had been able to outline with a few descriptive waves of his hand, was a mammoth project. At any given moment, furthermore, the number of soldiers actually digging seemed remarkably small. Somehow the visiting regiments managed to keep so busy with their own housekeeping that they had little time left over for fatigue duty. In some companies, moreover, the proportion of officers to men was absurdly high. Since officers did not dig, one might occasionally find more men supervising than working. There was a prodigious bustle of military activity—bugle calling, drum rolling, marching to and marching fro. It was baffling that so much activity could produce such limited results.

Manhattan's trees were disappearing at a rapid rate. Some of the wood was being used to build the fortifications, but much more was burned by the soldiers for cooking and heating. In normal times, New York City imported nearly all its firewood, but the visiting soldiers did not hesitate to chop down orchards and cultivated groves that represented years of labor and expense—the pity was that the green wood did not even burn well. Nicholas Bayard had a famous stand of cedars, and it was cut down. Oliver De Lancey's orchard suffered a similar fate. (De Lancey's estate was on the Hudson, at about what is now Twenty-third Street.) An anecdote was being told about the confiscation of De Lancey's fruit trees—and not a sympathetic anecdote, because De Lancey was frank in public about his British sympathies. (In secret, he was working on plans to recruit a battalion of American loyalists to join the British Army.) At any rate—so the story went—De Lancey had rushed out to try to stop the woodcutters by explaining to them that one-third of the land on which the orchard stood belonged to the Earl of Abingdon. Abingdon, besides being married to one of De Lancey's granddaughters, was fairly well known as a champion of the American cause in the House of Lords. The argument did not work. "Well, if he be such a great Liberty Boy," one of the soldiers was said to have said, "and so great a friend of our country, he will be quite happy that his wood was so happy for our use."

III. February to April, 1776

☆

A LARGER work force would have helped with the digging, but many of the New York civilians who might have been employed as laborers were being taken by the Continental Army's new recruiting drive. Immediately after hearing of the defeat at Quebec, the Continental Congress had called on the provinces to raise six new regiments. It planned a nine-regiment expeditionary force for Canada for 1776, and unrealistically supposed that two regiments could be formed of the survivors who were already there and, even more unrealistically, that there were enough sympathetic Canadians to form a third regiment, which Colonel James Livingston would command. (Livingston, who was a wheat merchant in Chambly, Quebec, and a cousin of the New York Livingstons, had managed to raise a force of about three hundred Canadians, and he and his men had taken part in the assault on Quebec. Most of Livingston's men had gone home. His chances of raising a new regiment—or even another three hundred men—were poor.) Of the other six, three were to be raised jointly by Pennsylvania and New Jersey; and Connecticut, New Hampshire, and New York were to supply one apiece. By now, a Continental regiment meant, ideally, four battalions of eight companies apiece—almost 2,500 men—so that New York Province was asked to provide nearly as many soldiers as she had raised starting in June, 1775. In conformity with the

distribution of population in the province, close to half of the
new soldiers were to be supplied by the city and areas around it—
eight companies from New York County alone, and seven more
from Westchester, Queens, Kings, Richmond, and Suffolk,
adding up to fifteen out of the thirty-two. The quota was large,
and the urgency was awesome. Colonel Gose Van Schaick's
Second New York, which had been raised in and around Albany
for the most part, and was filled with members of old Albany
families, Gansevoorts, Van Dycks, Ten Eycks, and Van Slycks,
had already been ordered to move toward Canada. The Second
garrisoned Albany and the forts north of Albany—Fort Edward,
Fort George, Ticonderoga, and Crown Point—so that its departure would leave a worrisome gap in the middle of the established lines until the new companies could fill it. The Continental
Congress emphasized this emergency by ordering that, in each
new battalion, the first two companies raised and equipped were
to march immediately for Albany without waiting for the rest
of the unit.

The Continental call thus put the defense of the Lake George–
Lake Champlain line ahead of the defense of New York City,
and there was some grumbling about it in town, and also out in
Suffolk County, where the most active Associators in Southampton, East Hampton, Shelter Island, and Sag Harbor considered
their area strategically crucial, and had asked for an adequate
Continental force of men, with ammunition, to bolster the local
militia. The Continental Congress had promised to help eastern
Long Island—its livestock and vegetables were temptations to
the British, and the food needed better protection, whether or
not Southampton was likely to become a major battlefield.
Another improvement the end of the island wanted—no
promises had yet been made—was a regular mail service from
New York City, so that Suffolk County patriots could have the

benefits of "the earliest intelligences." But Albany's requirements had been given priority over Suffolk's; instead of gaining
reinforcements eastern Long Island was asked to furnish recruits.

Considering how slowly New York City had answered the
first call for Continentals, the February response was surprisingly good. One distinct improvement was in the attitude of the
sons of the rich and socially prominent. (Not counting the few—
Captain Oliver De Lancey, Jr., the orchard owner's son, was
among them—who had enlisted with the British. De Lancey was
serving at Boston in the Seventeenth Regiment of Light Dra-
goons.) In a number of cases, well-to-do young New Yorkers
who had earlier decided that membership in one of New York's
independent companies, or something of the sort, was as much as
the situation required of them, were having second thoughts.
There was a good deal of angling for Continental commissions,
letters of recommendation and sponsorship flew back and forth,
and many of the successful officer-candidates bore prominent
New York family names—Avery, Brooks, Burnett, Dusenberry,
Forbes, Hammell, Van Hook, de Ronde, and the like. On the
other hand, when the New York Provincial Congress offered
Colonel Lasher's battalion, the First Independent New York, a
chance to transfer intact into the Continental Army, the officers
met at Captain Abraham Van Dyke's Inn, on Broadway, and
voted against the offer. Lasher himself favored the idea; he
believed that the Continental scale of pay—from five dollars a
month for privates to fifty a month for colonels—would attract a
better class of men. (His battalion did not get paid at all.) But
the majority of the officers were afraid that, as a Continental
unit, the battalion might be ordered to serve outside New York
County—as, almost certainly, it would have been. Still, by putting the question, the Colonel obtained a useful list of officers,
led by himself, who were willing, as individuals, to go on Conti-

nental service. It included Major Sebastian Bauman, Captain Henry Livingston (whose younger brother, William, had voted the other way), Captain James Alner, Captain Abraham Van Wicke, Adjutant Philip Brasher, and Lieutenants Gerardus Beekman, John Wiley, John Johnson, and Henry Tiebout.

Although each man's change of heart was an individual matter, New York's improved morale was general and noticeable. For instance, the new officers working to raise the new companies were finding recruits—though they still had to get prospects drunk and offer them bonuses besides. Lee's vigorous, belligerent presence had made a difference; his brash style had lifted up many of the young men's spirits. The transformation of the city into a garrison town had helped, too. The sight of hundreds of soldiers on the streets and camped all around the town made not being a soldier seem laggardly. Joining up was also a way of solving the problem of being unemployed. And then the effects of the news from Canada—further details were arriving constantly—were great beyond measure. The defeat had impressed New York with the seriousness of the war in a way that the actions around Boston could not have done. Montgomery's heroism and the exploits of many less prominent New York men were thrilling stories, and hearing them aroused the desire to make up for the failure in Canada. New York knew that Arnold, with some survivors, most of them New Yorkers, was holding a position outside Quebec, and needed help. It seemed right, in the minds of quite a few New Yorkers, that New York should have the leading part in Arnold's rescue and brave Montgomery's revenge, and these feelings helped a good many men overcome their natural fears and normal loathing for army life.

General Lee's health improved, and he seemed able to move about with less pain. As his appetite returned, so did his vigor.

On February 19, moreover, Lee got what should have been good news; his friend Robert Morris wrote that the Continental Congress had chosen Lee to assume command in Canada. Formal notification arrived two days later in a parcel of letters from Philadelphia that included congratulatory notes from John Adams, Benjamin Franklin, and Benjamin Rush. The appointment was what Lee wanted most—or so all his friends believed. His correspondents assumed that the General would be delighted, and Hancock ordered him to proceed north immediately. The Continental Congress promised Lee most of the matériel that he had said, when the search for Montgomery's replacement had first begun, he thought he would need. Twelve cannon (to be provided by New York) were included, along with at least eight tons of powder (to be drawn from supplies at Albany). All appeared to be well, and the next day, February 22, Lee wrote Hancock and accepted the command with what the General described as "zeal and alacrity."

But something irrational was troubling Lee. Just as his military career—his driving concern during the previous two years—was taking a great step forward, Lee seemed to lose interest in it. He did order a few supplies—barreled pork, rum, and some flour—to take with him, and so indicated that he really expected to go to Canada. But at the same time, he seemed indifferent, and the letters he wrote in the next few days were distracted. He returned to grumbling about his gout, and asked Hancock for permission to stay in New York City long enough to recover sufficiently "to be able to ride and walk with a tolerable degree of ease." However much pain Lee felt, he had not been making a great deal of it for some time. Furthermore, his letter of acceptance wandered off the point and dealt with old, irrelevant complaints. He described his disappointment, which the Continental Congress had already heard enough about, at not having been sent the battalion of Philadelphia Associators. He denigrated, as he had before, the Connecticut militiamen who had accompanied him to New York, saying that if he had been "as much acquainted with them when they were summoned as I am at present, I should have exerted myself to prevent their coming." At the same time, Lee had nothing to say about his hopes for the success of the Canada expeditionary force.

His new command might have crowded everything else out of Lee's mind, but instead he seemed to regard New York City's concerns as ever more absorbing; if anything, the energy with which he had been goading and inspiring the town increased, although, had New Yorkers been able to read Lee's mind, or even his official correspondence with Cambridge headquarters, they would have been aghast at Lee's pessimism. His February 19 report to Commander-in-Chief Washington said:

I wait for some more force to prepare a post or retrenched encampment on Long Island, opposite to the City, for three thousand men. This is, I think, a capital object; for should the enemy take possession of New York, when Long Island is in our hands, they will find it almost impossible to subsist. The Jerseys are too well manned, and Connecticut we know will not furnish them with anything. What to do with the City, I own, puzzles me; it is so encircled with deep navigable water that whoever commands the sea must command the town. Tomorrow I shall begin to dismantle that part of the fort next to the town, to prevent its being converted into a citadel. I shall barrier the principal streets, and at least if I cannot make it a continental garrison, it shall be a disputable field of battle.

The Provincial Congress had not thought the city was being made disputable, but defensible. It had also imagined, incorrectly, that it might satisfy Lee on the question of communications with the warships by tightening the existing regulations, and so, on February 17, it had reduced to thirteen the list of persons who could visit the ships without a special pass: the Lieutenant Governor, the Surveyor General, the members of the Council; the Council secretary, and the Council secretary's two clerks. The Provincial Congress had also appointed a port master, Mr. Elias Nixon. He was to station himself at the stairs leading down to the ferry slip, at the foot of Broad Street, and make sure that deliveries to the warships tallied exactly with the agent-victualer's accounts. Nothing the British ordered was to leave from any other place.

But, since the new arrangements, like the old, allowed Tryon all he really wanted, Lee was far from satisfied. Three days later, on February 20, Lee learned that the *Asia* and the *Phoenix* had been intercepting provision ships en route from Amboy to New York and stealing their cargoes. Surely, Lee thought, these piracies constituted an outrage glaring enough to convince the Provincial Congress that it ought to withhold all further supplies. "For my part," Lee wrote, "the measure of suffering ourselves to be plundered and at the same time feeding our plunderers, appears a degree of lowness of spirit which reflects dishonour, and must encourage the enemy to take still further liberties."

But the Provincial Congress, without comment on how high or how low its spirit was, replied immediately—on the afternoon of the day it received Lee's note—that it thought the provisioning should continue. The Congress reminded the General that the British could cut off New York City more easily than the other way around. The warships could stop water-borne provisions from reaching Manhattan Island, and imports of New Jersey corn, firewood, and hay were, as always, essential to New York. Also, the city was importing unusually large amounts of vegetables and meat from New Jersey, because New York's

ordinary supplies of barreled beef and pork from Westchester
had been diverted to the military, and Suffolk County, which
anticipated having to feed the Continental Army reinforcements
it had been promised, had stopped selling its produce to the city
in order to build up its own reserves.

Since the British could easily steal everything they needed by
raiding the shores or seizing cargoes, New York recommended
that the harbor traffic keep out of the warships' way. The Provincial Congress wrote to urge the New Jersey authorities to tell
the New Jersey shippers to stop using the Narrows and the Bay
and to leave for New York from Paulus Hook or one of the
several docks farther up the Hudson, and thus steer as far north
of the British as possible. The Provincial Congress also complained to Governor Tryon about the piracies. For the time
being, the provisioning arrangements remained as before.

If New York's pragmatic, low-keyed way of handling the
affair reflected dishonor, it did not encourage the British to take
further liberties. On the contrary, New Jersey boats were not
molested for several days, which was a hopeful sign—if no
assurance that the *Asia* and the *Phoenix* had permanently abandoned plundering. The news from London, covering developments up to about December 1, which appeared in Holt's *Journal*
and the *New-York Packet* on February 22, explained why the
British had suddenly taken to seizing boats, and it also made
Tryon's willingness to order a stop to the practice seem extremely accommodating. New York learned, three months after
the fact, that the Prohibitory Act had been passed. (Tryon and
the ships' captains had later information, thanks to a Royal Navy
storeship that had brought them word that the King had already
signed the Act, making it law. That news had not yet reached
shore.) Parliament had authorized His Majesty's ships to seize
any American vessel as a lawful prize as part of Lord North's

blockade. The captains of the *Asia* and the *Phoenix*, learning of the new rules, had evidently tried to take prompt advantage of them. And yet, somehow, Tryon had persuaded the warships to forgo their small New Jersey prize gains, in the interest of maintaining the peculiar understanding with New York. His success was remarkable; it was like persuading a cat to ignore mice.

Realization that Parliament, after full debate, consideration, and the required three readings, had given the King and his ministers complete and unprecedented legal support for their American policy should have destroyed all New York's hopes for a negotiated settlement. It did not do so. Many New Yorkers found shreds of comfort here and there. While they understood the gravity of the Prohibitory Act, most of those who had been optimistic before continued to nurse the idea that a negotiation was still possible. The news of the new Act, after all, was no surprise. The King's earlier addresses to Parliament had foreshadowed it. (This was a point that American belligerents, Washington included, had been using on the other side of the debate as proof that time for conciliation was long past.) Then, too, though the news was bad, it was, like all London dispatches, stale. Therefore it was possible to argue, if one had a mind to do so, that when the December, January, and February news arrived, New York might learn that America's friends in Parliament had not been completely routed. Indeed, the same editions of the newspapers carried a Philadelphia rumor that British peace commissioners were said to be on the way, and their number was not two, or three, but the magnificent total of thirty-nine. (The source for this untrustworthy concoction had evidently multiplied the number of colonies by three.)

In point of fact, the delayed London news would hold little or nothing pleasant for Americans. Lord George Germain had established himself as managing director of the British war effort. Even those ministers and secretaries on whose authority he had encroached, and who did not like him or his methods of amassing power, admitted that Germain was getting results, in spite of his concern with petty details. Part of Germain's war plan—the withdrawal of the British forces from Boston to Halifax, where they were to prepare for a move to New York City—was behind schedule, mostly because the British lacked ships. But Germain had successfully negotiated with several of the German states for mercenaries (and had personally ordered handsome boots for them, which were being made in London). He was demanding that the fleet for the expeditionary force that was to descend on New York be ready to leave Great Britain by April 7. (Admiral Sir Hugh Palliser was doing his best to assemble 52,000 tons of transports.) In all his plans, Germain took it for granted that General Howe would capture New York without serious difficulty. Germain had already ordered a supply of medicines to meet the ordinary requirements of a British garrison in New York City and was trying to decide who ought to be appointed the chief New York City medical officer.

On the evening of February 24, General Lee took time off from his problems for a party. Thomas Paine, the celebrity of the hour, was visiting New York, and dined with the General. Lee, a great admirer of Paine's new pamphlet, "Common Sense," found the author delightful. Lee had been among the first to read "Common Sense"—he had finished it not much more than a week after its appearance on January 9—and he had promptly recommended it to General Washington, writing that he had never seen "such a masterly, irresistible performance." In less than two months, thousands of others had seen it—the pamphlet was heading for a quick sale of more than a hundred thousand copies—and Paine had gone from anonymity (the pamphlet was signed, "By an Englishman") to fame.

Nothing quite like the success of "Common Sense" had occurred in American publishing. Nearly every literate American was at least aware of "Common Sense," and besides the thousands who had read the full text, countless others had seen one of the many newspaper abridgments. Paine had accepted some risk, no doubt, in admitting that he was its author; on the other hand, he was enjoying the attention paid him as a successful writer. Paine was thirty-eight, a stocky man with a ruddy complexion, and "an Englishman" in the sense that he had lived in America for only a year and a half. He had arrived in Philadelphia in the fall of 1774 with a letter of introduction from Benjamin Franklin, whom he had met in England, and had supported himself since then as a magazine writer and as an editor of a new monthly, Aitken's *Pennsylvania Magazine*. His journalistic output had been varied if not distinguished—literary criticism, historical pieces, poetry, articles on popular science, and editorials. Since "Common Sense" was so much better than anything Paine had written before, there was gossip that Franklin, or Dr. Benjamin Rush, or Samuel Adams, or David Rittenhouse, or any combination of them, had collaborated on the work. But the composition was all Paine's. (Rush had read the manuscript in installments, and thought he had suggested the title, but if he had, Paine neglected to give him credit for it.)

New York City booksellers and newspaper publishers, whatever they thought of Paine's arguments, were enchanted by the business his pamphlet was stimulating. Green's, Loudon's, and Anderson's bookshops were all advertising that they had copies in stock. The Philadelphia printers William and Thomas Bradford—the Continental Congress' official printers—called the attention of the readers of Holt's *Journal* to the completeness and cheapness of the Bradfords' edition. (Paine had left his first publisher, Robert Bell, and had gone over to the Bradfords because Bell had failed to make Paine's corrections and additions in the second printing; the Bradfords' version not only contained the new material, but was priced at one shilling instead of two, with discounts offered for bulk orders.)

Paine's arguments for separation, and the bold language he used, were exactly what New Yorkers—some of them, at least—had been waiting to read. "Common Sense" was more radical than any comparable brief before it, but it was advanced only a step or two beyond the ideas in many men's minds; if timing ever made a best seller, it made "Common Sense." The pamphlet ignored the convention of not attacking King George personally—it called him, among other things, a "Royal Brute" and "a hardened, sullen-tempered Pharaoh"—and it derided monarchy as an unnatural, insufferable evil; it denied that America had ever benefited from its dependence on Great Britain; it challenged even the notion that Great Britain was the colonies' mother country, and said, "This new world hath been the asylum for the persecuted lovers of civil and religious liberty from *every part* of Europe." Some of Paine's points, including this last one, may have been more tendentious than convincing, but on the whole he wrote with infectious certainty. "Common Sense" described separation as an affirmative good, not just an unavoidable necessity. "Everything that is right or reasonable," Paine wrote, "pleads for separation. The blood of the slain, the weeping voice of nature, cries, *'Tis time to part.*"

The controversy over "Common Sense" had grown more and more heated in the weeks after its appearance. One letter writer in Holt's *Journal*, praising the pamphlet to the skies, claimed that it had miraculously converted Tories into Whigs. That was undoubtedly an exaggeration, but Paine's essay had turned some doubting Whigs into convinced separationists, and had inspired a popular new toast: "May the INDEPENDENT principles of COMMON SENSE be confirmed throughout the United Colonies!" Needless to say, there were also many in New York who loathed "Common Sense," and it had indignant critics in all the other provinces, too. The Reverend Dr. William Smith, of the College of Philadelphia, for instance, called Paine's arguments an "*ignis fatuus* to draw the unwary into untried regions, full of precipices and quagmires," and Landon Carter, of Virginia, an old friend of General Washington, and by no means a timid man—he had contemplated complete severance of trade relations with Great Britain as long as two years before they had been terminated—regarded Paine's "rascally and nonsensical" thesis as a "disgrace" to the American cause. Perhaps more numerous than Paine's admirers and detractors added together were those readers who were not sure what to think. Henry Wisner, of Orange County, a delegate to the Continental Congress, wrote John McKesson, one of the New York Provincial Congress' secretaries, to ask what Orange and Ulster County delegates were saying about "Common Sense." Wisner also asked what John Morin Scott's reaction was. (Scott had not expressed a definite opinion one way or the other.) Some men praised Paine's literary style without agreeing, necessarily, that independence, total and entire, was America's appropriate objective; and, in fact, every middle-ground attitude toward the pamphlet had at least an adherent or two.

Furthermore, there were reasonable men in New York and everywhere else who agreed fully with Paine but were not saying so because they thought the time was not ripe. For instance, Sam Adams, of the Massachusetts delegation to the Continental Congress, admired "Common Sense" and Paine's conclusions as much as anyone in the country; and yet, as recently as January 15, Adams had maneuvered for postponement of a Congress debate on the desirability of making separation a war aim, for fear that the vote would be against it. The accuracy of Adams' estimate had been borne out, not long afterward, when the Continental Congress had asked a special committee, headed by James Wilson, of Pennsylvania, to prepare a declaration of nonindependence for consideration. Wilson had completed a six-thousand-word document to that effect, but in the time its writing had taken—from January 24 to February 14— many of the Continental Congress delegates had changed their minds. Even Wilson, a middle-of-the-road conservative and the chief among the Penn family's several lawyers, was no longer certain how he felt. He was not in favor of independence, but he was beginning to think that a negative declaration would serve no purpose. Partly on that account, Wilson's document had been tabled, and no one seemed interested in pressing for more conclusive action on it.

Lee had no reason to conceal his enthusiasm for "Common Sense"; he had been for separation long before he had read Paine. (Lee's remark, in his letter to Washington—"I own myself convinced, by the arguments, of the necessity of separation"—had been a private joke of understatement.) Paine, for his part, was one of Lee's greatest admirers. Paine knew only what he had read and heard about Lee, but Lee's reputation in Philadelphia was good. Any man who was working to bring New York City to its senses automatically had Philadelphia's best wishes. Furthermore, Paine was enthusiastic about the loyalty-oath device, and thought that Lee's Rhode Island campaign had been brilliant. Given all the chances that Lee and Paine had to congratulate each other, it was no surprise that their dinner was a success. The next day, Lee wrote to thank Dr.

Rush for arranging the introduction: "I am much oblig'd to you . . . he has genius in his eyes—his conversation has much life—I hope he will continue cramming down the throats of squeamish mortals his wholesome truths. . . ."

Compared to what New York had feared Lee might do, the General's anti-Tory actions had been few, but his passion for swearing non-Associators was undiminished. Lee could not understand why the Provincial Congress, especially now that he knew it better, had little or no enthusiasm for the Lee version of the Association oath and for the Lee style of administering it. The Provincial Congress, hearing testimony almost daily about inimicality and examining alleged inimicals by the score, realized that numbers of the local residents were astonishingly naïve about what they could and could not do. Lee thought offenders should be dealt with harshly, and counted on the effect of public example to deter other men from making similar mistakes. The Provincial Congress, in marked contrast, was inclined to treat inimicality—or apparent inimicality—leniently, and to assume, when it was at all possible, that the erring New Yorkers were misinformed rather than wicked. That was the spirit in which the Congress, on February 19, finally disposed of the cases of Colonel Heard's former prisoners, the Queens delinquents. Their number was down from nineteen to fourteen because Captain Jacob Mott and Joseph French had been restored and let go, and Samuel Clowes, George Weeks, and Gabriel Ludlow had been released on bond. (Ludlow's failure to appear as a New York County delegate to the Provincial Congress on February 12 had not been as mysterious as it had seemed; he had two residences, one in Queens and the other in New York; and he had been absent on account of being in jail as a Queens County inimical.) New York decided to let all the others go on bond, too. Each man was to post 500 pounds' security, swear to appear promptly if called, and pay his own confinement costs as soon as the bill was presented. Colonel Lasher was figuring out pro-rata charges for the guards he had supplied, and French, for one, questioned his bill even before he got it. (French agreed that he had been under guard for thirty-four days, but during the first three he had been confined to his own house, too sick to get out of bed. He did not feel he should be required to pay for what he considered an absurdly large guard around a sickroom— one officer and twelve enlisted men.) At the same time, the Provincial Congress voted to restore William Cock and his brother, Thomas Cock, of Oyster Bay, to their "former state and condition," just as Mott, their Manhassett neighbor, had been restored. (Through clerical error, presumably, Thomas Cock's name had not been on the original list of 788 Queens voters, but he had admitted having voted no.) The Cocks explained that they had made a misjudgment. They had changed their minds. They now thought that Queens should send delegates to the Provincial Congress, and they were ready to swear that, in the future, they would obey all orders of the Continental and the Provincial Congresses. The Provincial Congress felt that the Cocks' word was good enough. Many of the delegates thought, by this time, that blanket condemnation of the 788 (or 789, or whatever the correct number was) was legally weak, and the Provincial Congress was trying to retract, or at least soften the effect of, the previous session's drastic action. It explained, gratuitously and untruthfully, that "any former resolves of this Congress against the delinquents of Queens County were only intended to convince them of their error, and bring them to a just sense of their duty to the public."

In Lee's view, these releases and restorations were mad. "This measure must and ought to be considered an act of absolute idiotism," Lee wrote in a letter to Joseph Reed, Washington's military secretary, who was on leave from the headquarters staff at Cambridge, Massachusetts, to attend to his personal business affairs in Philadelphia. "The liberation of the notorious enemies of liberty and their country," he wrote the Provincial Congress, ". . . appears to me in our present situation, extremely ill-imagined. . . ." Lee predicted that as soon as the first body of British troops arrived, the 500-pound bonds would be forgotten. ("It is so far from a security that it is rather adding virus to their malignancy. . . .") What New York needed, Lee continued, was "some vigorous, decisive mode of discovering on whom you may depend, on whom not. The crisis will admit of no procrastination." The mode Lee was thinking about was the famous Lee oath.

Lee believed that a large number of the New York inimicals intended either to join the British armed forces or at least to assist the enemy in other ways. The Queens manifesto had boasted about a secret supply of arms—"means of protecting ourselves," the phrase had been—and Lee believed that these arms existed. Rumor said that Captain Richard Hewlett was in charge of the weapons cache, but no one had yet found him or the six other most dangerous men in the county. And, just as it was in the middle of releasing the Queens men, the Provincial Congress had a disturbing letter from Joseph Robinson, of the Queens Committee. In Robinson's opinion, some of the men who were being given their freedom were truly dangerous, no matter how reassuring their promises. Several had received and had passed out British gunpowder, Robinson said—an act that removed them from the class of misguided, or misinformed, political innocents. Robinson, however, refused to name the men. He said he didn't dare to, since he intended to go on sleeping in his own bed at night.

The continuing investigation of the cannon spiking at the King's Bridge, meanwhile, was making Westchester—Rye, Rye

Neck, and Mamaroneck, particularly—look unreliable, too. That crime, so baffling at the outset, had begun to unravel a few days later, when the proprietor of a brass foundry on Broadway, near St. Paul's Chapel, recalled having sold a number of second-hand flat files—just like those that had been used to make the spikes— to John Fowler, who ran the Farmer's Tavern, an inn on the Bowery near Collect Pond. When the Committee of Safety questioned Fowler, he said he had bought the files for William Lownsberry, a Mamaroneck farmer. (Fowler added that as soon as he had heard about the cannon spiking, he had suspected Lownsberry.) Lownsberry was arrested and questioned. All he would admit, at first, was that Fowler was telling the truth: Lownsberry had bought the files. But, Lownsberry claimed, he had not ordered them for any sinister purpose. He had only wanted his neighbor, Joseph Purdy, a blacksmith, to make some skeins, or metal caps for axles, for farm wagons out of them. But Lownsberry could not show the Committee the skeins or the files, and he could not say where they were.

At the same time, by coincidence, the Committee of Safety was investigating an old incident, the wreck of a small ship, the *Polly and Ann*, which had run onto Squan Beach (near what is now called Manasquan), New Jersey, in late December. The *Polly and Ann*'s cargo had been contraband for the British at Boston, including beef and pork, and Madeira addressed to General Howe himself. Furthermore, her captain, Godfrey Haines, of Mamaroneck, was wanted in New York as a jail-breaker who had escaped from the City Hall cells while await-ing a hearing as a flagrant inimical. And—alas for Westchester's reputation!—most of the *Polly and Ann*'s passengers were from Mamaroneck, Rye, and Rye Neck. Apparently they had been trying to travel, via Boston, to Halifax or England—a trip that few, if any, staunch Associators were making. Isaac Gidney was one of the passengers; the story was that he had previously owned the ship but had sold it to Haines. Bartholomew Haines, of Mamaroneck, Godfrey's cousin, was a member of the crew. The Committee of Safety suspected, although it lacked positive proof, that Governor Tryon had arranged for the *Polly and Ann*'s ill-fated trip, and that most or all of the costs, including the purchase of the cargo, had been paid for in English sterling.

While these revelations were coming out in testimony, Lownsberry was questioned a second time. He admitted that he and Joshua Gidney, of Rye, the son of Isaac Gidney, along with Josiah Burrell, of Rye Neck, and William Haines, Thomas Haines, and James Haines, Jr., of Rye Neck, three brothers who were related to Godfrey Haines, and several others had intended to spike the cannon. He admitted that the files had been purchased for that purpose. But, Lownsberry insisted, he and his associates had not spiked the guns because, when they reached Valentine's farm on the night of January 17, they had found that the deed had already been done. There had been a second cannon-spiking crew at King's Bridge, if Lownsberry could be believed. (It had already been established that he could not be.)

That was as far as the investigation had got. By admitting his intent while still denying the deed, Lownsberry could account for the most damaging evidence against him. But for practical purposes, Lownsberry's cleverness was not helping him much. To be on the safe side, the Committee of Safety had confined the men it suspected as the principal cannon-spikers to the prison cells in the Upper Barracks. The list included Lownsberry, Isaac Gidney, Joshua Gidney, Burrell, Thomas Haines, and Purdy. (Since there was no question that Godfrey Haines had, at the very least, broken jail, he had been sent to the Ulster County jail, at Kingston, New York.)

It was not clear whether Governor Tryon had been the insti-
gator of both the shipping and the cannon-spiking schemes or
just an enthusiast for projects that Westchester men had initiated; in either case the Americans' inimicality had gone well
beyond mere political confusion. There was some testimony that
the cannon had been spiked on Tryon's orders as part of the
preparation for the British attack on New York City; that the
Governor had confided the tactical attack plan in detail—it was
to start with simultaneous landings at Mamaroneck on the
Sound and at Philipse Manor on the Hudson River, with the
idea of cutting off Manhattan Island when the British forces
met each other—and had emphasized the importance of elimi-
nating the guns from the area where the link-up would occur.
And it was perfectly clear that the *Polly and Ann* had been
trying to deliver supplies to the enemy at Boston. Still, it hardly
mattered how influential Tryon had been, for New Yorkers had
committed dangerous acts, and no one in the Provincial Congress needed reminding, in view of what had happened, that
other dangerous acts might be in the planning stage. Even so,
the majority of the men in the Provincial Congress could not see
that indiscriminate Tory-swearing would help.

On February 29, Lee abruptly stopped trying to persuade
New York to adopt his policies. On his own authority, and
nothing else, he ordered the guards at the wharves to stop all
traffic between the shore and the British ships. He had just been
informed (he explained afterward) that one of the warships had
seized another New Jersey boat and another cargo. The *Asia*
had stopped a New Brunswick sloop, a violation of the unwritten
rules. She was loaded with bread, butter, and flour for New
York City, and the *Asia* had commandeered the cargo. But the
British had paid for what they had taken and had then released
the vessel. The New Jersey shipper's only complaint, it turned

out, was about the price. The British had paid eighteen shillings per hundredweight for the flour when the going New York City rate was nineteen shillings.

What struck the Provincial Congress as incredible was the fact that Lee failed to inform New York of his decision. As a result, no one had told Mr. Nixon, the new port master, about the change. The first he knew of it was on the morning of March 1, when the wharf guards began shooting at small boats in the vicinity of the Broad Street slip. Nixon thought they had gone crazy. A pair of Tryon's servants, who were bringing the Governor's dirty laundry ashore to be washed—an accommodation that had been part of the overall agreement—were arrested by Lee's soldiers and marched off, under guard, to the Lower Barracks.

Neither Nixon nor any other New Yorker had understood any of this. The Provincial Congress started to look into the queer situation. Meanwhile Lee, attending to last things first, had written a report to Washington, and had said—anticipating the facts by some twelve hours—that his order to cut communications with the British ships "has thrown the Mayor, Council, and Tories into agonies. Their propensity or rather rage for paying court to this great man [Tryon] is inconceivable. They cannot be weaned from him. We must put wormwood on his paps, or they will cry to suck, as they are in their second childhood." (Since Lee was concerned mostly with the courting propensities of the Provincial Congress, the omission of its name from his list was doubtless accidental. The Governor's new appointee, Mayor David Matthews, who had taken Mayor Hicks's place, like the members of the Governor's Council, had an obvious reason for paying court to Tryon—he had given them their posts.)

Lee was preparing another shock for the Provincial Congress.

He had decided to order a new Tory-swearing drive. He did not intend to ask for New York's consent. Lee knew that if he did, the Provincial Congress would not give it. He expected to miss the fun; before the swearing could begin, Lee thought, he would be on his way to Canada. Sears would be in charge, and Queens would be the main scene for the chase. (Lee recognized that Queens' inimicals had already had more than their share of attention; and that was part of what bothered him. The thought that Queens suspects had been released and, in some cases, restored, without having sworn to the Lee version of the Association oath was more than Lee could bear.) Sears, with a small patrol of men drawn from Ward's regiment, was already in Queens, near Newtown, at the head of Newtown Creek, looking into the possibility that supplies for the British ships were being smuggled by night from somewhere in that vicinity.

The wharf guards' shots were clearly audible at City Hall, and within minutes the Provincial Congress had an unconfirmed report that the soldiers not only knew what they were doing, but that they were doing it on Lee's orders. The New Yorkers could hardly believe it, but the seemingly preposterous development reawakened all their old fears, dating back to the days before the General's entry into the province. A committee to investigate the musket firings was appointed—Thomas Smith, Isaac Roosevelt, and Abraham Lott, the agent-victualer, who stood to lose the most by Lee's new orders. Another committee—John Morin Scott, John Hobart, and Peter Gansevoort—was to call on Lee to ask why communications with the British ships had been cut in direct contradiction to—if not defiance of—the Provincial Congress' resolutions. (An argument about the command issue was the last thing the New Yorkers wanted, especially when, with Harrison, Lynch, and Allen back in Philadelphia, no arbitrators were on hand. Even so, the Provincial Congress meant to do what it had to do. If Lee wanted to make trouble, New York intended to fight for New York's sovereignty.)

But when Scott, Hobart, and Gansevoort talked to Lee, the General seemed almost affable. He explained that he was, to use his word, "inhibiting" communications with the British ships as a way of making Tryon keep his part of the compact with New York, and that was all. If the Provincial Congress wanted to continue the daily supplies, Lee added, he would issue the necessary orders to the wharf guards. The one thing he could no longer permit, Lee said, was *personal* communications with the British; he could not allow anyone to go on board the ships or to come ashore from them. He said the shootings had been a mistake, a misunderstanding of his orders on the soldiers' part. Lee's friendly tone came as a relief to the Provincial Congress, although the General offered no excuse for having acted without consultation and still showed no sign of admitting that communications with the warships, personal or otherwise, were not his not to permit. (Lee also failed to use the excellent opportunity of his talk with Scott, Hobart, and Gansevoort to tell the Provincial Congress about his plans for the forthcoming Tory-hunt in Queens—an omission that the committee naturally was in no position to notice.)

The next day, Sunday, March 3, Lee's mail included a surprising letter from John Hancock. The Continental Congress had changed its mind. Lee was not to get the Canada command, after all, but instead was to take charge of the newly created Southern Department, a zone of potential military operations that included Virginia, North Carolina, South Carolina, and Georgia.

If Lee was disappointed, he hid his disappointment well. He did say, in a letter to Washington, that, ". . . As I am the only general officer on the Continent who can speak and think in

French, I confess it would have been more prudent to have sent
me to Canada, but I shall obey with alacrity, and I hope with
success." But otherwise he acted as if the Southern Department
had been what he had wanted, and, indeed, the command was at
least as remote from Washington's domination as Canada, which
was important to Lee. In time, the Southern Department clearly
could become an important military theater, although so far the
British threat to the South remained an unknown quantity to
everyone, including Clinton, who was at Hampton Roads,
Virginia, without an army, talking to Lord Dunmore, looking
anxiously for the fleet, and unaware that because of troubles of
all sorts, among them a bad storm, hardly more than half his
ships were on their way to America, with the leading vessels no
farther than Portugal.

Lee also had word from Cambridge—letters from both
Washington and General Nathanael Greene—warning that
General Howe was busy. The British had removed their
mortars from Bunker's Hill and Charlestown; they were putting their brass fieldpieces on board ship; they had taken all the
topsail vessels in Boston Harbor into the British service, by one
arrangement or another; their transports were hauled in to the
wharves; their sails were bent, and their water casks were filled;
and some of the officers' personal luggage had been loaded. All
these preparations for leaving, Washington explained to Lee,
might be a feint. But Washington intended to test Howe's
intentions by occupying Dorchester Heights, the high ground
just southeast of Boston. If the British failed to oppose the
American advance, Washington wrote, "I shall be confirmed in
my opinion that they mean to leave the town." By the time Lee
had passed this news along to the Provincial Congress, as he did
the next day, Monday, March 4, it was a week old—time
enough, New York imagined, for Howe's fleet to be well along

on its way to New York. In fact, the occupation of Dorchester Heights was still in progress and was scheduled for completion by dawn of the fifth, and Washington did not yet know what the British would do. Although no one had forgotten that Clinton's appearance at New York had caused a false alarm, the Provincial Congress took the new warning with the utmost seriousness, as was appropriate. Like most of Washington's council of general officers, the New Yorkers assumed that if the British were leaving Boston, they would proceed immediately to New York. Washington was almost alone in thinking that, as another possibility, Howe might first withdraw to Halifax to give his army a chance to rest.

The New York Provincial Congress, fearing that the British might appear at any moment, drew up a list of high-priority tasks in the emergency. The Southampton and East Hampton committees were notified, by letter, to watch for ships, and to let New York City know immediately when they saw them. Letters were also sent to all colonels of minute and militia regiments south of Albany "to hold their respective regiments in readiness to march with their arms, accoutrements, blankets, and five days' provisions on first notice of the invasion." The New Jersey Provincial Congress was given Washington's warning, and New York suggested that New Jersey's militia might be alerted, too. Westchester County's delegates were asked to buy 1,200 barrels of salt pork, and Albany County's delegates were asked to buy 1,850 bushels of "good peas." The Provincial Congress intended to establish several provisions depots north of Manhattan Island. Although the hour was late, the Provincial Congress wrote all six of New York's gunpowder manufacturers asking for up-to-date inventories of finished powder on hand, and urging the proprietors to make more as fast as they could. (Since June, the Provincial Congress had been doing its best to encourage New York gunpowder production, and was paying a bonus of five pounds per hundredweight, beyond the going price of twenty pounds, for powder made within the province—and noting, with dismay, that the going price was steadily creeping up. Judge Livingston had built the best mill, at Rhinebeck. Since his death, his son, Robert R., Jr., had continued to operate it, and had produced several thousand pounds of new powder, and had reconstituted a considerable additional amount that had accidentally gotten wet or had been spoiled. New York could hardly hope to defend itself with New York powder alone, but every little bit would help.) And, finally, the Provincial Congress ordered the Sandy Hook lighthouse blacked out. If the British fleet arrived by night, its navigators might not be able to find the Narrows—at least not until daylight the following morning.

These last-minute arrangements revealed how poorly New York City was prepared, but the men in the Provincial Congress showed no signs that they felt sorry for themselves. They were resolute, determined to do the best they could, and unaware that their best amounted to little. The warnings from Cambridge did not produce anything like panic, although some, but not many, New Yorkers were prompted to quit the city. (Renting a country place was even more difficult and expensive than earlier. A letter in Gaine's *Mercury* reported that some out-of-town rents were twice what they had been before the war, blamed unscrupulous landlords for taking advantage "of the times," and suggested a system of rent controls, to be administered by local Association committees.) Those New Yorkers who stayed where they were took comfort from a number of items of good news mixed in with the bad. One such was the designation of Lord Stirling, who had just been commissioned a brigadier general and was very highly thought of in New York, to take Lee's place, at least until some higher-ranking officer arrived in town. Also, Lee had persuaded the Connecticut regiments to stay and continue to work on the fortifications for a fortnight longer than they had promised—until March 25, instead of going home on the twelfth. The best news of all was a promise Washington had made in his warning letter to Lee: if the British were really leaving Boston, the Commander-in-Chief had said, and if New York City was really Howe's destination, a large part of the Continental Army would immediately be sent to New York's assistance. Whether the Continental soldiers could march fast enough to beat the British transports was a question, and Washington had not explained exactly how he would know where the British fleet intended to go. Still, the promise was reassuring as well as complimentary. The General, wedded to the military principle of concentration of strength, had never before been willing to divide his main army—not even to rescue the expeditionary force in Canada. His word that he would do so to defend New York lifted the city's morale and confirmed its high opinion of its military importance.

Civic pride was also increased by a local achievement. Christopher Colles, an inventor and engineer, invited all New Yorkers to inspect the city's marvelous new steam water pump in operation for the first time. Despite war worries and war duties, the demonstration drew great crowds—almost everybody who could possibly take the time. Colles had been at work on a city water-supply system for two years, and the steam pump, near Collect Pond, was to raise water from a well to a new two-million-gallon reservoir on the high ground just east of what is now Broadway and White Street. The steam engine, itself a novelty in America, had cost the city 9,000 pounds, but it promised to solve, once and for all, New York's chronic water shortage, although the wooden pipes, which were to carry the water throughout the city, had not yet been laid. The manpower for that big job might not be available before the end of the troubles with the British. Still, the working pump was a thrill. Lower Manhattan had many wells, both public and private, but the water from all but two or three of them had a bad taste, which got worse in drought years. Rather than drink it, or use it to make coffee, those New Yorkers who could afford to do so bought water, by the bucket or the bottle, from upper Manhattan's wells and springs. Colles was delighted with the way the pump functioned, and kept it running for several days. Whenever the engine was working, he flew a signal flag from a pole near the reservoir that could be seen all the way to Bowling Green.

On March 5, while the steam pump demonstration had New York's fascinated attention, Sears received Lee's orders for the march through Queens. Enclosed was a copy of the Lee oath, which began with a flowery, "I, ——, here, in the presence of Almighty God, as I hope for ease, honor, and comfort in this world, and happiness in the world to come, most earnestly, devoutly, and religiously do swear. . . ." In addition, Lee promised to forward to Sears a revised list of Long Island Tories as soon as possible. Meanwhile, Sears, working with the old lists, was to proceed at once, and he was to regard any refusal to take Lee's oath as "an avowal of hostile intention." Men who refused were to be arrested and sent, without delay, to Connecticut. The one exception was Daniel Hewlett, who was to be arrested and sent to Connecticut even if he was willing to take the oath. (It looked as if Lee was confusing Daniel Hewlett, who had taken the regular oath and was probably willing to take the Lee oath as well, with Captain Hewlett, whose first name was Richard.)

Like New York, Connecticut had not been informed about the Sears Tory-hunt, and had not been alerted to arrange to receive prisoners from Queens. A large bag of adamant inimicals might have been more than Connecticut's limited jail space could accommodate, but as it turned out, that problem did not come up. Sears was unable to find Daniel Hewlett, much less Richard. The men he could find, however hostile their intentions may have been, all took the Lee oath. On Wednesday, March 6, Sears swore what he called, in a report to Lee, "the four great Newtown Tories." He wrote that "they swallowed it as hard as a four-pound shot"; still, they swallowed it and that was that. Sears swore five more Newtown men the following day, and he also complained to Lee that he and his soldiers needed more horses. Sears believed that the most dangerous Tories were eluding him because their mounts were faster than his. He also estimated that one-half of all the men in Queens were potential traitors, but, as he moved through Hempstead, Cow Neck, and Great Neck, following in the footsteps of the Heard expedition, the *déjà-vu* quality of the Sears mission became increasingly obvious. Sears found only the men that Heard had found, former inimicals like James Cornell, Francis Davenport, and Jonas Valentine, to name a few. The Queens men were first frightened at being routed out again, and then relieved to find it was only for another oath taking. Many of them, after they had taken the oath, became indignant. They felt that, as respectable citizens, they did not deserve this senseless ordeal. Jacob Mott was among those sworn, and it was at least the third time he had taken the oath in one form or another, which gave him a record of some sort, if not one that he would have chosen to hold. Mott said later that he had offered Sears his two sets of official clearance papers, but that Sears had refused even to look at them. Under the circumstances, Mott explained, he thought that the easiest way out was to stop arguing and take the oath.

While Sears was accomplishing little or nothing, a New

Yorker named Samuel Gale had learned, at first hand, what it was like to be whisked off to Connecticut without delay. Before the war, Gale had been the Clerk of Cumberland County in the New Hampshire Grants. (That land, today part of Vermont, was part of New York, according to New Yorkers.) When the Cumberland County Committee had taken over as the effective government, and Gale was out of a job, he had protested against surrendering the county records. In the end, he had done so, but not happily. He had written several complaining letters to the Committee saying what he thought of it, and indicating that his opinion of congresses and committees in general was low. Gale had then moved to a town house in New York City, and there he had been arrested, in the middle of the night, by Lee's soldiers. He had been locked up in a cell in the Upper Barracks, and then removed, under guard, to the jail at Fairfield, Connecticut. His arrest, his deportation, and his confinement, Gale felt, were all outrageous. As he said in a letter to the New York Provincial Congress from his Connecticut cell, he thought that his opinions hardly merited the treatment he had been given. Gale had not been accused of anything, or tried by anyone, or been convicted of any crime. He was most uncomfortable in prison. He was the victim, he claimed, of "a wanton act of military power," and he was counting on the Provincial Congress to do something about it.

The Provincial Congress was distressed by Gale's letter, which it read on March 5. The delegates knew nothing at all about his arrest, because Lee had forgotten to mention it. Furthermore, the Provincial Congress could hear the port guards shooting again—a nuisance and a danger that Lee had promised would not recur. New York was angered by this combination of failures, and even though Lee was on the point of leaving—the formal transfer of his command to Stirling was scheduled for the evening of March 6—the Provincial Congress voted to inform Lee, officially, that he was finishing his New York tour of duty in an odious manner. Smith and Hobart quickly drafted the note. Its hard tone was, in itself, a reprimand. The Provincial Congress demanded to know what the Gale affair was all about. It reminded Lee that the Provincial Congress—not Lee, or any other visiting troop commander— had the right and the responsibility, delegated to it from the Continental Congress, of apprehending, trying, and punishing citizens "who violate the resolutions of Congress, or who act inimical to the liberties of America." And it informed Lee that the provisioning arrangements for the British ships were to remain as they had been.

New York had never before laid down the law to Lee with such blunt concision. The General was anything but cowed. When the note was delivered to him by messenger, Lee brushed it aside with a comment about its being Stirling's concern. But then, after the messenger had left, Lee had second thoughts. He wrote the Provincial Congress a fairly long letter, a mixture of arrogance and false modesty, in which he claimed as his justification that his most recent instructions from the Continental Congress—"to use every means in his power for the defense of the city"—implied everything he had ordered. (The shootings were the exception; Lee insisted that they were accidental.) Lee declared that furnishing the enemy with the necessities of life was not the way to defend New York. He said there was no practical way of preventing the provision-boat crews from smuggling intelligence to the British. As for Gale, Lee admitted that the man's arrest had been "irregular," but said it was not prudent to allow a single man to stay in New York who would not be willing, in the emergency, to take up arms in the province's defense. Furthermore, Lee wrote, he had the assurances of "many respectable men" that Gale was a most dangerous man and "ought not to be suffered to remain on Long Island, where an enemy is perhaps more dangerous than in any other spot of America." (Was Lee confusing Gale with another person? Gale had been living in the city, not on Long Island. Nothing in the record or Gale's letter suggested that he had been offered the Lee oath or that he had refused to take it. What made Lee think that Gale would not take up arms in New York's defense?)

Then Lee's letter revealed his major surprise for New York: "I must now inform you, Sir, that in consequence of the last instructions from the Continental Congress . . . I have ordered Colonel Ward . . . to secure the whole body of professed Tories in Long Island. . . ."

It was interesting that Lee should mention Ward, whose regiment had only supplied the detachment of men with which Sears was conducting the Tory hunt, instead of Sears, who was actually doing the job. Lee finished off with a flourish of insincere self-criticism: "If I have done wrong, and I confess the irregularity, I must submit myself to the shame of being reputed foolish, rash, and precipitate. I must undergo the censure of the public, but I shall have the consciousness in my own breast that the most pure motives of serving the public cause, uncontaminated by pique or resentment to individuals, have urged me to the step."

With that, Lee was gone. He left the city late in the afternoon of Thursday, March 7. New York did not give him any formal farewell—not an escort and not a word of thanks. Lee appeared indifferent to New York's discourtesy. Besides his favorite, Spada, and a few other dogs, he was accompanied by his two aides, Otway Byrd and Lewis Morris, Jr., the son of the Continental Congress delegate; his secretary, Mr. Nourse; and a private guard, the escort that had marched with him from

Cambridge at the start of his Connecticut recruiting campaign. (Lee acted as if these soldiers had been permanently assigned to him. Actually, they were not, and Washington wanted them back.) Lee also took with him a French civil engineer named Le Brun, an expert who might prove useful in the Southern Department. Lee had employed Le Brun without the authority to do so, and without having asked for it. Conceivably, Lee felt that one or two more irregularities added to those he was already guilty of could hardly matter. He left behind a scattering of personal belongings, including some uniforms at the tailor's, and several unpaid accounts. Among New Yorkers, Mrs. de la Montaigne may have been one of the number who were sorry to have Lee go, for, according to her reckoning, he owed her rent money. Lee's answers to New York's reprimand—if they could be called answers—made New York angrier than before. The Provincial Congress' one recourse, which it immediately voted to take, was to furnish the Continental Congress with a complete, detailed complaint about Lee's transgressions. While that document was being written, New York hoped, Stirling might be persuaded to countermand several of Lee's last orders. Perhaps the provisioning arrangements could be reestablished before the British ships began stopping the boats that supplied the city; perhaps Ward's men could be called off the Long Island Tory-hunt before too many men had been harassed and humiliated. There was no "body of professed Tories" on Long Island, the Provincial Congress thought, and it followed that whatever Ward's men were doing was illegal, morally wrong, and a waste of manpower needed for the fortifications.

Hard as it was to imagine, Lee was much more nearly correct than the Provincial Congress. Lee lacked proof of his suspicions, and his term "professed Tories" made no sense, but, in fact, the pine barrens of Long Island and the marshy wilderness along its south shore, indented with bays, inlets, and coves, were teeming with true inimicals. The dangerous men were not at home on their farms waiting for Sears's or any other posse. They were in hiding, camping in the woods, moving their campsites constantly, and staying clear of roads and beaten paths. Some of them had formed small bands. Many had boats, and were spending their days on the water, not far from shore, coming in at night for fresh water and provisions. They were armed, and they had a certain amount of ammunition cached away. There were many more of them than Lee imagined, and they were not just local men. Long Island, Staten Island, and parts of New Jersey had become assembly points for Tories from miles around who were waiting for the British to come and meant to join them when they did. No one had a count, or even a good estimate, of their total number. It was smaller, by far, than Lord George Germain hoped—and much bigger than the Provincial Congress dreamed.

From the first hour of his new command, General Stirling proved himself enormously agreeable. He wanted to confer frequently with the Provincial Congress (rather than, like Lee, abuse it by letter), and a special committee that the Provincial Congress appointed to meet with Stirling (Smith, McDougall, Van Zandt, Yates, Randall and Ten Broeck) reported on Friday, March 8, that in a single meeting compromises had been found for all points of contention between the province and the military. Stirling agreed that, for the time being, there was no sensible alternative to provisioning the British ships in the harbor. All he asked was that goods delivered should be carefully limited to the list of authorized necessities; that the provision boats' crews not board the warships (and reveal all they knew about the city's defenses); and that no extra hands be carried in the supply boats (they might be escaping Tories). Stirling promised to stop random firing by the port sentries. Governor Tryon's two servants and the Governor's laundry, which was still dirty, were to be sent back to the *Duchess of Gordon* by the next boat. Stirling agreed that Samuel Gale's arrest was entirely the Provincial Congress' concern; if it wanted to ask Connecticut to release Gale, that was all right. (The only objections to Gale, as far as Stirling could discover, were the old, complaining letters Gale had written to the Cumberland County Committee. Copies of them were in the hands of one of the Cumberland County delegates to the Provincial Congress, Major William Williams, and it did not take much imagination to think who had persuaded Lee that Gale was dangerous.) Stirling also assured the Committee members that no civilian in New York City or New York Province would be arrested or thrown into jail or deported to Connecticut by the military. Every case of inimicality that his men found, Stirling promised, would be referred to the proper authority, the Provincial Congress. Stirling said his purpose was to aid New York's civil government, not to interfere with it.

New York was delighted by Stirling's attitude, although not entirely surprised, because many of the delegates knew him well and considered him at least half a New Yorker. Stirling had been born and brought up in the city, and had lived in New Jersey for only a little more than a decade. Now fifty years old, he was a good-looking, well-mannered, and convivial man. His father, a successful New York City merchant, had left him a fortune in New Jersey and New York real estate. Stirling was married to Sarah Livingston, a daughter of the second Lord of the Manor and a sister of the third. He had made the mistake of thinking that he ought to be able to live like his in-laws, who lived like English lords. That fancy depended on finding reliable tenants for his property, which was anything but easy; and Stirling, having accumulated spectacular debts, had been reduced to selling his land—or watching the sheriff sell it—piece by piece to calm his creditors. (Stirling did not seem greatly concerned, even though he was getting Continental dollars, which were depreciating, for land that was growing in value.) Stirling had not been to college, but he was a member of the King's College Board of Governors. He was not much of a reader—except of books on his hobby, astronomy—but, as a member of the New York Society, he had helped found the city's first library, in 1754. (The New York Society Library, at 53 East Seventy-ninth Street, after several removals, still has a few books from its original collection.) Stirling's personal style was as polished as Lee's was rude, but, on the other hand, as Stirling was the first to point out, he was only an amateur soldier. He had served in the French and Indian War as one of General William Shirley's aides—he was an amateur who had at least seen several battles—and any professional would have been proud of the job he had done raising and training the New Jersey regiments. Still, Stirling chose to classify himself as "a rank beginner." After Lee, New York fully appreciated Stirling's lack of military pretensions, even if it was false modesty.

The Provincial Congress never bothered to finish writing its formal complaint against Lee to the Continental Congress. It concentrated, instead, on assisting the new commander. Including the thousand Connecticut men who were scheduled to go home, Stirling's strength was not more than three thousand, and Stirling calculated that, with eight thousand men, he might complete the city's basic fortifications by the middle of May. Reports of British sails on the horizon began to come in to his headquarters on the first day of his new assignment. Stirling kept calm. When confirmation of the reports arrived, Stirling said, it would be time enough to sound the alarm. So far, confirmation had never come. (In every case, anxious lookouts had misidentified American ships in the distance.) Stirling's first definite word about the British arrived on March 13, in a letter from Cambridge dated March 9, saying that the enemy was surely leaving Boston, probably for New York. The writer was one of Washington's aides, Stephen Moylan. He said that armed schooners would try to follow Howe's fleet and report back as soon as they could tell what course the British were setting:

If they steer west you may expect a large reinforcement from this army, and in all probability the main body will soon follow. You will please to communicate this to the Provincial Congress or Convention, who, the General doubts not, will coöperate with you in using every endeavor to prevent their forming a lodging before His Excellency can come or send to your assistance. The fate of America depends upon this campaign, and the success of this campaign will a good deal depend upon your exerting yourselves with vigor upon this occasion.

Stirling also learned, almost simultaneously, that New York could expect reinforcements from Pennsylvania and New Jersey, for the Continental Congress, having studied Lee's military report on New York's defenses, had ordered three Pennsylvania regiments (General William Irvine's, Colonel John Shee's, and Colonel Robert Magaw's) and a New Jersey regiment (Colonel Elias Dayton's), as well as a few smaller units—to the magic total of 8,000 men—to march to the city. New York knew that all these reinforcements needed time to get ready and time to travel. Still, the two promises added together meant that New York was to get practically all the troops of the United Colonies except the regiments intended for Canadian service.

Stirling took Washington's advice about vigorous exertions literally, and in his first order as commander in New York he called out the entire male population of the city to work on the fortifications. Every man, including indentured servants and slaves—the three thousand blacks included about eight hundred males over sixteen years old—who was physically capable of fatigue duty was to work every third day under the direction of Colonel Smith, Stirling's chief engineer. Men who could afford to could send substitutes—a servant, a hired man, or a slave—provided that it was not the substitute's day to work on his own behalf. The work project began on March 15, after one day's delay because of bad weather—driving rain, mixed with snow. The escape clause was not abused. Many well-to-do New Yorkers—those serving on the Committee of Safety, for instance—had compelling reasons to take advantage of it, but among the hundreds of pairs of hands that were added to the fortifications job there were quite a few that had not held a spade, a shovel, or a pickax for a long time. Slaves, servants, and hired men were numerous, but the militia units—soldiers who had been alerted for duty but not yet called—provided the bulk of the emergency labor force. Still, New York's rich and powerful men did report for work, and the sight of them digging—the able-bodied members of the Walton family, for instance—was an unusual inspiration. There was one complaint: the hardworking civilians wanted a rum allowance, like the rum allowance members of the military units got. The Committee of Safety thought that fair, and voted a ration: six ounces of rum or one quart of ship's beer or spruce beer per man per day.

According to the latest reports, the work on the Highland forts, after so many false starts and delays, was at last headed in a sensible direction. Progress had been made on the sod-and-fascines ramparts on the summit of Popolop's Hill, and it was beginning to look as if the British might have more difficulty sailing past Peekskill than Tryon had indicated in his letters home. New York's chronic gunpowder shortage was slightly relieved, or about to be relieved; a shipment of 1,500 pounds of powder had docked despite the British warships, and Nicholas Low, as the consignee, was dickering with the Committee of Safety over price. He wanted thirty pounds per hundredweight, which was high but not outrageous, plus a special 45,000-pound export permit for his own use, but no one doubted that, in the end, New York and Low would come to terms. Low was trying to take advantage of an interesting special exception to the Continental Association's rules against ordinary shipping activities. He and a few others, like Philip Livingston and Jacobus Van Zandt, for instance, knew that if they could bring in shiploads of any of the items on the list of critical shortages, such as gunpowder, New York would issue them, as a reward for patriotic risk-taking, a permit that would allow them to export goods equal to the value of those they had brought in. (Low wanted to use his permit to ship a cargo of flaxseed and lumber to Ireland.) Within a few days, the Provincial Congress agreed to Low's full price, and, almost at the same time, New York heard from Philadelphia that the Continental Congress was sending the city 5,000 pounds more than New York had lent Boston, a total of about 7,000 pounds. The Continental Congress was also helping New York with money. Francis Lewis, the delegate, rode in with 47,000 Continental dollars, divided for traveling purposes into two large packages. Many of the province's pressing debts could be paid off right away. Abraham Lott, the agent-victualer, was also New York's Treasurer and in charge of disbursements. While the cash was most welcome, New York realized that it would soon need more money, even if it postponed paying interest on the royal administration's old bills of credit. (The interest on the 1771 issue was already due.) So it both put off the payment on the province's debt and ordered another printing of New York currency—$137,500 worth in fractions of a dollar (one-eighth, one-sixth, one-fourth, one-half, and two-thirds) and in $1, $2, $3, $5, and $10 denominations. That would be the equivalent of 55,000 pounds sterling, as New York figured the current exchange rate—at least until Gresham's Law and inflation began to erode the New York dollar. Sam Loudon, whose staunch support of the Association had earned him a privileged position, was given the large printing order. The job was so big—213,400 separate bills—that Loudon would probably have to farm out some of the work to other printshops. The Provincial Congress realized that the printers and engravers might be tempted to print a few extra sheets of money or engrave an extra plate or two, so an elaborate affidavit form was prepared for all the workmen to sign, and Isaac Roosevelt, the supervisor of the project, was ordered to do his best to prevent counterfeiting. While the Provincial Congress was on the subject of printing, someone remembered the Rivington case and pointed out that Connecticut had never returned Rivington's stolen type fonts, and had not compensated the man, either. New York therefore resolved, on March 8, to remind Connecticut. Since the first claim, addressed to Trumbull, had been completely ignored, this time New York addressed its note to the Connecticut delegation in Philadelphia.

For a day or two after Stirling's assurances that inimicality would be left to New York's civilian authorities, Sears nevertheless continued to operate in Queens. A few more of the much-harassed men on the old list—despite his promise, Lee had never sent the revised one—were resworn, but when Sears finally heard about the policy change, the unprofitable hunt came to an end. Lee's report to the Continental Congress had mentioned the prevalence of "professed enemies of liberty" on Long Island and Staten Island, too, "nested" where they could do the most harm. But the General had not boasted about Sears's Tory-swearing expedition, or even recommended the Lee oath. By the time he reached Philadelphia, Lee was enthusiastic about a new device for coping with inimicals: "I should therefore think it prudent to secure their [the professed enemies'] children as hostages. If a measure of this kind (hard as it may appear) is not adopted, the children's children of America may rue the fatal omission." Meanwhile, however, Christopher Duyckinck had told the Provincial Congress a disturbing new story about Long Island inimicals. Duyckinck swore that a group of New York Harbor pilots, including Frank James, were working for Captain Parker of the *Phoenix*, "decoying" American ships as they approached the port. Duyckinck was considered reliable. He was a prominent member of the Mechanics Committee, the strongly pro-Association group of artisans, clerks, and working men, most of them unable to meet the property requirement and therefore not qualified to vote, who had organized to give themselves a voice in the protest movement. The moderates in the Provincial Congress thought that Duyckinck and the Mechanics Committee were a shade too radical, but more sensible than the old Sons of Liberty. And, furthermore, Duyckinck's charges rang true. Most ships approaching New York took on a harbor pilot to steer them through the channel from Gravesend Bay to the New York City docks. James and his colleagues, according to Duyckinck, had been boarding ships in the usual fashion, but then, before the ship captains realized what was happening, had been steering not for New York's docks but for the *Phoenix*. Once within range of the *Phoenix*'s guns, a ship would hardly dare defy an order to stop. Duyckinck's allegations, if true, would explain how the *Phoenix*, in recent months, had managed to take several American ships, including the *Sally*, the *Frances*, and the *James*, with unbelievable ease. Duyckinck added that he knew where the pilots' secret shore camp was—he could not name the particular cove on Jamaica Bay, but he knew how to get there. On hearing all this, the Provincial Congress sent McDougall right over to talk to Stirling, and within a few hours, Colonel Ward had Stirling's orders—"in the utmost confidence of secrecy"—to send two officers and forty men, with Duyckinck acting as their guide, to raid the camp and arrest the pilots. If James resisted arrest, the soldiers were "to destroy" him. (A possible death sentence for James, on nothing more than Duyckinck's unverified word, was rather more excessive than Lee's worst irregularities.) But the raid was a failure. When Ward's men reached the campsite, on the night of March 9, the pilots were gone. The chances were that they had been warned, had taken to their boats, and were either on board the *Phoenix* or tied up alongside her.

By now, New York had acquired one naval vessel—the schooner *Schuyler*, which had been fitted out for patrol duty with three small guns. The Provincial Congress ordered her captain, James Smith, to sail back and forth between Egg Harbor, Long Island, and Sandy Hook in an effort to discourage any further decoying. Captain Parker promptly made a countermove. He announced to every New Yorker who visited him, or who saw him on the *Duchess of Gordon*, that the *Phoenix*'s tender was being armed. As soon as she was ready, Parker said, the sloop would go into service off Egg Harbor as an anti-patrol patrol.

The men in the Provincial Congress knew that at some point a complete break with the British ships and Governor Tryon would have to occur. An engagement between the *Phoenix*'s tender and the *Schuyler* would surely be an unacceptable incident, but in New York's view there was no advantage in trying to define the limits or in guessing what was going to happen next; each day's problems, in themselves, were sufficient. In that spirit, on March 11, the Provincial Congress, as before, issued passes to the members of the Governor's Council (only De Lancey, Apthorpe, Smith, Wallace, Cruger, and Axtell were still in town), to Sam Bayard, Jr., and to one clerk to go down to the *Duchess of Gordon* for a routine meeting with Tryon. Acceptance of ship decoying and pilot subversion was in no way implied by the permissions. On the contrary, the issuance of the passes—on most days a *pro forma* business item—touched off a peppery debate. Fifteen voted to issue the passes, but with ten opposed and John Morin Scott abstaining, the Provincial Congress had come to its first serious division on the question.

Passes were also issued for John Foxcroft, the Crown's New York Postmaster, and several of his staff to go aboard the packet *Swallow*, just arrived from Falmouth, England, to collect a large batch of mail even though, since the royal mails had stopped functioning in America, the Provincial Congress regarded Foxcroft as an anachronism. The new New York Postmaster, Ebenezer Hazard, of the Constitutional Post Office system, would not do because the captain of the *Swallow* had orders to deliver the mail to Foxcroft or not to deliver it at all. Also, postage was due, letter by letter, to the huge total of 500 pounds—the result of a mean-spirited increase in the British rates on letters to America.

Foxcroft and his men went aboard the ship, sorted the mail and made a list of the addressees. They returned to the city, and handed the list to Hazard. Then Hazard and his helpers found out, one name at a time, which New Yorkers were willing to pay the postage due—as almost all of them were. Hazard collected the money, and it was his job, after the letters that had been paid for were released, to make the deliveries, but before he did so Hallett and Sands, as a Provincial Congress committee of two, opened and read all of the letters that, in their opinion, looked "suspicious." (No one was greatly shocked by that invasion of privacy because the royal mails had been unsafe all along, and if the Constitutional Post Office was any better, it was only because its employees were pressed for time. They expected to earn tips by passing along information they had learned by reading other people's mail, just as Foxcroft's mail handlers had; and none of the New Yorkers' English correspondents had thought that their letters would not be read by strangers—which explained why many of them were written in language so oblique that they could hardly be deciphered, even by their proper recipients.) But Hallett's and Sands's time was wasted; they found nothing in the letters that was worth the Provincial Congress' attention.

The Provincial Congress was about to adjourn for another round of elections, and the sense that a crisis was impending—so the majority thought—made new elections more, not less, important. A new Committee of Safety was appointed to govern during the interim, and it was more powerful and larger than any of the earlier interim bodies, with specific authority to do nearly everything the Provincial Congress could. (As New York City became more and more of a garrison town, governing it had become easier. Stirling, like Lee, was carrying a great part of what had formerly been the Provincial Congress' work.)

The Provincial Congress wrote the Fairfield County Committee asking that Samuel Gale be released, as Stirling had agreed would be proper. It announced a long list of money prizes, from ten to four hundred pounds, for completion, before certain dates, of gun, gunpowder, and gun-barrel factories in New York Province, but not in New York County, or in the counties immediately surrounding it, or on Long Island—there was no sense building munitions factories where the British might capture them—and a prize to the processor who could distill the most salt from sea water, beyond a minimum of twelve hundred barrels, before December 1, 1776. Then, on Saturday, March 16, the Congress adjourned. The new Committee of Safety, which started sitting on Monday, March 18, decided, as a first item of business, to let John Murray deliver five hundred pounds of bread to the *Duchess of Gordon.* Since that seemed like a lot of bread, however, Murray was not to get another permit until he produced an account of just what was in the ship's larder. (The *Duchess of Gordon* was not supposed to store more food than the ship's officers, crew, and guests could eat within a reasonable length of time.)

Captain DeWitt, who was in charge of the particular work party, wanted to fine John De Lancey for not having taken his turn at fatigue duty, and for not having sent a substitute. The Committee of Safety appointed a subcommittee to look into the case, which must have settled it somehow, for the matter was never brought back for the full Committee's further attention.

Loudon misgauged what were, by now, the permissible limits of public political discussion, and learned an expensive lesson on March 19. Although his press had more work on the New York currency order than it could handle, and the *Packet* was doing reasonably well, Loudon had recently been looking for printing to keep his shop busy. Some weeks earlier, a New Yorker— Loudon refused to name him—had brought in an anonymous manuscript, written by a "gentleman" living some distance from New York, entitled "The Deceiver Unmasked; or Loyalty and Interest United." It was an attempt to answer "Common Sense." The gentleman wanted Loudon not only to print it but to publish it, and Loudon, having satisfied himself that the manuscript was written "with decency," had decided to go ahead at his own expense. If the pamphlet sold well, Loudon estimated, he might make a profit of 150 pounds. When the first edition's press run was almost finished, Loudon had begun to advertise "The Deceiver Unmasked," beginning with a notice in Gaine's *Mercury*. (His shop also had rhubarb for sale, and Loudon advertised that, too.) Considering that he had been selling "Common Sense" most energetically, and given his standing as a good Associator, Loudon undoubtedly thought no one would regard his publication of "The Deceiver Unmasked" as evidence that he personally disagreed with Paine; and he took it for granted that a well-reasoned note of dissent would interest all those interested in the subject at all. That was where Loudon was mistaken. "To my great surprise," Loudon said afterward, "I soon found that the advertisement had given disgust to some of the inhabitants, who highly resented it."

Chief among the resentful was Duyckinck, who had returned from the unsuccessful raid on the pilots' camp and was busy, as usual, with Mechanics Committee affairs. Loudon was invited to attend the Mechanics Committee's next evening meeting, where various members, in turn, told him how little they thought of his publishing venture. Loudon defended it. None of the Mechanics, he pointed out, had read "The Deceiver Unmasked." He offered to send the Committee proofs. More than that, he offered to refer the question to the Committee of Safety. If it thought "The Deceiver Unmasked" should not go on sale, Loudon said he would abide by that decision. But the Mechanics Committee was in no mood to accept Loudon's reasonable terms. Some of its members were convinced that the anonymous author was none other than Tryon. That was not true, but Loudon refused to tell who the writer was, and the meeting broke up with nothing settled. Loudon went back to his shop on Water Street, a block east of Hanover Square. Some time after ten o'clock, Duyckinck appeared at the shop with about forty men, most of whom were members of the Mechanics

Committee. Since Loudon could not stop them, they entered and made off with all the finished copies of "The Deceiver Unmasked," about fifteen hundred pamphlets. Besides Duyckinck, Loudon recognized John Gilbert, Thomas Pratt, John Buchanan, a tavernkeeper, and Malcolm McEuen, a pewterer. Loudon was not sure of any other names. The gang did not harm Loudon, but it carried all the pamphlets to the Commons, heaped them in a pile, and burned them.

Loudon immediately complained to the Committee of Safety not only that he had been robbed but also that freedom of the press had been insulted and infringed. He wanted New York to help him get back his out-of-pocket loss, which he estimated at seventy-five pounds, a temperate claim since he was forgetting the profit he had hoped for. The Committee of Safety listened to Loudon, but, to his dismay, it postponed taking action on his appeal for one week, and then for another week. Loudon slowly realized that New York was going to solve the affair by ignoring it.

Tryon, shortly after, had a lesson to match Loudon's. Among the letters the *Swallow* had brought were several from Germain to the Governor. One of them contained the news that the government would soon be sending peace commissioners to grant pardons and confer with the colonies about the restoration of peace. (The gap between what New York and Germain thought the term "peace commissioner" meant had not narrowed in the slightest.) By some quirk, Tryon thought the information was extremely important. He wanted to issue a proclamation about it, but his councillors did not agree. They urged Tryon not to do anything, saying that New Yorkers despised proclamations and that Tryon would only "irritate the multitude." Tryon appeared to bow to his Council's judgment, and the councillors left the *Duchess of Gordon* believing that he had dropped the idea.

On thinking it over, however, Tryon decided to address a

communication to New York—something slightly different from a proclamation—for publication in the newspapers. Mayor Matthews was to handle the practical arrangements. As printed, Tryon's communication urged that "honest but deluded" New Yorkers submit now and hope for pardons later, when the peace commissioners arrived. Since Tryon knew this suggestion was impossible, not to mention irritating, he may have been acting with only his formal record in mind—a handful of newspaper clippings to show how much he had done for peace might eventually prove valuable. Besides, Tryon may have thought that the peace commissioners would reach New York within the next few days or weeks. (Germain's letter halfway implied as much.) In that case there would not be any time to lose. (Lord Howe, the Admiral, who was still in London, had been offered the commission, but he had not yet accepted it. Howe was asking for more latitude in dealing with the colonies than Germain wanted to give him—not that Howe dreamed of offering the Americans much. General Howe was considerably closer to New York, but his commission depended on his brother's, a point that still had not been made clear to him. All in all, Tryon had no reason to act hurriedly.)

Tryon's communication appeared on March 21 in both Loudon's *Packet* and Gaine's *Mercury*. His advice to New York happened to come at a time when the town was disturbed by two scatter-brained reports, each with a grain of truth. Thomas Vernon, a hat seller with delusions of grandeur who talked too much for his own good, was locked up in the city jail. Vernon had been telling his fellow prisoners that Tryon wanted him to serve as the captain of an armed cruiser, manned by fifty or sixty deserters from the Continental Army, to be fitted out at Tryon's expense. Vernon said he meant to do it, if he ever got out. He was going to sail the East and Hudson rivers looking for provision ships to seize. The Committee of Safety soon heard about Vernon's boasts. What might otherwise have been dismissed as absurd fantasy had to be taken seriously because, not long before his arrest, Vernon had in fact purchased a small sloop. It could conceivably serve the purpose he had described. On account of that one item of tangible corroboration, the Committee of Safety was wasting hours of valuable time looking into the rest of Vernon's story. (Vernon, as far as the Committee could ever find out, was making up all the rest of it.)

The second disquieting report did not implicate Tryon in anything, but it worked against Tryon's communication. One of the *Swallow*'s passengers was William Temple, of Boston, the brother of John Temple, the Lieutenant Governor of New Hampshire. Before hurrying on to Philadelphia with what he claimed were secrets for the Continental Congress, Temple told a number of New Yorkers, including some members of the Provincial Congress, that it was obvious in London that the King and his ministers really wanted peace with the colonies. (Temple's new story sounded much like Drummond's old one.) Temple had seemed extremely nervous, and looked as if he had been ill, but the gist of his conversation was interesting: if the Americans could hold out through the summer, the North Ministry would be replaced by fall. Temple said that twenty peace commissioners were en route, traveling in an enormous 90-gun warship; and that their instructions were to settle the dispute as best they could. Confusingly enough, Temple also reported that, in addition to 10,000 German mercenaries, the British had hired 20,000 Russian soldiers for the coming offensive against America. He explained that the unusually large buttons on his coat contained letters to the Continental Congress from Dr. Arthur Lee, the London agent for Massachusetts, the Duke of Grafton, the Duke of Richmond, Lord Shelburne, Charles

James Fox, and a few others. And Temple's buttons were indeed very large. (New York's hope that Temple might be right ended a week or so later. He told the Continental Congress substantially the same story, but when he was asked to open his buttons and produce the correspondence, Temple showed the delegates just one tiny scrap of paper. It may, or may not, have been written by Dr. Lee. All it said was: "The troops are to sail from Ireland.")

These unsettling stories—Vernon's fantasy and Temple's odd reports—combined with Tryon's communication to agitate New York. No sooner were the newspapers on sale than a mob began to form. By noon, several hundred men began to march through the streets, carrying a crude dummy of the Governor with a sign around its neck: "William Tryon, late Governor of this Province, but now a professed rebel and traitor to its dearest rights and privileges." It was the first time, since Tryon's return to the city, that New York's fears, frustrations, and anger had been directed against him personally. One marcher carried a placard that read, "Behold the bloody tool of a sanguinary despot, who is using his utmost efforts to enslave you! 'With how secure a brow and specious form, he gilds the secret traitor.'" The parade, like nearly all of New York's demonstrations, wound up at the Commons. Tryon's effigy was hung on a mock gallows, leaders of the march made speeches, and the crowd milled about for a time. Finally the dummy was cut down and kicked around the parade ground until it came apart. Not counting the blows to Tryon's self-esteem, the only permanent damage done was to the wooden sign over the door of a tavern called Tryon's Arms. The sign was ripped from its brackets by the marchers and smashed to pieces. It was time, in any case, for the establishment to think about changing its name.

Before the end of the month, the Richmond County Committee was pleased to report that, at long last, Staten Island had been divided into militia beats, that field officers had been picked, and that the Committee expected that it could soon forward a roster of militia captains and lieutenants.

A letter from the New York delegation in Philadelphia explained what had previously seemed a surprising coincidence: on March 9, just when Sears had been starting his operation in Queens, the Continental Congress had passed a resolution that: ". . . no oath, by way of test, shall be imposed upon, exacted, or required of any inhabitants of these Colonies by any military officer." New York's copy of the resolution had come too late to have any practical value, for by the time it arrived, New York and Stirling had come to their own agreement on the question. But now, the Committee of Safety learned, Lee's boast to Hancock, written before the Queens march began, had provoked the Continental Congress' action, and what had looked like a coincidence was explained as cause and effect. When the New York delegates in Philadelphia had read about Lee's plan, they had been "much alarmed":

> We could not . . . be silent upon so momentous a point, though we were not favored with your sentiments or instructions, nor informed of what, or whether anything, had passed between you and the General respecting the disaffected inhabitants. We took up the subject on general principles. There can be no liberty where the military is not subordinate to the civil power in everything not immediately connected with their operations.

As the New York delegates had pointed out to the Continental Congress, Lee could easily have applied for proper authority before issuing orders, since both the New York Provincial Congress and the Continental Congress were sitting at the time. They also reminded the Continental Congress that "a similar effort" by Lee in Rhode Island had passed unnoticed—a mistake on the part of the Continental Congress, in the New Yorkers' view: "Reiterated precedents must become dangerous. We therefore conceived it to be our unquestionable duty to assert the independence and superiority of the civil power, and to call the attention of Congress to this unwarrantable invasion of its rights by one of their officers."

The Continental Congress had agreed with the New York arguments, and the resolution had been the result. It was, in effect, a reprimand for Lee—"a thundering stigma," was how Lee himself described it. The General, who was in Philadelphia when the resolution was passed, managed to take his scolding with considerable grace, admitting that at the time he had seen the irregularity of his order. His excuse for having gone ahead, anyhow, was the emergency: he had had "reason to expect the enemy every hour." Above all, Lee wanted the episode forgotten. "I confess that I expected a reprimand, but flattered myself that it might have been conveyed to me in a less severe manner than by a public resolve. As I consider the Congress as the most respectable sovereign in the world (indeed, in my opinion, it is the only legitimate one), their public censure sinks deep in my spirits."

New York's most important news was the word that the Continental Army—or part of it, at least—was at last marching to New York from Cambridge, starting with a brigade of infantrymen (called "riflemen" in the military usage of the day, although almost all of them carried muskets, not rifles) commanded by Brigadier General William Heath, of Roxbury, Massachusetts. The post of military commander at New York automatically went to the highest-ranking general present, and it now began to change hands rapidly. Stirling lost the title (but continued to supervise many of the projects under way) on

March 21, when Brigadier General William Thompson arrived. A week later, on March 28, Thompson was superseded by Heath, and Heath realized that he would be in charge only as long as it took General Israel Putnam to come down from Boston—unless Washington happened to arrive ahead of Putnam.

Washington was still not certain of General Howe's intentions. The British had withdrawn from Boston on March 17, but ten days later the whole British fleet was still in sight in Boston's outer harbor. Howe had told his troops, before embarkation, that they were going to Halifax, and his men had passed the word on to various Bostonians, who had informed Cambridge headquarters. Washington had no good reason to doubt the story—Howe's soldiers did need some rest after living under siege for a long time, there were many Boston Tories who needed a safe place to live, and Halifax was the only British base on the Atlantic seaboard as long as New York was unavailable—but the Commander-in-Chief remained a little suspicious until the British fleet sailed from Nantasket Beach, on the afternoon of March 27. (Howe was, in fact, headed for Halifax.) Starting two days later, Washington dispatched the main body of his army, a group of units at a time, to New York—General John Sullivan and six regiments on March 29, General Nathanael Greene and five regiments on the thirty-first, and General Joseph Spencer and five regiments on April 4, along with Colonel Henry Knox and the artillery. With good weather, a marching unit was expected to average about twenty miles a day, or twelve days for the whole trip. Washington himself started south on the fourth. He wanted to go by way of Providence, and then down the Post Road through all the Connecticut shore towns, because so many of them, at one time or another, had requested Continental Army reinforcements and Washington had felt compelled to say no to every appeal. A personal visit, the General hoped, would assuage their hurt feelings. Washington's wife, Martha, who had joined him at Cambridge in December, traveled the more direct route, through Hartford.

In New York City, meanwhile, Colonel McDougall was looking for a suitable place for Washington's headquarters, a residence and an office combined. Because the five or six members of the General's personal staff of aides—his "family," as they were called—had to live in the same building that the General lived in, or right beside it, a large house was required. In effect, Washington's aides were all on duty all the time. The headquarters group also needed a large stable—every man had at least one horse—and quarters nearby for the General's guard. McDougall was also looking for a good housekeeper and a cook and a steward. The Colonel passed over James De Lancey's estate in favor of Abraham Mortier's beautiful mansion and grounds, the next place north of Leonard Lispenard's. The house stood on the crest of a considerable hill, called Richmond Hill, and had a splendid view of the Hudson. (If Mortier's mansion still existed, it would be close to the intersection of Varick and Charlton streets.) McDougall did not know the exact date of the Washingtons' arrival, so, in case the General arrived before the Mortier house was cleaned and in order, William Smith's town house on lower Broadway, at the corner of what is now Exchange Place, was picked as a temporary lodging.

New York was both excited and worried about Washington's arrival. After so many months of feeling helpless under the *Asia's* guns—not that that had changed—the city welcomed having more military assistance than it could easily accommodate. As the leading Continental Army units arrived, property owners quickly realized that the ten thousand men in Washington's army, added to the three thousand militiamen on hand (the Connecticut troops had again postponed their departure), plus the promised eight thousand men from New Jersey and Pennsylvania, might wreck the city in their off-duty exuberance before General Howe's British forces arrived. Merchants, retailers, and tavernkeepers, on the other hand, looked forward to an unprecedented business boom, despite their low stocks. Although the fighting around Boston had not amounted to much, and many of the soldiers had not seen any action at all because they were newly enlisted, all the new arrivals were looked upon as veterans who had been at Lexington, Concord, Bunker's Hill, Dorchester Heights, and so on. And those who had in fact been in a battle were the first, except for the handful of New Yorkers who had returned from Canada, who could tell what fighting the British was like.

In the middle of the town's bustle of welcoming the Continental Army, the lookouts on top of the Kennedy mansion saw something peculiar happening on Bedloe's Island. For more than a month, New York had suspected that the British had some interest in the place. The city already knew that the British were using Governor's Island, when the weather was fair, for an exercise ground. That occupation of New York territory dated back to the days before the tightening of the provisioning rules, when Governor's Island had been a supply transfer point. Goods had been delivered to the island, and the British had collected them at their convenience. But what, if anything, the British were doing on Bedloe's Island, where there were four or five buildings, including a house and a very large shed, among the trees, was not clear. Since the *Asia* had taken up a position no more than a half-mile north of the island, no one had been anxious to make a reconnaissance. Now the signalmen could see with their spyglasses that a British work party was digging along the Bedloe's Island shoreline. Tryon's idea was to present New York with the *fait accompli:* a small British strongpoint, with entrenchments, in the middle of the harbor. He needed the space as a temporary sanctuary for Americans with British sympathies—inimicals who had waited all this time to leave the country and no longer felt safe where they were, inimicals who wanted to join General Howe's army when it arrived, and various others. The *Duchess of Gordon* had already taken on as many persons as it could hold. As of April 1, there were more than one hundred men, women, and children concealed on Bedloe's Island.

There had been earlier whispers around town—too fantastic to be believed—that a large colony of Tories had been assembled on the island, less than two miles off the Grand Battery, but the visible digging moved General Heath to action. He did not take time to consult the Committee of Safety. Major De Hart, the veteran of Heard's Queens expedition, and two hundred men of the First New Jersey, Stirling's old regiment, volunteered for the mission. They landed on Bedloe's Island at midnight on April 2, prepared for a fight. They found no one there except forty women and children. In spite of Heath's quick decision, Tryon had been warned in advance, and from the deck of the *Duchess of Gordon,* close by the *Asia,* the Governor was watching De Hart's attack. Tryon did not intend to make a fight of it. The British entrenching party had returned to the *Asia,* and the sixty male Americans who had been on Bedloe's were aboard the *Lady Gage,* a merchant ship the British had stolen from her Staten Island dock earlier that day. De Hart's raiders, left with little to do, spoiled the half-finished trenches as best they could and collected the British entrenching tools, a considerable stock of overcoats and white shirts, and a flock of chickens that Tryon was saving as a present to welcome

Howe. De Hart then herded the women and children into the house, for safety's sake, and set fire to all the other buildings and a large haystack. The flames rose into the early morning's dark sky. As the Americans pulled away from the island, leaving the women and children behind, the *Asia* fired two shots. Both rounds splashed harmlessly into the water. The booming noise did remind De Hart and the city that the *Asia* was on station, but New York had not forgotten that fact for a moment throughout the whole year.

The next day, the Committee of Safety routinely let the provision ships take out thirteen hundred pounds of beef to the *Asia*. The *Phoenix* got a thousand pounds of beef and eighteen shillings' worth of vegetables, which did not speak well for the sailors' diet balance. The *Duchess of Gordon* and the packet *Swallow* got food and supplies, too, and visitors' passes were issued to Mayor Matthews, Mr. Murray, and to a Michael Conner, of Philadelphia, who wanted to go down to the *Phoenix* and demand the return of the brigantine *Mary*, which, Conner said, Captain Parker had seized. But this unruffled maintenance of the old system was a sham. The Committee of Safety took it for granted that, after the Bedloe's Island affair, the British would not take long to intercept New York's provisions. It wrote Samuel Tucker, president of the New Jersey Provincial Congress, asking him to ask "all persons supplying this Colony with any kind of necessaries to be as speedy as possible in sending articles to this market, especially hay and fuel, as a great number of horses are daily expected from the eastward." Suffolk County took it for granted that the British would start stealing from eastern Long Island when the city stopped provisioning the warships. Since Suffolk had not received the Continental reinforcements it had more or less been promised, but had almost finished raising three companies of men for Continental service, it asked for permission to keep its own men to guard against raids. The Committee of Safety asked Heath what he thought. Heath replied that New York should decide the point for itself. If the three Suffolk companies stayed near home, Heath reminded the Committee, they would not count in New York's effort to fill its Continental Army quota. Nevertheless, the Committee of Safety voted in Suffolk County's favor. At least for the time being, the Long Island men could stay where they were.

Connecticut's favorite son, General Israel Putnam, arrived on the evening of April 4, and took over command from Heath. New York immediately felt the impact of Putnam's energy and drive. The barrel-shaped, fifty-eight-year-old veteran of the French and Indian War was a natural leader of men with a powerful personality and questionable judgment. Even so, Washington counted on him to manage the battle for New York, should it begin before Washington arrived. That possibility no longer seemed likely, given the course of Howe's fleet, but Putnam was elated by the Commander-in-Chief's expression of confidence. (Washington was not making a mistake, for Putnam's strength as a field officer and his ability to rally men to stand and fight, as he himself was ready to stand and fight, was exceptional. For a day or two, in case the shooting started, his courage was likely to count as much as any skill.)

Putnam was shocked to hear that New York's Continental Army quota was not yet filled, and he started out by giving the Committee of Safety a dressing down. As for the game that New York was playing with Tryon, Vandeput, and Parker, Putnam was incredulous. None of it made the slightest sense to him. Word came that a small boat from one of the British warships had landed on Staten Island. The Committee of Safety, left to its own devices, might have spent an afternoon deciding the appropriate response to the challenge. No such debate took place, because Putnam ordered immediate action. He sent down three rifle companies "to scour the shores" for the intruders.

A fog hung over the Narrows that morning—April 6—but it did not hamper Putnam's men, for the British were in plain sight at the Watering Place, a beach just south of what is now the town of St. George, then Ducksbury Point. They were getting fresh drinking water from the wells nearby, filling up casks and loading them into two small boats, as they had done many times before. They had no formal permission for this practice, but Tryon and New York both felt that it was a logical extension in the spirit of the provisioning agreement. The pilot boat *James* and the sloop-of-war *Savage*, with twenty guns, were standing just offshore, waiting to take the small boats in tow when the water casks were aboard.

Putnam's companies landed some distance away and approached the British from the land side. The *Savage* fired a warning shot, and then, since the Americans kept advancing, the ship began to shoot in earnest to cover the work party's withdrawal. The Americans fired on the retreating sailors. One of the small boats got away from the beach, although Putnam's men believed they had hit two or three of the eleven men she carried. The other boat and ten sailors were captured. One American was wounded, though not seriously. After the fight, New York watched the *Asia* more apprehensively than usual. The *Duchess of Gordon* had set sail earlier in the day, and had moved down through the Narrows to the outer harbor—Tryon had glimpsed the Staten Island engagement as he went by—but apart from that repositioning, there was no other British activity.

Then Putnam learned that the fortifications planned for

Governor's Island—gun emplacements of great importance in Lee's overall artillery plan—had not yet been begun. The Committee of Safety had to confess that the British were in the habit of using Governor's Island as a playing field. It was hard to say which revelation outraged Putnam more. The *Asia* was not much farther from Governor's Island than she was from Bedloe's Island, but for once New York had the discretion not to mention the threat of the ship's guns—its habitual excuse for every failure. Putnam wasted no time issuing another order. On April 8, just after candle-lighting time, a thousand soldiers drawn from several regiments were ferried over to Governor's Island. They were to dig, and dig hard. The island was empty, and no one disputed the landings or tried to interfere with the work party's night labors. By dawn, Putnam's men had dug trenches and piled up breastworks—a good start on the gun emplacements that were to follow. The soldiers saw, moreover, that they had worked faster than necessary. The *Asia* was gone. During the hours of darkness, Captain Vandeput had weighed anchor and had followed the *Duchess of Gordon* down through the Narrows. For the first time in months, there was not one British warship inside the upper bay.

It looked as if Putnam's boldness had forced the withdrawal, but that was not so. Captain Parker, as the senior naval officer at New York, had for a long time recommended that Tryon and the *Duchess of Gordon* move to, say, Gravesend Bay, because Parker thought the proper place for his little fleet of warships was the open waters south of the Narrows. Tryon had always argued against the move. He wanted to stay as close as possible to New York City, in order to exert what political influence he could and because he believed it fitting for the Governor to be at, if not in, his capital. Wherever the *Duchess of Gordon* was, the warships, in their role of protectors, had to be. Parker had finally persuaded Tryon to stop valuing proximity so highly.

The Governor, downcast, had guessed that the provisions delivered just before the doings at the Watering Place, on April 6, were the last the British ships were likely to receive. (The sailors could live for something like three months on what had been accumulated, but the menus would be boring.) Tryon was right. On April 7, after the Staten Island skirmish, Putnam wrote the Continental Congress: "Hostilities are now commenced." On the eighth, Putnam ordered all communications with the British stopped. New York concurred by not disagreeing. Henceforth, any person who went on board the *Duchess of Gordon* or any of the warships, or was even found near them, would be treated as an enemy. Broadsides to that effect were distributed all over town, so no New Yorker could claim that he had never heard of the new rules. Starting April 11, the newspapers all published the order. And, with some exceptions, all communications with the warships and the *Duchess of Gordon* did stop. The Governor's Council, with Mr. Bayard, got special permission to meet Tryon again. Mr. Nixon was allowed to go down to the *Swallow*, as the ship got ready for her return to England, with provisions for twelve gentlemen who had booked passage on her. (Eighteenth-century ship passengers customarily supplied their own food.) A few other special passes were issued, but the provisioning was at an end; and to make sure of it all oystermen were now required to obtain special new fishing permits from Captain James Alner, who was stationed at Beekman's Slip. (Beekman's Slip was near what is now the eastern foot of Fulton Street.) It was believed, or at least hoped, that no oysterman, after registration, would attempt to smuggle fresh New York oysters to the *Duchess of Gordon* no matter what Tryon offered for them.

The news from Philadelphia was exciting. After seven weeks of on-and-off debate, the Continental Congress voted its response to the Prohibitory Act, in which Great Britain had closed all the American ports. On April 6, the Continental Congress, with a defiance that matched the edict, declared that all the American ports were open to the ships and products of every country in the world—except, of course, Great Britain. This resolution swept away the whole structure of trade ties with the mother country, eradicated all the Acts of Trade and Navigation—the economic foundations of the British colonial system— and thus said, though not in so many words, that the American colonies were colonies no longer. American merchants were now free to import whatever they chose—not just war materials— from any non-British port. (The one exception, contained in the resolution's last paragraph, was that "no slaves be imported into any of the Thirteen United Colonies.") American restrictions on the export of scarce war materials remained, but that was quite another question, and the United Colonies' own restraint. The Continental Congress hoped for a lot of trade with France and Spain, and Silas Deane, a delegate from Connecticut to both the First and Second Continental Congresses, a lawyer, and a shrewd businessman, was on his way to Paris as an agent of the United Colonies. He was to see whether he could buy arms and ammunition, and, if possible, to arrange for a French loan. If the French Foreign Minister, the Comte de Vergennes, seemed friendly, Deane's further instructions were to ask him a hypothetical question: In case the American colonies should be forced to form themselves into an independent government, would France be likely to acknowledge it as such and receive an ambassador, or enter into a treaty or an alliance with it? The Continental Congress had also authorized American privateers to capture any British ship they could, and had established prize courts to deal with the disposition of the spoils. The Continental Congress had advanced almost as far as it could toward economic separation; only a parallel political declaration of freedom was missing.

Most New Yorkers, including New York's delegates in Philadelphia, believed that the Continental Congress' April 6 resolutions went further than necessary—not that the merchant traders minded the prospect of trade revival under the new rules. But, for the time being, New York as an open port looked discouragingly like New York closed. Captain Parker's repositioned fleet had better control than ever over every ship that left or entered the Narrows, just as he had been telling Tryon it would, and departures and arrivals were at his pleasure. Lord Drummond, who was willing to admit that his hopes for arranging a peace were gone, and who was feeling poorly besides, presented his physician's recommendation and asked the Committee of Safety for permission to go to Bermuda. It was granted without any hesitation: ". . . . it is hereby recommended to all the friends of America not to interrupt him on his passage, but to let him pass in safety without molestation." Tryon's physician, Dr. Middleton, also wanted to go. The Committee of Safety approved his request, too, and Drummond and Middleton together engaged the sloop *Charming Polly* for the trip.

General Washington, General Horatio Gates, the Adjutant General, their aides, and Washington's guard rode into town on Saturday, April 13, a little past noon. The party was all business, and there was no welcoming ceremony. Washington, anxious to get to work on several different projects, went straight to the Smith house. Quebec was almost as much on his mind as New York. He still did not have confirmation of Howe's arrival at Halifax, but, assuming that the English were there, he thought that they might plan to reinforce Quebec by sending troops around Cape Breton and up the St. Lawrence River. Washington shared the Continental Congress' concern over Canada, and the Congress intended, one way or another, to make Canada the fourteenth of the United Colonies. That ambition was hardly realizable unless Continental forces could take Quebec and hold the province. A special commission of the Continental Congress—Benjamin Franklin, Samuel Chase, and Charles Carroll —was on its way north, trying to decide what to do and how to do it. The commissioners had reached Albany, where they were talking to General Schuyler. They were going on, and they planned to stay in the north indefinitely as civilian administrators of whatever policies the Continental Congress finally adopted. Washington, meanwhile, had orders from the Continental Congress to detach four regiments from his army at New York and send them to the Northern Department "as soon as he shall be of the opinion that the safety of New York and the eastern service will permit." Orders were orders, but the proviso was absurd. The safety of New York was more than Washington knew how to arrange.

Washington wanted to think about that question, and he wanted to inspect New York City's fortifications. He intended to review Lee's plan, now that he could examine the unfamiliar terrain in person. He also needed to grasp the New York political situation as quickly as possible; whatever was coming, he felt that he had to have the cooperation of the New York Provincial Congress, and, indeed, of all New Yorkers. This last ambition made the General wish, more than ever, that Joseph Reed, who had been his military secretary until the end of October, would rejoin his staff. Washington had not forgotten the poor impression the New Yorkers had made on him in June, but he did not underrate the intelligence of the men in charge of New York's affairs. He hoped he would not have to argue with New York. If he had to, Washington thought, Reed's diplomatic manner— an asset that Washington thought he himself lacked—and

Reed's knowledge of the law could match the New Yorkers' debating skills. But Reed was on leave, taking care of some law cases in Philadelphia, interesting himself in Pennsylvania politics, and showing little interest in returning to Washington's headquarters.

The Committee of Safety had no thought—at least not now—of anything except cooperation. John Morin Scott, Abraham Brasher, and John Van Cortlandt, as a committee, called on the General to offer, formally, whatever New York could provide. Their offer was more than a polite gesture. In the nine and a half months since New York had last seen him, the Commander-in-Chief had become a symbol of the American cause to such a degree that New Yorkers, like the residents of all the other colonies, had partly forgotten that he was only a man. This concerned Washington, but not enough for him to try to counteract it. He was aware that his battlefield achievements so far were negligible, and he knew that his success in driving the British out of Boston had depended largely on Howe's desire to withdraw. Still, these truths did not prevent Washington from enjoying the exaggerated letter of commendation from the Continental Congress that Hancock had signed on April 17:

> The disinterested and patriotic principles which led you to the field, have also led you to the glory: and it affords no little consolation to your countrymen to reflect that, as a peculiar greatness of mind induced you to decline any compensation for serving them, except the pleasure of promoting their happiness, they may, without your permission, bestow upon you the largest share of their affection and esteem.
>
> Those pages in the annals of America will record your title to a conspicuous place in the Temple of Fame. . . .

The Massachusetts Provincial Congress' address to Washington had been at least equally flattering; Harvard had given the

General an honorary Doctor of Laws degree; and if he had accepted all the invitations he had been offered on his trip to New York, the journey would have taken many weeks. Added to these honors, all of which delighted him, Washington found when he got to New York a confidential letter from John Adams saying that the Continental Congress had voted to give the General a gold medal—the first the United Colonies had ever bestowed. Adams was chairman of the medal-design committee. He wondered whether Washington had any ideas about how the medal ought to look. Whatever the committee thought best, Washington replied, would be "highly agreeable."

At forty-four, Washington was physically well suited to the role of hero in which his fellow Americans cast him. He was six feet two inches tall (more unusual then than now), and he weighed well over two hundred pounds. Besides being taller and broader than most of the men around him, Washington was in excellent condition. He exercised often in the company of his aides, a relief from the hours of desk work he had to do, and he rode constantly. For a large man, he moved with remarkable grace. He was fairly handsome, too, with a long, full face and strong features. Washington was concerned with appearances, and wanted to look the man his admirers imagined he was. One of the many lessons he had learned at Cambridge had a bearing on that; he knew he could not afford to share his anxieties. Even within his military family, his attitude determined the moods of the other men and set the upper limits on their optimism. And so he tried to conceal worry and to avoid mentioning his fears so far as possible. For instance, he had appeared calm in January, after the expiration of the original Continental Army enlistments, even though at the time he had thought the Army was on the verge of disintegration. His own determination, combined with very hard work, had kept it together, and for that achievement alone, perhaps, he deserved the Continental Congress' gold medal. If New York imagined that Washington could manage the unmanageable, the General was not going to shake its confidence. In the past, Washington had felt that candor was a virtue, but, having since learned that everything he wrote or spoke—jokes included—was likely to be taken with great seriousness, or misunderstood, or misquoted, Washington had cultivated reserve.

Mrs. Washington reached New York City on April 17. The Mortier house was ready, and Washington moved there from Smith's house that same day. The General's appointment calendar was crowded—it looked as if every man in New York needed a private word or two with him. Washington gave all his callers their fair share, or more, of his time. Mostly he listened. When he gave answers they were cautious. He was scrupulously courteous. His manner fitted the role of great man, which was what he intended, but it was a bit deceptive. When Washington wrote Reed or John Augustine Washington, his younger brother, who was managing the Mount Vernon farm for him, he sounded like another personality. He said mean things about his subordinates, used slang, made jokes, and expressed all kinds of rash opinions. His brother and Reed both knew, by letter, a man different from the Washington New York saw.

Coming from Cambridge, where the American Army had taken everything, and Boston, where the British Army had taken everything, the Washingtons found the New York City stores and markets—half empty though they were—full of wonderful things. They went shopping. They bought quite a lot, including a feather bed, pillows, some bed curtains, crockery, and glassware. The General ordered two elaborate tents from Plunket Fleason, with three folding walnut mess tables and eighteen walnut camp stools, all of which fitted into special cases, for use in the field. The bill, charged to the Continental Congress, was sixty-four pounds. As Washington looked the town over further, he was bothered by the large number of bars, inns, taverns, saloons, and grogshops. More specifically, he was upset by the drunks, both civilians and soldiers, he observed staggering around the streets. Washington liked to drink, and he regarded the moderate use of strong liquor—the gill of rum per day, say, that was part of the Continental soldier's ration—as beneficial. But he despised drunkenness, and New York, as even New Yorkers admitted, was the hardest-drinking city in America. Someone had once figured out that a man could get a drink in every eighth building in Boston. In New York, no one needed to go that far. New Yorkers were fond of wine, particularly Madeira, from the islands off Morocco, and that taste had made the importers Richard and Theophylact Bache, who specialized in Madeira, extremely well-to-do. But New Yorkers also liked claret, burgundy, sack, port, champagne, beer, porter, brandy, West Indian rum, New England rum, cider, and a variety of home brews and concoctions. A few New York specialty markets sold nothing but lemons, limes, and, occasionally, pineapples, all to be used in alcoholic punches. Many of the visitors to Manhattan admired the profusion of carefully tended fruit trees without fully understanding that when the fruit was picked it was made into wine, cider, or brandy. New Yorkers themselves were less concerned with drunkenness than with the fast-rising prices of alcoholic beverages. A bottle of American rum, which in January had sold for sixpence, now cost almost a shilling.

At Washington's request, Colonel Thomas Mifflin, his former aide-de-camp and now Continental Quartermaster General, appeared before the Committee of Safety to ask whether some of the city's bars and taverns—those that, in the Committee's opinion, were not "necessary"—could be closed. The General had been in town for only four days, and the Committee of Safety wanted to prove that New York was as full of good will and cooperation as it claimed; yet Washington's suggestion raised an unanswerable question. If there were too many liquor sellers, how could anyone decide which were unnecessary? The best the Committee of Safety could do, as it did immediately, was to suspend the granting of new liquor licenses, thus freezing the number of legal bars and taverns. Washington was not satisfied, but he did not press the question. The Committee of Safety, for its part, knew that its gesture meant little or nothing, for what was legal and what was going on had for years been two different matters, and there was no way to stop a man who lacked a proper license from selling a soldier a drink.

The Committee of Safety's failure to close down any bars did not mean that New York liked drunken soldiers as well as it liked sober ones. Soldiers' rowdiness—fighting, minor rioting, and shouting—had been a nuisance for a long time. Just how much of it could be blamed on rum was not clear, but no one thought excessive drinking made for peace and quiet. Putnam had established a nine o'clock curfew for all the troops under his command, and had tried to insist that all soldiers be in their barracks or encampments from then until reveille. The hour Putnam picked was too early. The soldiers did not like it, but the complaints about the curfew came mostly from New Yorkers. It was very hard to tell a soldier from a civilian in the dark. The street lighting—oil lamps on ten-foot posts every fifty feet—left something to be desired, and the uniforms Putnam's men wore, in many cases, were indistinguishable from ordinary farmers' or workingmen's clothes. As a result, the Provost's guards, who were stationed throughout the city to enforce the curfew, looked with suspicion on all males, except, perhaps, those dressed formally as gentlemen. As a result, an ordinary civilian could hardly walk a block after nine without being halted, challenged, asked the password, which changed daily, and having to establish his right to be out.

Washington changed the curfew to ten o'clock—a more convenient time in the opinion of both the town and the soldiery—but that did not solve any of the disciplinary problems. Most of the men the General had brought down to New York were New England farm boys, and since only a few soldiers had been allowed to enter Boston in the few days between the British withdrawal and the Army's departure, partly for fear of the smallpox epidemic, many of them had never before seen a real city. For an army, the Continentals behaved reasonably well. For instance, Loudon's *Packet* commented, on April 18, that the New England men seemed remarkably interested in going to church: "They attend prayers, with their chaplains, evening and morning regularly, in which their officers set the example. On Lord's day, they attend public worship twice and their deportment in the house of God is such as becomes the place." And many of the soldiers, in off-duty hours, merely wandered around like tourists inspecting the New York sights: the steam pump; the view from the cupola on top of the Province Arms (formerly the King's Arms) Tavern, the tallest building in town; the large gilded equestrian statue of George III, dressed as a Roman emperor, in Bowling Green; Fort George (with its north wall torn down); the Grand Battery; the Rhinelander and Livingston sugar warehouses; the new DeBrosses distillery; and all the rest. One form of temptation stepped forward to meet the visitors. All over town, unscrupulous New Yorkers waited, cash in hand, ready to buy any or all of the Continental soldiers' equipment, especially their firearms—often the family musket, with powder horn, which had been taken down off the farmhouse wall when the boy had set out to enlist. Since the fair price was fantastically high, the New Yorkers' offers sounded good to anyone who had not tried to buy a musket lately. Washington's officers could not stop their men from selling, but the Committee of Safety attempted to prevent New Yorkers from buying by forbidding "any inhabitant to receive or purchase, from any non-commissioned officer or soldier, any goods, clothing, or other article whatsoever," unless the soldier could produce a certificate, signed by his company or regimental commander, stating that the specific item was his to sell.

And then there was prostitution. It was not new either to New York City or to the Continental Army, but it gave Washington and his officers constant trouble; and the Committee of Safety did little or nothing to help, possibly because the New Yorkers did not know of a remedy. The brothel district, popularly known as the "Holy Ground" because most of the land belonged to Trinity parish, was a dreadful slum of shacks and dilapidated buildings just west of the Commons. Whenever soldiers got involved in brawls, the odds were that the Holy Ground was the place, especially Robinson Street (now Park Place) in the block from Broadway to Church Street (where the Woolworth Building now stands). According to one estimate, five hundred prostitutes ordinarily lived and worked in the Holy Ground, and, whatever the number was, the arrival of the Continental Army had not reduced it. The Grand Battery promenade and Broadway were notorious as the walks where most solicitations occurred—information that many of the soldiers acquired before they knew anything else about the city. Perhaps the Holy Ground was no worse than comparable sections of Philadelphia, Boston, and Charleston, but there was nothing like it in an average New England village. Colonel Loammi Baldwin, an apple grower from North Woburn,

Massachusetts, was shocked by the district when, as officer of the day, he and his guard had to patrol it. He wrote to his wife: "The whores' . . . unparalleled conduct is a sufficient antidote against any desires that a person can have that has one spark of modesty or virtue left in him." But the incidence of venereal disease in the regiments, worse in some commands than in others, proved that Baldwin was exaggerating.

Even Lee's little army had been too big for New York's regular barracks space, and it went without saying that most of Washington's men would have to live out of doors in tents, if tents could be provided, or in whatever other kinds of shelters could be improvised. Two large bivouac areas had been marked out and were being improved. One was not far north of the built-up areas in the vicinity of the Bayard estate—approximately Canal Street in present-day terms. The other was on the eastern slopes of the high ground above the Brooklyn ferry slips (now Brooklyn Heights). New York was also clearing out space in various buildings to use as temporary barracks rooms. The new city hospital building, begun by Governor Tryon in 1773 and not yet finished, which stood on a five-acre plot of open land at the northwestern edge of town (near the intersection of what are now Duane and Hudson streets), was turned over to the military. So were the King's College buildings on Murray Street in the second block west of the Commons, in the heart of the Holy Ground. First, however, the college library's books were all carted away, some to City Hall and the rest to St. Paul's Chapel, for fear that the soldiers, instead of reading them, might burn them for warmth. The college officials objected, but their protests were in vain. They believed that the Committee of Safety was punishing the college because many of the members of its 1775 faculty had been pro-British. Actually, student enrollment had fallen off, and only six King's College seniors expected to be graduated in June—assuming that their classes were not interrupted before then. Furthermore, the Committee of Safety was providing a perfectly good, if small, substitute college building: Leonard Lispenard's town house at No. 13 (now No. 60) Wall Street. The top two floors of Cruger's big sugar warehouse near the waterfront between Coenties Slip and Old Slip were cleared, not for troop quarters but for additional ammunition-storage space. Other business and loft buildings were commandeered for one military purpose or another, and soldiers were installed in all the empty, boarded-up mansions. The damage riflemen could do was remarkable, as Washington's headquarters quickly heard. Soldiers were reported to be chopping up parquet floors for firewood, throwing refuse out of the upper-story windows, and ruining fireplaces beyond repair. The General was not pleased. The complaints were painfully similar to those of American householders during the years when British soldiers had been quartered, without invitation, in private homes. Washington told the Barracks Master that a suitable proportion of officers would have to be quartered with the enlisted men in any building the Army used. He ruled that all the soldiers in any given house would have to pay for wanton damage. And he promised "severe corporeal punishment"—whippings, that meant—for future offenses.

Poor troop discipline caused other points of friction between New York and the Army. Some farmers had started spring planting, for instance, and they complained, doubtless with justification, that the soldiers were carelessly trampling their newly sown fields. But as time passed and the regiments settled in, however uncomfortably, the city and the Army began to get used to each other. The soldiers had their complaints, too, of course, among them that ferryboat owners tried to charge them full fare. Just the military traffic back and forth from Manhattan to Brooklyn might have made the ferrymen a small fortune, but Colonel Mifflin said he would establish a ferry system owned and operated by the Army rather than allow such profiteering. The commercial operators, realizing that Mifflin was in earnest, decided to carry soldiers free.

The Committee of Safety was enchanted by Washington's polite, firm manner of negotiation, and the General's skill at getting what he wanted in the easiest possible way was marvelous. A perfect illustration was Washington's success in making sure that New York did not backslide into provisioning and communicating with the British ships. Putnam's orders had effected the break, but Washington wanted more than that; he wanted the Committee of Safety to agree with what Putnam had done and to think it necessary and correct. Therefore, Washington was the first, among all the military commanders at New York, to go to the civil authorities and ask them to help him by ordering all traffic ended. He did not scold, as Lee had done. Instead Washington pretended to be sympathetic to New York's side of the long story. (In reality, he thought New York's timidity under the *Asia*'s guns had been spineless.) In his request he wrote: "In the weak and defenseless state in which this city was some time ago, political prudence might justify the correspondence that subsisted between the country and the enemy's ships of war; but as the largest part of the Continental troops is now here, and as many strong works are being erected and erecting for the defense of the city and harbor, those motives no longer exist."

These words of understanding were worth a thousand harangues. The General was forthright in his appeal. The colonies were at war, though not a declared war, he pointed out, because no man could think they were in a state of peace when the ports were shut, trade destroyed, property seized, towns burned, and citizens captured and suffering cruel hardships. And Washington admitted that it was his duty, on military grounds, to stop all future "correspondence" with the warships, whether New York approved or not. He added, however:

In effecting the salutary purposes above mentioned, I could wish for the concurrence and support of your Honorable Body. It will certainly add great weight to the measures adopted, when the civil authority coöperates with the military to carry them into execution. It will also redound much to the honor of the government and of your Committee in particular, for the world are apt to judge from appearances; and while such correspondence exists, the reputation of the whole Colony will suffer in the eyes of their American brethren.

It is, therefore, gentlemen, that I have taken the liberty to address you on this important subject, relying on your zeal and attachment to the cause of American liberty for your assistance.

Minutes after Washington's letter had been read, the Committee of Safety began writing its own resolution outlawing all traffic with the warships. The Committee passed it the following morning, April 18, and sent a copy to the General with an appreciative covering note: "We cannot sufficiently thank your Excellency for your most delicate attention to the civil government of this Colony, and beg leave to give you the strongest assurance that we most eagerly embrace this, as we shall every other opportunity of coöperating with you, in every measure which shall come recommended to us with the argument of public utility."

It was too much to hope that New York's enthusiasm for Washington's delicate attentions could last forever, but no commander, with the possible exception of Stirling, had started with such finesse. New York's readiness to cooperate may also have owed something to the shocking testimony it had been hearing from Lieutenant Edward Tylee on the morning of the day

Washington's request arrived. Tylee was one of the Americans (the number, which had reached eight, was now down to seven) who had been held prisoner on the *Asia*. He had managed to escape. During the seven months he had been held prisoner, he had been able to see much of what went on aboard the *Asia*, and he was the first man who could tell New York, of his own knowledge, that a procession of American spies had been visiting the ship more or less regularly and informing Captain Vandeput of all they knew. Tylee named names. He said that Lawrence Hartwick, of New York City, for one, had been a constant visitor and a bearer of tidbits of military intelligence. (The Committee of Safety recalled that Hartwick, who had been arrested and held as a suspected Tory in January, had been released when five of his friends—James Reid, Robert Leonard, Francis Cunningham, John Burns, and Francis Dominick—had posted a bond for him and had guaranteed that Hartwick would appear whenever New York called for him; but that in March, when the Provincial Congress had wanted to interrogate Hartwick, neither he nor any of his five bondsmen could be found.) Tylee identified John Noble, also of New York City, as another informer; Tylee himself had heard Noble telling in advance about the plans for the Bedloe's Island raid—which explained why Putnam's raiders had found no one there except women and children. All in all, Tylee's account documented one of Washington's arguments against sustaining the British warships, and it made the Committee of Safety realize that perhaps, in the past, New York had not taken spying seriously enough.

From Tuesday, April 16, through Thursday, April 18, the voters in the city and the province of New York were choosing a new Provincial Congress. Once again, the purpose of the elections was to strengthen the Provincial Congress' authority by making certain that the delegations represented the counties' latest views; and, with a political consensus as a goal, the old Provincial Congress had voted a daring, democratic experiment: qualified non-Associators, as well as Associators, could vote. (November's liberal redefinition of the property qualification, which included tenants, was still in effect.) To prove that New York really wanted to get out the non-Associators' votes, written ballots were accepted at the polls. The old viva-voce system had been hard on men with minority views who did not care to have their neighbors learn their opinions. Ballots were anything but secret, since voting booths were not provided, but they did allow some degree of privacy, and with the polls open for most of three days—the polling place in New York City was at City Hall—a voter could register his choices at a convenient time. The political-rally aspects of elections were greatly reduced.

The risk involved in trusting the New York electorate as it had never before been trusted was genuine but slight. New York's conciliationists were not organized, and the lists of candidates, in any case, were dominated by middle-of-the-road names. By offering signs of respect to those voters who were least happy with the way things were going, the cautiously belligerent majority improved its reputation—just as the old Provincial Congress had calculated. No one could estimate how many non-Associators went to the polls, but in contrast to the fiasco of November, 1775, the total turnout was large, and the test of New York sentiment was more accurate than any for a long time.

The New York voters made some changes in their representation, but the new Provincial Congress, like the old, was to be dominated by moderates. The result was a vote of confidence for the way the Provincial Congress had been managing New York's affairs. Fourteen of New York County's twenty-one delegates were reelected—Abraham Brasher, Jacobus Van Zandt, John Van Cortlandt, James Beekman, John Morin Scott, Isaac Roosevelt, Joseph Hallett, Anthony Rutgers, Comfort Sands, John Jay, Philip Livingston, John Alsop, Francis Lewis, and James Duane. In the other counties, most former delegates who were willing to serve again were also reelected. Many men—in New York County's case, ten out of the twenty-one— had served in the Provincial Congress from the outset, since April, 1775. Lawyers were not as numerous as they had been, and all seven of New York County's new delegates—William Denning, Evert Bancker, John Broome, Isaac Stoutenburgh, Henry Remsen, Thomas Randall, and Peter P. Van Zandt— were businessmen. They had all served or were serving on the New York City Committee. As far as it was possible to judge, the New York County delegation and the new Provincial Congress as a whole would be a trifle more belligerent than before. But the substitutions were in the middle of the political spectrum—to the right of John Morin Scott on the left, and to the left of John Alsop on the right.

Isaac Sears had not been a candidate. The one surprising upset—surprising, at least, to the incumbent—was Colonel McDougall's defeat for reelection. His pride was wounded. Since he had always been on the belligerent extreme with Scott and Sears, his failure looked like a victory for the conciliationists, but that was not so. New York voters felt that McDougall had failed in belligerence by not leading his regiment to Canada, and had failed again by not following it after it had gone. His defeat was partly a rebuke for those failures. Then, too, McDougall had been quarreling with Christopher Duyckinck. The Mechanics Committee had been greatly interested in the election, and even though many of its members were not qualified to vote, it had published a list of the candidates it supported. At an earlier period, McDougall might have been the Mechanics' second or third favorite. This time, he had not been on their slate.

Although the electorate had expressed general approval of the Provincial Congress, the election results were ambiguous on the question that most interested the delegates to the Continental Congress. By mid-April, eight of the thirteen delegations in Philadelphia had received instructions from home to vote in favor of independence, should a resolution to that effect be offered. (Ever since the news of the Prohibitory Act, such a resolution had seemed possible.) New York, New Jersey, Pennsylvania, Delaware, and Maryland were the five colonies that were not ready to declare for separation. New York and Pennsylvania were the unreadiest of the lot. Yet the Provincial Congress delegates just chosen were to serve for a year, until May, 1777, and if New York was going to instruct the New York delegation to vote for independence, these were the men who would make the decision. Nevertheless, their opinions on the subject, individually and collectively, were hardly known; they had stood for election on their general reputations. Henry Remsen, to take one example, had not spoken in favor of independence, and he had not spoken against it, either. He was just a man who was greatly esteemed in New York. He had done extremely well running his dry-goods store, at No. 8 Hanover Square (119 Pearl Street, as the numbers now run). He was rich, though not in the same financial class as James Beekman, say, or Philip Livingston. Remsen cared deeply about the city and the province, and New York voters could expect Remsen to do his serious best, on one issue after another, to represent their interests.

The city's vote for successful businessmen of moderate views might be interpreted this way or that, but its meaning remained unclear as far as any specific policy was concerned. Nevertheless, the conciliationists were pessimistic. General Howe's schedule was unknown, but an attack on New York, obviously, would make a negotiated settlement more difficult than it already was. Dr. John Jones, the Provincial Congress' medical adviser, had always managed to maintain some hope that an alternative to separation could be worked out. On the eve of the elections, however, he had to admit that the chances looked painfully slender. In a letter to his good friend James Duane, Dr. Jones summed up his opinion: "If they [the British peace commissioners] come quickly and offer you [the Continental Congress] something like a *carte blanche*"—Dr. Jones did not think that was likely—"perhaps we may have peace upon the footing of reconciliation; otherwise, from the rising spirit and temper of the people, I presume you will be under a necessity of declaring independence."

Governor Tryon was another who recognized that his ideas for New York's future were not going to be realized. The *Duchess of Gordon* had moved down to Sandy Hook Bay because it was still possible to steal fresh water near there, and the Governor, who had never stopped trying to preserve the legal continuity of the New York Assembly, wanted to hold a session on board his ship so that, on the assemblymen's advice, he could prorogue the legislature. But he saw that he would be asking those New Yorkers who might have tried to attend, by stealth, to sacrifice too much: they certainly could not have returned safely to their New York City homes. This was, Tryon wrote Germain, "A strong evidence of the little attention that is now paid even towards preserving the form of a legal and constitutional representation of the people." So the Governor dissolved the New York Assembly for the second time in five months— not, however, as a prelude to new elections, but forever.

IV. April to June, 1776

NEW YORK's interest in the subject of independence was
evident. Its opinion was unclear. "Common Sense" was
selling as well as or better than ever. (The pamphlet's total sales
by mid-April had reached 120,000, not counting pirated editions,
and the New York bookshops had disposed of their fair share.)
The word "independence" was no longer shocking. The newspapers' letters columns were dominated by contributions to the
debate, mostly pro-independence and, in many cases, remarkably
well written. A good letter, wherever it first appeared, was likely
to be picked up by at least one editor in most of the other cities,
and the six Philadelphia weeklies, which had, as regular con-
tributors, James Cannon, a mathematics instructor at the College
of Philadelphia, Sam Adams, John Witherspoon, President of
the College of New Jersey (now Princeton University), and Dr.
Benjamin Rush, among others, initiated more reprintable copy
than the papers in any other place. The man writing letters to
the Pennsylvania *Packet*, who signed himself, "The Forester,"
and whose work was reprinted in New York, wrote exactly like
Paine. He was Paine. But New York writers added some excellent letters to the pro-independence production from Philadelphia. The New Yorkers who signed themselves "Essex," "An
Independent Whig," and "Spartanus," to name a few, guarded
their anonymity. Still, their propaganda and their arguments

were in no way second rate. By April, the vogue in pro-independence essays was for statistics, calculations, and computations—the high cost of maintaining membership in the empire, the number of sailors that could be recruited for an American navy without hurting farm production or manufacturing output, and so on. These served to paint the argument with a surface of realism, to make independence sound practical; but while the writers' arithmetic was good, their premises were mostly guess-work.

From April 6, the day the Continental Congress had authorized privateers, the New York Committee of Safety, on behalf of the Provincial Congress, and various individual New Yorkers, on their own accounts, had been working to get private warships out of the harbor and into action. Privateering was risky. A ship's owner could lose everything if, instead of taking, his privateer were taken. But the chances for big profits were enticing, and the government was ready to help investors by supplying guns, fittings, and supplies. It even looked as if New York might insure against loss. Comfort Sands had lost two ships, the *Sally* and the *Polly*, together worth 1,150 pounds. They had not been privateers but the blockade runners that the Provincial Congress had engaged earlier in the year. As Sands read his contract, New York had agreed to pay for their loss in case anything went wrong, and he thought the Provincial Congress would pay him—as, eventually, it did. The Continental Congress was the authority that commissioned privateers, and Colonel McDougall had applied for a commission, on New York's behalf, for the patrol boat *Schuyler*. A second New York ship, the *Montgomery*, commanded by Captain William Rogers, which carried a crew of sixty men, received its commission on April 17. Thomas Randall had applied for privateer's papers for a third sloop, the *General Putnam*, Captain Thomas Creiger commanding. And various other men, including Sands, planned to make applications as soon as they could qualify. Besides an armed ship, a captain, and a crew, one needed to post a $5,000 bond, if the privateer was one hundred tons or less, and a $10,000 bond if it was larger.

The Continental Congress not only approved of privateering but in some instances was willing to subsidize the ventures by paying the crews' salaries. The pay rates were slightly lower than the Continental Army's, but the New York recruiting campaign was nonetheless suffering from the competition. Unemployed merchant seamen, who might otherwise have drifted into the Army, signed aboard the privateers instead. The crews were to share in whatever prizes the ships succeeded in taking, and, with luck, this could much more than make up the difference between a soldier's and a sailor's base pay. Extra incentive bonuses were also being offered—a double share, for instance, would go to the man who first sighted a British ship that later became a prize, and a triple share to the first crewman to board a resisting prize ship.

The privateers' owners expected their ships to operate on the high seas, although, legally, all British ships everywhere were fair game, including shipwrecks, provided only that they were below the high-tide water mark. But Washington, while admiring the New Yorkers' eagerness to get into privateering, thought of New York's growing fleet of armed vessels primarily as a useful addition to American seapower. The American Navy proper had gained substance during the winter. Since November, the Continental Congress had had a Naval Committee, with John Adams as its leading member; formal rules for the naval service had been adopted; Esek Hopkins, of Rhode Island, had been appointed naval Commander-in-Chief; captains had been named, in order of seniority, starting with Dudley Saltonstall,

Abraham Whipple, Nicholas Biddle, and John B. Hopkins (Esek Hopkins' oldest son); a special category of seagoing soldiers, the Marines, had been established; and the Continental Congress had bought eight merchant vessels and converted them into warships—the *Alfred* (twenty-four guns), the *Columbus* (twenty), the *Andrea Doria* (fourteen), the *Cabot* (fourteen), the *Providence* (twelve), the *Hornet* (ten), the *Wasp* (eight), and the *Fly* (eight). General Washington was pleased with all this—it was, among other things, an endorsement of his own initiative in having organized a little fleet of raiders at Boston—but, since Hopkins' fleet, of 110 guns, was opposed, in American waters, by at least seventy-five British warships with about 2,000 guns, sea battles were, for the moment, to be avoided. On April 6, this point had been emphasized in a humiliating manner. Hopkins, with five of his warships, encountered a lone twenty-gun British frigate, the *Glasgow*, off Block Island in the middle of the night. The *Glasgow*, commanded by Captain Tryingham Howe, should have been an easy victim. Instead, ignoring the discouraging odds against her, the *Glasgow* had sailed circles around the Americans. At the end of a three-hour engagement, the *Glasgow* had not only escaped but had put the *Alfred* out of action temporarily with a hit on the *Alfred*'s wheel block, and had inflicted twenty-four casualties on the Continental Navy while suffering only four. Hopkins was discouraged, and the Continental Congress was disappointed in him, although his one other action, a lucrative raid a month earlier on New Providence (now Nassau) Island, in the Bahamas, had been a sparkling success, and had added more than a hundred cannon and mortars to the United Colonies' arsenal.

Washington had once again organized a little navy of his own, a squadron of gunboats to operate in and around New York Harbor. Its commander, Lieutenant Colonel Benjamin Tupper

—he was called "Commodore," in deference to his special assignment—was under Washington's command, whereas Hopkins and the Continental fleet took their orders directly from the Continental Congress and could not be counted on to support the Continental Army. (For the time being, Hopkins was protecting Providence, Rhode Island, not New York.) Tupper had made a name for himself at Boston, where he had had a similar assignment. He was thirty-eight years old, a Dorchester, Massachusetts, man, originally, who had moved to the western part of the colony; and, while he had been many things—a farmhand, a sergeant in the French and Indian War, and militia lieutenant, a schoolteacher—he was not an experienced sailor. But the Commodore was aggressive, enterprising, and an excellent troop leader—qualities that Washington treasured because they were uncommon.

Washington wanted Tupper's squadron—four armed sloops (the *Hester*, the *Spitfire*, the *Shark*, and the *Whiting*) and a few whaleboats, rafts, and small boats—to prevent the British from going ashore and to prevent Americans from going aboard the British ships. Tupper had to watch the New Jersey coast, especially between Sandy Hook and Amboy, as well as the shores of Staten Island and Long Island. Sandy Hook and the lighthouse there, which had been dismantled on New York's initiative, were a special—and especially difficult—case. The spit of land was within the range of the *Phoenix*'s guns, and the British openly drew fresh water from a well near the lighthouse, confident that the *Phoenix*'s firepower was greater than any the Americans could bring to bear on the site. The British, on Tryon's orders, had burned down the house that had stood beside the light, to the dismay of the lighthouse keeper, Adam Dobbs, in order to keep New Jersey militiamen from using the structure as a fort. (Dobbs had not been hurt, and he was waiting for New York to send down a boat for him, his servants, and his possessions—as Tryon had agreed to let New York do.) A British guard—one sergeant and twelve marines—was posted by the well at night to prevent the Americans from spoiling the well water under cover of darkness. And, all in all, though Sandy Hook was a no man's land during the day, it was more nearly under British than American control at night.

By coincidence, Tupper's best-known success at Boston had involved a lighthouse, the one on Great Brewster Island, at the entrance to Boston Harbor. It had been dismantled by the Americans in an effort to make navigation more difficult for the British. A British work party of carpenters and mechanics had been trying to repair it, with a detachment of thirty-three British marines guarding the operations, when, on July 31, 1775, Tupper's raiders had attacked. The Commodore's force of three hundred soldiers, traveling in whaleboats, had not only halted the repair work but had captured the entire British group. So Tupper, in a limited sense, was a lighthouse specialist. He was itching to do something dashing at Sandy Hook, despite the proximity of the *Phoenix*. And while Washington wanted no senseless risks taken, he had not told Tupper that an attack on Sandy Hook was absolutely forbidden.

Washington did want Tupper to have some more armed sloops, however. As the General explained to Thomas Randall, a member of New York's special committee for marine affairs, it would be helpful if, instead of sending the *Montgomery*, the *Schuyler*, and the *Putnam* out to sea in search of prizes, New York would lend its navy to Tupper for patrol duty. Randall reported his conversation with the Commander-in-Chief. The Committee of Safety was upset. New York was looking forward to a return on its investments in the ships, and while the *Schuyler* had originally been armed for patrol duty, the Committee of

Safety had changed its mind about how the ship might best be used at the moment privateering had been made legal.

By merely talking informally to Randall—Washington could have made his request as a formal, written demand, and sent copies of the letter to the Continental Congress—the General may have been misleading New York. In any case, the Committee of Safety interpreted Washington's manner as an indication that New York could dicker about the ships. Would the General be content, the Committee asked, through Randall, with taking one, or maybe two, of the sloops "on the Continental account" and letting one or two go? The Committee, in other words, was asking Washington to buy instead of borrow. New York realized that the *Schuyler* was probably too small for successful privateering, and furthermore, as of April 24, Captain Smith's crew was short eighteen men. Would the General, by any chance, be willing to buy just the *Schuyler*, and allow the *Montgomery* and the *Putnam* to start their privateering cruises?

New York was mistaken in trying to bargain with Washington, as Randall was quick to learn, but before that point was made, a larger and more important misunderstanding came up. When Washington got his first all-inclusive count of his Army's strength at New York, he was discouraged to learn that, as of April 23, it was low. Besides 674 officers, 588 sergeants, and 293 drums and fifes, he had only 8,301 enlisted men present and fit for duty—something like 2,000 men fewer than the full theoretical total. There was no mystery about the figures. Washington knew that quite a few men had deserted, and when he subtracted the 1,133 men who were sick, 692 on special assignments, and 64 on furlough, the returns made sense. By this time, all the New York and Connecticut militiamen (including Colonel Isaac Sears) had been dismissed—subject, of course, to recall in an emergency. And four regiments (Poor's, Paterson's,

Greaton's, and Bond's), under Brigadier General William Thompson—about 2,000 men—had started on their way to Canada, in compliance with the Continental Congress' directions. The exact count made Washington feel that it would be dangerous to reduce his army at New York any further.

Just as the General reached that conclusion, the Continental Congress sent word that Canada needed six more regiments, and it wanted Washington to supply them. That, Washington believed, was going much too far. He got the bad news on April 26, and he immediately replied that he could not afford to lose another three thousand men; but he also began to obey his orders before he got an answer to his protest against them. He designated the regiments he would send—Irvine's, Wayne's, Stark's, Dayton's, Winds's and James Reed's—if he had to send them. General John Sullivan would go as the group's commander.

In the meantime, Washington had been wondering where New York's four Continental regiments were. The recruiting, which had started briskly in February, had petered out. Washington put his question to the Committee of Safety on April 24: "It being necessary that I should know the number of troops to compose the army here, I must request the favor of your honorable body to inform me how many regiments are raising in this Province for the Continental service, by order of Congress, and what their state is as to men and arms."

The Committee of Safety, confused by the General's smooth style, again imagined that it had an opportunity for a little dealing with Washington, and so its reply was as disgraceful as its attempt to sell the Continental Army a fraction of New York's three-ship fleet. New York was raising four Continental regiments, the Committee of Safety wrote in reply, adding—as if this were a well-known fact—that they were "destined by Congress for the protection and defense of this Colony." The Committee mentioned Van Schaick's regiment (the old Second New York) "for the Canada service," as a contrast to the other four. The Continental Congress had made no such agreement with New York, as Washington knew.

As to the units' readiness, the Committee of Safety said, Washington had no cause for concern: "Congress has thought proper to put them under our immediate direction . . . we have taken the necessary steps for filling up the battalions and for enforcing a return of their present state, with which we will furnish you as soon as we are possessed of them."

The Committee of Safety went on to say that it might have a little difficulty furnishing arms for the men, because:

When the affair of Lexington proclaimed the war, this Colony was extremely destitute of arms; our brethren of New England, who were first called on for the defense of American liberty, had purchased many arms from our inhabitants; our Colony troops were supplied last year with arms at our Provincial expense; most of those still remain in the Canada service. These considerations, together with our ineffectual attempts to obtain foreign supplies, increased the difficulty of arming our battalions. We are not, however, without hopes of succeeding; we have made several contracts already with manufacturers; we have published encouragement for people in that branch. We shall continue to make as many contracts for the purpose as we shall, from time to time, have in our power; we have also directed the committees in the several counties to purchase arms. The number already furnished by our Commissary is 311; he has still on hand a few. We have reason to believe many of our troops will come provided; and upon the whole, we hope we shall not be very deficient in so material an article.

All of this was inexcusable. New York did not need an up-to-the-minute report to find out how badly off the four regiments were; the implication that Washington need not be concerned about them was rude and incorrect. McDougall's new outfit was less than half full. James Clinton's regiment appeared to be more nearly up to strength, but New York was still trying to do exactly what Heath had explained was impossible—to count the three Suffolk County companies toward its Continental quota when it had left them at home for Suffolk's defense. And the Committee of Safety's assurances that the province expected to be able to supply the regiments with weapons was preposterous. Rudolphus Ritzema, who as McDougall's lieutenant colonel in 1775, had led the First New York to Canada, survived, and been rewarded with his own Continental regiment in 1776. All of Ritzema's eight companies had enough muskets for one—a shortage that would worsen as the unit approached full strength. And the Committee of Safety knew that New York gun manufacturers, in perhaps a year, would do very well if they could supply Ritzema with guns for the other seven. The other New York battalions were almost equally underequipped.

Finally, the Committee of Safety asked Washington to advance New York 6,000 pounds. The province, it explained, was "some weeks" behind in its bookkeeping, and, "though the balance is not yet struck, we are sure it must be considerably in our favor." New York would ask the Continental Congress for the money "without delay," the Committee of Safety assured the General, but it needed an advance because it could not wait to get the money from Philadelphia; it had not "one farthing of Continental money" on hand, and it did not want "the public service under our care" to suffer as a result.

Washington received New York's inept letter with perfect calm. The General was well informed on all the matters the Committee of Safety had fibbed about. His answer—still polite —was brilliant, judged by the results it produced. It pointed directly at the foolishness of New York's attempt to pretend that New York Continentals were on a different footing from any other Continentals. Washington picked out the clumsy phrase the Committee of Safety had used about the New York regiments being under New York's direction. The General wanted to know what that was supposed to mean:

If the four battalions which were directed to be raised under the command of Colonels McDougall, Clinton, Ritzema and Wynkoop are placed under the immediate care of the Committee of Safety for this Colony by Congress, I should be glad to know how far it is conceived that my powers over them extend or whether I have any at all. Sure I am that they cannot be subjected to the direction of both, and I shall have no small reluctance in assuming an authority I am not vested with powers to execute; nor will my solicitude, (further than as a well wisher to the cause,) on account of arms for and returns of these regiments continue, if they are not considered as within the lines of my command. It becomes, therefore, my indispensable duty to be ascertained of this matter, and to know whether these regiments cannot be ordered out of the Colony, for instance, to New Jersey, if necessity should require.

As for the loan, Washington expressed his regrets, but "the low state of our cash" made it "altogether impracticable at this time." The General did add, however, that he would see if Heath and Thompson could pay back the sums they had borrowed from New York.

The General's short, rather stiff answer brought the Committee of Safety back to its senses. And, in fact, New York's next contribution to the correspondence, dated April 29, was almost fawning:

We are sorry to find there is a possibility of misunderstanding the passage in our letter respecting the four battalions raising in this Colony. Be assured, Sir, that we never considered them as under our direction except so far as concerned the forming and equipping them; and if you will be pleased to refer yourself to our last letter, the distinction taken therein between the four battalions and Van Schaick's regiment will convince you that we meant nothing more than in obedience to Congress to have the completing of them for the command of the Continental general. . . .

If Washington was pleased to refer back, he saw that he had read the reference to Van Schaick's regiment correctly the first time—as a tangential argument that the four new regiments were not to go to Canada.

. . . nor do we esteem them so pointedly under our direction in in this respect as to exclude your solicitude as Commander-in-Chief to have them speedily completed and armed—a solicitude highly becoming your station, and which, instead of affording the least ground for umbrage, serves to heighten the opinion which your former conduct has invariably taught us to entertain of your vigilant attention to the important duties of your office. . . .

On and on the Committee of Safety went, retracting, one point at a time, the advantages the first letter had tried to establish for New York. The General had an "unquestionable right" to know the state of the four regiments. The Committee enclosed a rough return of McDougall's outfit, and confessed that it was "most deficient." And of course, the Committee agreed, the four regiments were liable to service anywhere in the Colonies—the British fleets and armies were to be considered as much New York's enemies while they were on "the coasts of Connecticut, New Jersey, or Carolina, as if they lay in the East River." One sticking point—about service in Canada—did remain. New York admitted that some of its recruiting officers had been promising prospects that they would not be sent there. How many enlistments had depended on that impossible, illegal condition, no one knew.

Since New York had no right to promise any limit on the

obligations of Continental Army service, it was the province's good fortune that Washington regarded the question as academic. He had already sent more regiments from New York to Canada than he felt he could spare. The Continental Congress had rejected Washington's opinion, and the six additional regiments did have to go; in fact, Stark's and Reed's were already started north. But, given their poor condition, McDougall's, Clinton's, Ritzema's, and Wynkoop's regiments were in no danger of being sent to Canada in the near future—not even if the Continental Congress, in some emergency, insisted that Washington send more reinforcements. The question in the General's mind was whether the New York regiments were even worth keeping on the Continental payroll. Since unequipped soldiers could not fight, might it not be more economic—especially in the case of Ritzema's unit—to dismiss them? The weight of the argument, Washington felt, was against dismissal. Weapons might be found in some unforeseen place. If not, the regiments could easily be sent home later. But if they were dismissed now, and then wanted later, it might be hard to reassemble them. Washington was sufficiently unsure of this opinion, however, to write to Philadelphia for advice. Two weeks later, the Continental Congress agreed that the regiments should be kept.

The General did not mention the dismissal possibility to New York. In his letter of April 30, he managed to apologize and, at the same time, gently smothered New York's idea that it could fill its quota of Continental troops by providing regiments with conditions attached to them:

I perceive by the tenor of your favor of yesterday, that my letter . . . has given umbrage, which I am sorry for. . . . Three things led me to suspect that the York battalions were not upon the same establishment of the other Continental troops—current report, an implied exception in the order detaching six more battalions to Canada, and that part of your letter signifying that four of these battalions were to be raised under your immediate direction, which intimation, coming in corroboration of the two first reasons, (for I never had any information of this matter from Congress) led me to believe that you intended it as a genteel hint that I was not to consider them in the same light as I did the others. It was not to be wondered at, therefore, that I should wish to know the extent of my authority over them, (that my conduct might be regulated thereby) or that I should be so solicitous in arming regiments raised for local purposes as those for the general service, when the latter are also greatly deficient in this essential point. These were the ideas that filled my mind at the time of writing. If the extreme hurry, occasioned by a variety of business which is continually pressing upon me, clouded the meaning I wished to convey, I can only add that it never was, and I hope never will be, my intention to give unprovoked offense. Of this your Committee may be once for all assured —that it is my earnest wish to coöperate with them in every measure which can conduce to the general good, and that if I should, at any time, differ from them in the means, I shall feel my share of the concern.

Washington's explanation may have confused the Committee of Safety, but there was no mistaking the General's friendly intent. That was what counted most. There had been a showdown between Washington and New York, and yet, by leading the Committee of Safety into exposing its own failings, Washington left the New Yorkers with no sense of grievance. The Committee had not been scolded or maligned; on the contrary, it had been praised and flattered. Washington had taken trouble to spare the New Yorkers' feelings, but his devices had won what he wanted, and the General had increased New York's esteem for him. (The Reverend Joseph Treat, chaplain of New York's Second Independent militia regiment, baptized Mr. and Mrs. Alexander Anderson's twins on Sunday, April 29; the children were named George Washington and Martha Dandridge.)

Washington got some satisfaction from the steady progress on the trenches and gun-battery positions. The digging was helped by an improvement in the weather during the first week in May. April had been as cold and raw as an ordinary March. As the temperature rose, the soldiers, who had been doubled up in every available square foot of emergency barracks space, were ordered out of the city to various encampments. General Nathanael Greene's brigade (Varnum's, Hand's Hitchcock's, and Little's regiments) moved over to Brooklyn Heights, and other units filled up the big Manhattan camp. The General was happy to empty most of the town houses the Army had been compelled to borrow, because their owners, or agents speaking for their owners, had been pestering Headquarters with claims of property damage, often justified.

Inimicality was on Washington's mind. The inimicals had been inconspicuous since the General's arrival—perhaps that was more than mere coincidence—but Washington feared that they might make serious military trouble. He wanted to forestall that. He also wanted, as in every other matter, New York's cooperation and approval, and so he had suggested that the Committee of Safety appoint a semi-secret subcommittee on "intestine enemies" which might be able to work out a practical plan of action. Washington was thinking that New York might point out the really dangerous Tories in and around the city, and that the Continental troops could then arrest them and turn them over to the civilian authorities for hearings, punishment, and, possibly, confinement. The Committee of Safety had obliged. It asked Gouverneur Morris to head a small subcommittee to draft and present such a plan. Morris' subcommittee was baffled by the conundrums that had faced all previous efforts of the kind—especially the question of knowing how to order an arrest on suspicion before the suspect's side of the story had been heard. The year's experience had been disheartening. The Provincial Congress had listened to thousands of hours of testimony, and had never been able to arrive at a regular procedure that seemed safe and just. And, yet, as the subcommittee members realized, while they were thinking about legality and fairness, the intestine enemies were busy at their dangerous work. For example, the Committee of Safety as a whole heard a distressing story from Henry Smith, of North Castle, Westchester, about the effectiveness of British recruiting in the New York area. Smith himself had been recruited in his home town by a man named Thomas Gibson, of Fishkill, and, with five other young men from his own neighborhood, had been led, by Gibson, through Westchester County to Long Island Sound, across the Sound to Long Island, and across Long Island to the east side of the Narrows, where a boat from the *Lady Gage* had picked them up. Smith did not seem at all ardently pro-British, and in fact he and two other New Yorkers had changed their minds about wanting to serve in the British Army, had deserted from the *Lady Gage,* and had turned themselves over to the New Jersey authorities—which explained why the Committee of Safety had the opportunity to hear what Smith knew. Like his fellow recruits, Smith explained, he was "a country boy." What had persuaded him to sign—and he was not sure just what he had signed—was not his admiration for King George, but Gibson's promises that he would get a bounty (3 pounds, 14 shillings), good pay (20 shillings a month), and, above all, a bonus of two hundred acres of land after Great Britain had won the war.

According to Smith, the clandestine route from North Castle to the Narrows was well organized, and relied on the complicity of New Yorkers who lived along it. Smith's party had hidden by day and traveled at night. They had spent the first day in the woods. On the second day, Gibson hid the five recruits in Purdy's barn, not far east of White Plains—Smith was not sure which Purdy, but Smith did believe that the owner knew what his barn was being used for. At Hempstead, Long Island, where the group had hidden for more than a week, they had used Daniel Denton's house part of the time and one of the Hempstead taverns the rest of it, with Gibson paying all bills. (Daniel Denton was a captain in Ritzema's battalion, the only man with a full company. Young Smith may have confused his Dentons, or Daniel Denton's house, in his absence, may have been used without his knowledge.) On the *Lady Gage*, Smith estimated, there were one hundred Americans, recruits for the British Navy as well as the Army—presumably including the sixty men taken off Bedloe's Island just before Putnam's raid. Smith had recognized several and had heard the names of others. William Lownsberry, of Mamaroneck, was there. Lownsberry and Joshua Gidney, after having been jailed as suspected cannon-spikers, had escaped from the Upper Barracks and had disappeared. Smith had also seen a couple of men named Gidney, but he was not sure which ones. (Joshua, possibly? Smith had certainly not seen Isaac, Joshua's father, because Isaac was in jail in White Plains, begging the Committee of Safety to let him go home to look after his wife and seven children—an exaggeration because, however much he needed looking after, one child, Joshua, was not at home.) Smith had also recognized several Haineses, but, again, could not give their first names with any certainty. (Godfrey, at least, was still locked up at Kingston.)

The fact of British recruiting was not news to the Committee of Safety, but Smith's detailed report made it seem especially threatening, and the reminders of the January cannon sabotage were unpleasant, too. (Even so, the Committee of Safety, a few days later, took pity on the Gidneys: it voted that Isaac had been in jail long enough; that Joshua would not be re-arrested if he came out of hiding; and that both the father and the son could go home, on security, for the time being.) Among other reports on the enemy's recruiting efforts, there was one from Jonathan Sturges, of the Fairfield County (Connecticut) Committee. According to Sturges' information, Redding, Connecticut, was an assembly point for British recruits. Small parties of young men, like Gibson's group, were being led from there to the shore, across the Sound by boat, and on across Long Island to places where small boats from British ships could pick them up. Sturges wanted Washington's help with Connecticut's efforts to cut this route. One of Connecticut's warships, the armed brig *Defence*, had captured a party of eight such recruits in the middle of the Sound, and much of what Sturges knew about the system he had learned from his prisoners. Washington answered that he was more than willing to help, but he needed to have specific names and places. Long Island was big, and the General could easily have scattered his whole army on random patrol duty.

Washington and the Morris subcommittee imagined that inimicals were managing to supply the *Asia* and the other ships, despite the published prohibitions and Tupper's squadron's efforts at enforcement. Tupper, as a result of Washington's efforts, now had another ship, the *Putnam*, on loan from New York Province. A man who intended to take food to the British and who got caught in the act by the Americans could easily claim that he had not meant to approach the enemy fleet, but had been captured by it. That almost undisprovable excuse had been used repeatedly all winter, and a case in point came up on May 5. Peter Puillon, of Staten Island, was arrested by Lieutenant Docherty, commander of the picket guard on the Long Island side of the Narrows, who had seen Puillon coming in his

boat from the *Asia*. Puillon looked guilty, especially to Docherty, but when Puillon testified before the Committee of Safety
he swore he was innocent. He admitted that he had indeed
carried something like three pounds' worth of provisions to the
Asia, but only because the *Asia* had fired a warning shot he had
not dared ignore. Puillon said he had been hugging Staten
Island's south shore, doing his best to avoid the British. He was
not aware, at the time, of the new rules; if he had been, Puillon
insisted, he would not have taken his boat out at all.

Who could say, for certain, whether Puillon was telling the
truth? A witness who remembered hearing the *Asia*'s shot
would have strengthened Puillon's case, but Puillon did not
have one. However, he did produce several Staten Island character witnesses who said he was "a friend to the liberties of his
country." Puillon spoke with what the Committee believed was
candor. Also, the Committee discovered, the proclamations
against corresponding with the British had not, in fact, been
published on Staten Island until Friday, May 3, which allowed
Puillon only two days to have read them. All in all, the Committee of Safety decided that the whole affair was an unfortunate accident, and that Puillon was "entirely innocent." In
conclusion, the Committee said:

And it is earnestly recommended to the said Peter Puillon, not only
to be very cautious himself, but also to endeavor to prevent any other
inhabitants of Richmond County from attempting to come with any
provisions within reach of the guns of the said ship, or of any other
Ministerial ship or vessel which may be in that channel, and to use his
best endeavors to make the regulations adopted with respect to the
said ships publicly known in Richmond County.

Though Washington lacked positive proof for his suspicions,
he feared that Governor Tryon was still being kept informed of
everything important that was happening on shore. On the day
of Puillon's arrest, Captain Caleb Gibbs, commander of the

Headquarters Guard, took into custody a spy suspect named Joseph Blanchard, of New York City, who was known to several members of the Committee of Safety and was not, in their opinion, an inimical. But Blanchard was a friend of Tryon's son-in-law, Colonel Fanning, and Blanchard had boasted to several of Washington's officers that it was still possible—if one knew how—to correspond with the British warships. He had hinted rather vaguely that either Tryon's former housekeeper, Mrs. Hatch, or, perhaps, an unnamed woman who lived at Mrs. Hatch's, was a courier—an allegation that Mrs. Hatch, at the first opportunity, firmly denied. Besides Blanchard's chatty self-incrimination, there was one piece of tangible evidence against him: a copy of one of General Sullivan's brigade orders, in Sullivan's handwriting, which Captain Gibbs had discovered on the table in Blanchard's room in the course of making the arrest. At that moment, Blanchard had said to Gibbs that he couldn't imagine how Sullivan's orders happened to be there—a comment as damaging as the document's presence. By May 7, however, when the Committee of Safety interrogated Blanchard, he had collected his wits. He had an explanation for everything. He had indeed been in regular correspondence with Fanning for a long time, but—except for a single letter asking Fanning for money—the correspondence had all taken place before the new regulations were announced, during the time when Mr. Nixon, as the city's port master, had been making frequent trips out to the *Duchess of Gordon* with New York's permission. Blanchard said that all his letters had been left unsealed for inspection. He had sent Fanning a few supplies, such as a small memorandum book, twenty-five goose quills, a small bottle of Turlington's balsam oil, and other sundries. As for the copy of Sullivan's orders, Blanchard said he had finally figured out what must have happened. He remembered having seen the orders at a

Lieutenant Fisher's apartment, and, as an old friend of Sullivan, Blanchard had picked the paper up, just out of curiosity, to study the handwriting. Blanchard claimed that he had not thought of taking the document, but he realized now that he must have unintentionally put it in his pocket. The explanation was thin, but Blanchard had in his favor the point that there was nothing secret about Sullivan's orders. They had been, as Blanchard expressed it, "as public as anything in town." Therefore he could not see any evil purpose that the possession of a copy could serve. (Blanchard did not seem to realize that what was public in town should have been unknown on board the *Duchess of Gordon*.) Again the Committee of Safety was lenient. It decided to let Blanchard go.

Among other rumors and reports which the Committee of Safety was not, or not yet, able to investigate was an assertion that, in Rockaway, Captain Hicks was drilling a company of 140 Americans to join General Howe when he arrived. The woods around Brookhaven and Moriches were said to be full of "skulkers"—would-be British Army recruits. A report from Hempstead stated that nearly all of the five hundred men who lived in the vicinity were pro-British, no matter what oaths they had taken. It was also said that, at a recent Hempstead sheep-shearing, fresh lime punch had been served. Since limes were not available in local markets, had the fruit come from one of the newly arrived British ships? It was a good deal easier to feel certain, as Morris and his associates did, that all sorts of dangerous acts were being committed than to devise a plan to prevent them, which was what Washington expected.

The Committee of Safety looked forward to the start of the new session of the Provincial Congress. There was much more work than the smaller group of men could manage. A circular letter to all delegates had been sent out, urging them to come to town as quickly as they could, and delegates had been arriving daily and getting right to work. The clerks discovered on May 8 that, by this gradual process, a quorum was present at the afternoon assembly. The new session of the Provincial Congress was therefore called to order without any ceremony. Money was the first order of business. The New York treasury had been empty for three weeks. After Washington had refused to help, a few of the individual Committee members had lent the province some cash, enabling it to pay its most pressing bills, but that was not a proper way to run a government. On checking the accounts, happily, the Provincial Congress discovered that about $37,500 of the March 1 issue of New York dollars had not yet been delivered to the treasury. Isaac Roosevelt, the delegate who had been chosen to supervise the printing, explained that he had the printed money, all right, but that hand-numbering the bills, and getting each one signed twice, as his instructions required, was a slow business, particularly because of the preponderance of small bills, which were intended to take the place of silver coins as change. A ⅛-dollar bill took as much hand work as a ten-dollar bill. New York had been spending faster than he and his colleagues could authenticate the paper. Roosevelt's report came as a relief: New York, for the time being, did not have to authorize another issue. The Provincial Congress ordered Roosevelt to hurry, and twenty-four hours later, he delivered $30,000 in small bills, all properly numbered and signed. And, Roosevelt said, he thought the balance would be ready in a few days.

No sooner had the Provincial Congress settled down—several days went by before a reliable quorum began to attend regularly—than the Continental Congress presented New York with a question more difficult by far than money embarrassments. On May 10, the men in Philadelphia voted a recommendation—not

an order—that all colonies without adequate governments proceed at once to establish them. The delegates did not define
adequacy; their phrase was "sufficient to the exigencies of their
affairs," and if that had been all, New York might have replied,
with some justification, that the recommendation did not apply
to the Provincial Congress. Most of its members believed that
their improvised government had done well, although numbers
of problems needed to be worked out. But the Continental
Congress' preamble to the May 10 resolve, which was not
passed until May 15, was more controversial than the recommendation itself:

Whereas his Brittanick Majesty, in conjunction with the Lords
and Commons of Great Britain, has, by a late act of Parliament,
excluded the inhabitants of these United Colonies from the protection
of his Crown; And whereas no answer whatever to humble petitions
of the Colonies for redress of grievances and reconciliation with Great
Britain has been, or is likely to be, given; but the whole force of that
Kingdom, aided by foreign mercenaries, it is to be exerted for the
destruction of the good people of these Colonies; And whereas it
appears absolutely irreconcileable to reason and good conscience for
the people of these Colonies now to take the oaths and affirmations
necessary for the support of any Government under the Crown of
Great Britain; and it is necessary that the exercise of every kind of
authority under the said Crown should be totally suppressed, and all
the [powers] of Government exerted under the authority of the people
of the Colonies, for the preservation of internal peace, virtue, and
good order, as well as for the defense of their lives, liberties, and
properties, against the hostile invasions and cruel depredations of their
enemies: Therefore . . .

In short, the Continental Congress was less interested in
sufficiency than in independence, and its resolution asked the
New York Provincial Congress to transform New York from a
colony into a state.

The Merchants' Coffee House—renamed the New York

Coffee House, and under the new management of Cornelius Bradford—had reopened on the first of May and was operating almost exactly as before, and there, as well as everywhere else that New Yorkers met to discuss the exigencies of their affairs, the statehood suggestion became the major topic of debate. Men upset by the resolution considered it a declaration of war. Those who liked it replied that declarations were unimportant compared with facts, and that the United Colonies had in fact been at war for months. Some men felt that the language of the preamble was excessively belligerent, but that the suggestion itself was good. As the Provincial Congress had grown in power, assuming one function after another by necessity and forming countless special subcommittees for still other functions, the machinery of government had become strained. New York agreed in principle (with Tryon) that it needed a governor, or a chief administrator, and it was remarkable that the Provincial Congress had managed to function so long without any executive more powerful than its presiding officer. New York had accomplished most of what had been required, but no one thought that it had done so as efficiently as a more regular government could. And the Provincial Congress had not attempted to replace the old legal system. That subject was crying for attention because, with some exceptions, by now the courts had stopped functioning. Governor Tryon himself had been at the head of the province's legal system. He had been Chancellor of the Court of Chancery, Judge of the Prerogative Court (for wills, estates, and marriage licenses), and with his Council, Tryon had constituted the last court of appeal before Parliament. Further, he appointed the judges. New York had no substitute for Tryon in his judicial capacities, and none for the Attorney-General, John Tabor Kempe, who was still a refugee with Tryon on the *Duchess of Gordon*. Some judges of the courts of common pleas, sheriffs, clerks, and justices of the peace were still carrying out their duties as best they could, but many were not. Many had gone to Nova Scotia or to England. Others were lying low for fear that, as members of the civil establishment, if not, in most cases, Crown officers, the local committees might assume they were inimical—as many were. The Provincial Congress had not appointed new judges or tried to reconstitute the courts.

The idea of improving New York's government had everyone's support. (The most conservative of the Provincial Congress delegates favored good government as a defense against anarchy.) But there was also a disturbing suspicion—Robert R. Livingston, in Philadelphia, had raised the point—that the Continental Congress' militants were trying to sneak a disguised declaration of independence past the hesitants. Livingston was right. The pro-independence majority of eight colonies was impatient with the middle five, none of which was ready to vote for independence outright, though all of them, New York included, were edging in that direction. The May 10 resolution was partly a product of that impatience. All sorts of men, by now, were trying to persuade Maryland, Delaware, Pennsylvania, New Jersey, and New York to see the light—or, as William Smith, in his diary, put it, "to encourage the rising Bias towards the general Independency." The Virginia delegates had formal instructions, dated May 15, to take "the initiative" in this work, but they were doing no more than numerous New Englanders, without instructions, had been doing for months. The heaviest pressure was on Pennsylvania, where John Dickinson and his supporters, who still favored conciliation, remained in control. Since the Pennsylvania Assembly agreed almost perfectly with Dickinson—even after its enlargement, on March 14, to make room for seventeen additional men—Dickinson had no reason to try to improve Pennsylvania's government. Yet even Dickinson saw that conciliation was not likely to succeed internationally, and he had been compelled to recognize the existence of a threat to his policies within the Assembly. Washington's former military secretary and confidant, Joseph Reed, was using all his considerable skill to organize a pro-independence clique of assemblymen. The clique's first object was to rescind the Pennsylvania delegates' instructions to vote against an independence resolution, if one should come up.

As the pro-independence strategists saw their campaign, a change in Pennsylvania's opinion would affect Maryland's—not to mention New Jersey's and Delaware's. Maryland, on the other hand, felt perfectly competent to make up its own mind. Maryland had moved slightly farther toward independence than Pennsylvania. On May 15, Maryland, on its own initiative, had voted that all Maryland office-holders were to dispense with oaths of allegiance to the Crown; Maryland affirmed its right to manage its own internal government, to tax itself as it saw fit, and to take military action against any force that was trying to make Marylanders submit to unjust taxes. Nonetheless, Maryland still did not want the Continental Congress to vote for independence. Maryland's delegates were instructed to vote no. They were to withstand any political stampede—to keep their heads even if, for a specific example, all the twelve other delegations voted yes. If Maryland delegates were tempted to do otherwise—if they did think it was absolutely necessary to vote yes—they were ordered to refer back, for new instructions, to the Maryland Convention.

New York's view was not far from Maryland's, although by this time the New York Provincial Congress was not quite so set against independence. But New York, like Maryland, was determined not to be unduly influenced by other colonies. New York intended to make up its own mind in its own time. Since the militants in Philadelphia had scrambled two important, semi-separate questions—state government was one idea, independence another—in one resolution, New York's decision might be slow. Some men, James Duane among them, felt that New York might gain by not hurrying, as he explained in a letter to John Jay: "I would first be well assured of the opinion of the inhabitants at large. Let them be rather followed than driven on an occasion of such moment. But, above all, let us see the conduct of the middle Colonies before we come to a decision; it cannot injure us to wait a few weeks; the advantage will be great, for this trying question will clearly discover the true principles and the extent of the union of the Colonies." Duane was by no means the only New Yorker who wondered what the population thought about making New York a state. Most of the delegates to the Provincial Congress, although they had been elected only a month earlier, were uncertain about how their home counties felt, for the question of statehood had not come up until the Continental Congress had raised it. New York had hoped that the new Provincial Congress could sit for a whole year, until the second Tuesday in May, 1777, without the trouble and expense of another election—and yet here, only two weeks into the new session, was an issue of such far-reaching significance that nearly all the delegates thought they needed advice from their counties on how to vote.

Friday, May 17, was set aside for the second observance of the Continental Congress' twenty-four hours of humility, fasting, and prayer. The city came to a standstill. All business stopped. Services were held in all the churches for the dual purpose, as the New York City Committee's instructions phrased it, "of asking for peace, or let the Americans win the war." No one was permitted to ride the ferries, ride, or even walk the streets for amusement. Parents of children and masters of servants were particularly enjoined to prevent "playing and straggling" around town. In contrast to 1775, New York's compliance with the rules was exemplary. The Continental troops—though technically exempted from the observance—were excused from fatigue duties. Washington ordered the regiments to parade in the morning on their various parade grounds, and then, a little before ten o'clock, they marched to services conducted by their respective chaplains.

For all its outward appearance of calm meditation, New York was actually agitated about more matters than any one man could keep in mind, starting with the ever-present fear that the lookouts, at any hour, might report the sails of Howe's fleet. Then, at Cold Spring, Long Island, four men—Isaac Ketchum, Isaac Youngs, John Henderson, and Henry Dawkins—had been arrested on suspicion of counterfeiting Massachusetts, Connecticut, and New York paper money. A considerable amount of incriminating physical evidence had been seized. The inclusion of Dawkins' name, as the story broke in Loudon's *Packet* in the May 16 issue, was enough to alarm every reader, because Dawkins, whose shop was on Broad Street, was not only the best engraver in the city and one of its best silversmiths but the man who had engraved the plates for the New York issue just completed. Another cause for concern was the Provincial Congress' order of May 10 requiring "every male inhabitant of the city and county of New York" between the ages of sixteen and forty-nine who had left Manhattan Island since June 1, 1775, to return immediately. The Congress was trying to enforce the compulsory militia-service rule, and to catch New York County men who were evading their duty by staying away. But the resolution, as it stood, made no exceptions at all—not for sickness, religious scruples (Quakers were not asked to serve in the militia), or any other reason. And the order also disturbed the many prominent men who had been able to move away—to Westchester or Dutchess counties, say, or to the New Jersey shore—during the recurrent alarms. Quite a few of these men had already made their military commitments in their country neighborhoods. Christopher Smith was one of the first to question the resolution's blanket nature. He wrote from Jamaica, Long Island, where he had been spending most of the past two years. Smith, who still felt that he was primarily a New York County man, said that because of an "infirmity" he had been excused from all civic duties for the past eighteen years. If the order did not apply to him, could he please have a letter from the Provincial Congress saying he could stay in Jamaica? For lack of careful drafting, the Provincial Congress' order was arousing needless apprehension.

The cost of living was going on up. Not long after the Continental Congress had declared the ports open, it had removed the old price ceilings on articles that had been listed as forbidden imports. These controls had been imposed by the Association in 1775 in an effort, mostly successful, to keep the prices of old stocks on hand from rising. Now the economic problem was to encourage merchant speculators—"adventurers," as the Continental Congress resolution described them—to hunt for new sources for the goods formerly purchased in British markets. Unless the adventurers could look forward to prices considerably higher than prices had been, they would have no incentive to accept the added expenses and new risks of importing—particularly the risk of capture by the British Navy.

One ceiling price remained—on green tea. It was six shillings a pound. All the other stocks of forbidden imports had dwindled to almost nothing, but there was a lot of tea in various warehouses. The tea had been bought, originally, to sell at four shillings sixpence per pound, so six shillings was not an unfair price. Some of the men who owned tea in bulk, however, had sold it slowly, if at all, speculating on a rise in its value and assuming that eventually the price ceiling would be lifted. The demand for tea in New York was great, despite the old campaign of 1773 to make consumers regard the drink as unpatriotic. Some retailers imagined that, without price control, they could get twenty shillings a pound. Within two or three days after the other ceilings were lifted, on April 30, the rumor spread through Connecticut that New York shops were illegally charging eight shillings for tea right under General Washington's nose. As a result, legal tea sales in New Haven stopped; no one wanted to sell for six shillings if he could get eight. Isaac Sears, who had returned to New Haven, his adopted hometown, after the Connecticut militiamen had been dismissed, and who was speculating in tea futures on a modest scale—he had twenty-nine chests of tea on hand, having sold ten—was one of those who had heard the story. Sears wrote directly to Washington, arguing that the ceiling price ought to be held, but adding, with a suspicion of pride, that he, Sears, stood to "advance my estate largely" if tea-holders were about to be allowed to charge what they liked. Washington replied, coolly, that he agreed with Sears that "the resolves of Congress should be strictly adhered to," but that since the price of tea was New York's concern, not the Continental Army's, he would turn Sears's letter over to the Provincial Congress.

Over the weekend of May 18, while New Yorkers were concerned with statehood, counterfeiting, and the price of tea, Washington was studying the latest bad news from Canada. Sir Guy Carleton, reinforced, had marched out of his Quebec fortress with a battery of artillery and fewer than a thousand soldiers, and had routed the American "besieging force"—as the optimists in the Continental Congress had liked to think of it. General John Thomas, who had just taken command there, had been forced to leave two hundred sick Americans to the mercy of the British and to abandon his guns and powder. He had halted the remnants of his army at Deschambault—forty miles up the St. Lawrence from Quebec—but then, after a council of war, had withdrawn farther, to Sorel. General Thompson was supposed to have arrived at Lake George with his troops, and General Sullivan's brigade was supposedly on its way from Albany to Lake George. In numbers, their combined strength was considerable. Holding the position outside Quebec, however, had been essential to American plans, and the Continental Congress' commissioners, Franklin, Carroll, and Chase, at Montreal (they had reported the disaster to General Schuyler, who had sent their news on to Washington), saw that the American supply system was not good enough to maintain the men who were already in the province of Montreal, let alone reinforcements.

On that same Saturday, Washington got confirmation, from an escaped prisoner of war, George Merchant, of the rumor that Germain had hired about seventeen thousand German mercenaries during January and February. A letter in Merchant's possession—it was addressed to Lieutenant Governor Cadwallader Colden—predicted that by late June the British expeditionary force, including the Germans, would number about thirty thousand. Then, on Sunday, May 19, Washington got a letter from the Continental Congress telling him to come down to Philadelphia to confer. Washington felt that discussion was necessary, but he had hoped that General Horatio Gates, who had all the information Washington had, could represent him. Even though all the bad news, in Washington's phrase, added up to an "alarming crisis," Washington would not have left New

York City without the Continental Congress' request when there was a possibility that the British might appear at any time.

When the Continental Congress issued an invitation, on the other hand, Washington did not refuse. The dispatch rider who brought the Congress' letter to Washington also brought the news that Gates and Thomas Mifflin, one of Washington's former aides and now his Quartermaster General, had both been promoted, Gates to major general and Mifflin to brigadier general. Washington was pleased by both advancements. The only drawback was Hancock's accompanying note, requesting that both officers be assigned to duty in Massachusetts. Washington did not believe that Howe was going to return to Boston, and he did not want to waste the talents of two of his best men on garrison duty. But perhaps that question could be settled in Philadelphia.

The General immediately prepared to leave, taking Gates and Mifflin with him, and once again putting General Putnam in charge of the New York City defenses. Washington had already explained to the Provincial Congress, by letter, that he was including the New York militia regiments with the Continental troops in the assignment of posts in case of alarm, and that therefore he would appreciate an order from New York, in advance, instructing its militia commanders to obey him and to obey the other Continental generals. Washington did not want to have to reargue the old command-authority question (on which New York had been first prickly and then deceitful), after Howe's troops had started to go ashore. Washington's general orders for Sunday, May 19, reminded everybody, including civilians, what the alarm signals, agreed on earlier, were: two cannon shots fired from the Fort George rampart and a flag (or, by night, two lanterns) hoisted to the top of downtown headquarters, No. 1 Broadway. Once again he asked the

Provincial Congress to try its hardest to find weapons and entrenching tools for the New York troops. And, to make sure that Putnam kept everything in mind, the Commander-in-Chief handed him a long memorandum. Putnam was to try to hurry along the fortifications under construction—especially the Long Island, Governor's Island, and New York City works—and to finish them before starting any new projects. Then, if Colonel Knox had cannon to mount there, but not otherwise, Putnam was to start on forts that had been proposed at Paulus Hook and at the Narrows. Washington wanted Putnam to check up on the alarm-signal system, to try to get the powder magazine in order, and to have as many cartridges made as possible. If there was any time, Washington thought a good man should be sent up to inspect the Highlands forts—Knox or Stirling or Colonel Rufus Putnam, of the engineers (General Putnam's cousin). Putnam was to open all Washington's business mail. The Commander-in-Chief said nothing about specific tactics in case of a military emergency. Washington thought he could return from Philadelphia quickly enough to take charge of a battle, if New York was attacked. But Washington had started to worry that Howe's fleet might outflank all the prepared defenses and sail up the Hudson as far as "the woody grounds above Mr. Scott's." (John Morin Scott's country place, in present-day terms, was on the Hudson, around Thirty-fourth Street.) If Putnam managed to finish everything else, therefore, Washington suggested that he might have the men throw up some "flushes"—hasty entrenchments—above Scott's, just in case.

Although the semi-secret subcommittee on intestine enemies had not yet decided on a plan, Washington wrote Putnam, on a separate sheet of paper, that he had "reason to believe" that the New York Provincial Congress was planning to arrest all the principal Tories on Long Island, in the city proper, and in the

country around New York. When New York approached him
for help, Washington wrote, Putnam was to give the Provincial
Congress anything it asked for. Since Long Island would probably be "the most active area," Greene's brigade would be the
command most likely to furnish troops; Putnam should confer
with Greene as soon as New York made its request. Meanwhile,
Washington cautioned, Putnam was to keep the whole matter—
including the fact that Washington thought he knew what New
York would decide before it had reached the decision—completely secret.

On Tuesday, May 21, Washington started for Philadelphia
by way of Staten Island and Amboy, where he inspected local
defenses. (They needed more work.) Mrs. Washington had
gone on ahead to Philadelphia in order to be inoculated for
smallpox. If the procedure worked properly, the patient usually
got very ill, with a "light case" of smallpox, but did not die.
While the "light case" was running its course, however, the
patient could infect others. Therefore, inoculation was forbidden
to anyone in the Continental Army, and it was against the law in
New York City, too. It was too dangerous. (In Mrs. Washington's case, and in the cases of the many other well-to-do persons
who had been inoculated, it was taken for granted that she
would be looked after in an isolated sickroom, and that no one
would come near her except persons who were immune or those
who knew the risk they were taking.) A smallpox epidemic was
a terrifying possibility. Some cases had been reported in New
York since the Continental Army's arrival, and the sick had
promptly been sent to Montresor's (now Randall's) Island,
which Washington had designated as an isolation area. Smallpox
was raging in the American Army in Canada—there was no
knowing, as yet, what part the disease had played in the defeats
there. And smallpox had taken a dreadful toll in Boston during

the British occupation. Washington and the Army's chief physician, Dr. John Morgan, were determined not to let smallpox or any other disease capture New York. But despite all orders to the contrary, soldiers who believed in inoculation (many did not) had little difficulty in finding a battalion surgeon or a private doctor willing to perform the simple skin-scratching operation. Dr. Azor Betts was a New York enthusiast for inoculation, and he had been in trouble with the authorities for a long time because he had been inoculating patients regularly. An Army investigation showed that a number of the officers in Prescott's regiment had been inoculated, contrary to Army regulations. Betts was summoned before the New York City Committee, and he admitted, without much chagrin, that he was the guilty physician. (He excused himself by saying that he had been "overpersuaded.") The doctor was committed to the city jail, where he had spent time before on the same charge, for an indefinite sentence, which stopped him from practicing but did not persuade him that inoculation was medically wrong. And General Putnam, distressed by the Betts case, announced what the punishment would be in the future for officers who broke the inoculation rule: "Any officer in the Continental Army who shall suffer himself to be inoculated, will be cashiered and turned out of the Army, and have his name published in the Newspapers throughout the continent as an enemy and traitor to his country."

The details of the Cold Spring counterfeiting scandal, as they emerged, provided the excitement of a serious danger mostly averted. The counterfeiters, with one exception, were jailed before New York heard what had happened, and the crime could have been much worse than it was. The plot had been foiled so quickly that the number of fake bills that had actually passed into circulation, it appeared, was not very large, and the counterfeits were Connecticut, Massachusetts, and Continental bills, not New York money. As the story came out, New York learned that Captain Jeremiah Wool, of Colonel Malcolm's regiment, with a small detachment of soldiers, and acting on orders from the Provincial Congress, which had a tip from Westbury, Long Island, had raided Isaac Youngs's house at Cold Spring one Sunday morning at dawn. Henry Dawkins was not there at the time, but in the room where he was staying one of Captain Wool's sergeants had spotted a secret door in the wall behind the head of Dawkins' bed. It led to a narrow flight of stairs that went up to a concealed garret with one small window. There Captain Wool had found a little print shop with a rolling press, a basin of water filled with papers cut to the size of Connecticut bills, and, on the floor, an imperfect printing of a Connecticut forty-shilling bill. Further search of the house, including the rooms that Israel Youngs, Isaac's brother, and his wife occupied, had turned up engravers' tools, plates (both blank and engraved), paper, ink, and several more bills, including some Massachusetts forty-two-shilling notes, dated December 7, 1755, which looked very realistic but had not been signed or numbered. Captain Wool's men, meanwhile, had found Dawkins, Isaac Ketchum, and John Henderson (one of the men who had tipped off the Provincial Congress); and when the whole group was assembled for questioning at Williams's Tavern, in Huntington, Dawkins was soon ready to talk. On his own initiative, Captain Wool said later, Dawkins had written out a brief confession and had signed it. The other men, in various ways, argued that they were more nearly innocent than guilty.

In later testimony, Dawkins' description of what had happened was far more convincing than the excuses the other men offered. Without minimizing his own guilt, Dawkins said that

Israel Youngs had been the leader of the ring. Dawkins also added a new name to the list the Provincial Congress already had: Townshend Hulet, Isaac Youngs's brother-in-law, who, for the time being, was missing. Dawkins explained that his own debts had driven him to crime. Israel Youngs had approached him several times, starting not long after Dawkins had engraved the plates for the New York issue. Dawkins, honoring his oath not to engrave any extra plates, had always refused to work for Youngs. But then Dawkins, unable to pay the rent on his shop, had had to go to debtors' jail, and Youngs had visited him there. Youngs had promised to get Dawkins out if he would change his mind, but still Dawkins had refused. Then, a few weeks later, after Dawkins had been released, without any help from Youngs, Youngs had approached him again. Once more the rent on Dawkins' shop was due. Youngs had paid it. Moreover, though the men had entered into no agreement about counterfeiting, Youngs had persuaded Dawkins to move to Cold Spring with his small son and to stay in Youngs's house. Youngs had taken the Dawkinses there in his boat, and not more than three days later, Dawkins had engraved—reluctantly, so he said—the two plates for the front and back of a Connecticut forty-shilling bill, and, because Youngs was so eager, and the rolling press had not yet arrived, Dawkins had rubbed off a few poor proof copies with a burnisher.

Later, Dawkins set up the press in the garret and taught Youngs how to run it. Dawkins engraved two more sets of plates—for a Massachusetts forty-two-shilling bill and a Connecticut thirty-dollar bill. He made tiny corrections in his plates for the Connecticut bill because Gaine's *Mercury*, in an article on the fakes in circulation, had pointed out that two small crosses in the design were not properly joined; and Dawkins was working on the plate for the front of a Continental two-dollar bill at the time of his arrest. Dawkins emphasized that he himself had run off only a handful of bills. On the other hand, he said, the speed with which the handle of the press had turned black with printer's ink showed that the Youngs brothers and Hulet must have worked fairly steadily for about a month. Ketchum's main function, as Ketchum admitted, had been buying suitable paper in Philadelphia and Brunswick, New Jersey. Ketchum knew what the paper was for, but felt that he had kept his conscience clear by warning the Youngses that counterfeiting was hazardous. The Provincial Congress, however, felt that Ketchum was as guilty as the others. All the men were continued in jail, and Hulet would have been jailed, too, if the Provincial Congress had been able to find him.

Dawkins' downfall made many New Yorkers sorry. His business may have suffered lately, but his work was greatly admired. He had designed beautiful bookplates for a number of prominent men, including former Mayor Hicks, as well as countless company letterheads, trade cards, bills, coats of arms, and seals. His colored engraving of the college at Princeton, done in 1763, was as handsome as any of the pictures of the place. Nevertheless, Dawkins, like the others, was kept in the City Hall jail, and put into leg irons. No one was allowed to visit any of the prisoners without a special pass from the Provincial Congress. Since the men were only suspected of counterfeiting—they had been interrogated but not tried—their treatment was harsh. But the Provincial Congress was growing more and more worried about maintaining the value of American money. Since the Youngses admitted next to nothing, and since Dawkins could not even guess how many bills had been printed and passed, the Provincial Congress could not deny Tory whispers that the numbers had been huge. Confidence in American money had been low before the scandal, but after Dawkins had corrected his

Connecticut bill, all his counterfeits were almost undetectable—his work was that skilled—and this cast suspicion on all paper money, good and bad. Dawkins said he had not made any plates for a New York bill, but who could be sure that he had told the whole truth?

The business before the Provincial Congress on Friday, May 24, was so important that some of the counties with poor attendance records—Richmond, for one, which was now being treated as if it had never been proscribed—had been sent letters asking them to make a special effort to have their delegates present. As a result, the Assembly room at City Hall was well filled for the reading of the report of the Committee on Intestine Enemies. That group, with John Alsop as its acting chairman, was no longer secret. Its recommendation, as General Washington had anticipated, urged the Provincial Congress to order the immediate arrest of all "known Tories" in and around New York "for their own safety as well as the safety of America." A list of names of known Tories, including all the men in the area who held military or civil commissions from the Crown, was attached. (That part of the report was confidential.)

The Alsop report also suggested that the Continental Army units should make the arrests, if their commanders were willing. The Committee recommended that Tories who, after having been taken, were willing to swear that they would not act against the colonies, and would give security for their oaths, should be allowed to "go at large." If they would not give security, the report added, perhaps they could be deported to a "neighboring Colony" on their unsupported words of honor.

For practicality—or, at least, simplicity—the plan was just what Washington had asked for. In every other way it was as far from the ideal as all the earlier schemes. Still, times had changed, and the new Provincial Congress was no longer so concerned with the harassment of a hypothetical dissenting but peaceably behaved citizen, and it did not automatically assume that the Continental troops, guided by the Committee to Detect Conspiracies, as it was to be called in the future, would abuse their power. The Alsop report, in short, only recommended what seemed unavoidable. It was approved with a minimum of discussion.

The Provincial Congress went right on to the Continental Congress' state-government proposal. The delegates were little, if any, better informed than they had been about their constituents' wishes. They quickly agreed to appoint a subcommittee to report, which would give the house a motion to consider. John Morin Scott, John Jay (who was not present, but was on his way from Philadelphia, and was expected by the following day, Saturday, May 25), and John Haring were entrusted with that task. They worked fast. On Monday, the twenty-seventh, their report was ready. Since Jay had been enthusiastic for improving the New York government, and Scott was among the minority of delegates with no misgivings about the Continental Congress' preamble, the subcommittee's favorable report was anything but a surprise. Scott, Jay, and Haring wrote that "the right of framing, creating, or new modeling civil government is, and ought to be, in the people," and they felt that it had become "absolutely necessary" for the people of New York to "institute a new and regular form of internal government and police," in which the supreme legislative and executive power should, "for the present," wholly reside within New York, in "exclusion of all foreign and external power, authority, dominion, jurisdiction and preëminence whatsoever."

But, the subcommittee added, there was a serious doubt whether the Provincial Congress, at present, had the authority to frame such a new government. Only the voters could resolve that question. The report suggested that the question be put, county by county, in a new election. If a majority of the counties authorized a new government, then the Provincial Congress should frame one.

Gouverneur Morris moved that the report be adopted. His motion was seconded, and in a short discussion before the vote John Morin Scott argued, though not very hard, that the doubt about the Provincial Congress' authority amounted to little; Scott thought the delegates could go ahead and act without a referendum. But most delegates preferred the county-by-county vote, and the report was approved, with Scott voting for it, and only two votes against it—those of John Van Derbilt, and of Rem Cowenhoven, both from Brooklyn. The new elections would take time. The Provincial Congress specified that the new house would be convened on the second Monday in July, which would fall on the eighth, six weeks away. This delay did not appear very important. The latest news from Maryland was that its Convention had rejected the Continental Congress' resolution, and Pennsylvania was reported to be so divided on the statehood question that prompt action of any kind was unlikely. As long as those two were as slow as, or even slower than, New York—as Duane had imagined they would be—the Provincial Congress felt entitled to take the time to be assured of the opinion of New York's inhabitants.

In the midst of this discussion, the City Committee formally cleared John Alsop's name of a slander. A story had been in circulation for some little time to the effect that Alsop, whose company had considerable stocks of tea, had evaded the ceiling price by charging extra for bags and twine, which, by custom, were free. Furthermore, it had been said, Alsop was asking that at least half the price be paid in hard money, instead of Continental or provincial paper.

The City Committee was forced to investigate. Many New

Yorkers believed the charges, partly because the men who made them, Colonel Abraham P. Lott and one of his in-laws, Peter Van Alstyne, were creditable; besides, if a Continental Congress delegate, not to mention the acting chairman of the Conspiracies committee, could break two Provincial Congress resolutions with impunity, neither would be enforceable. Alsop welcomed a chance to confront Lott and Van Alstyne. A fundamental difference between the rumor and the sworn testimony was that no transaction had taken place. Lott and Van Alstyne, Alsop agreed, had called on him. Van Alstyne had wanted to buy tea to resell at retail. The wholesale price, Alsop had said, was six shillings. When Alstyne had then asked how he could make a profit, since the retail ceiling price was six shillings, Alsop had replied—according to Lott and Van Alstyne—that he had heard some persons were charging for bags and twine. Alsop did not remember having said that. If he had said it, he had not meant it as a recommendation that Van Alstyne do the wrong thing. Alsop admitted that he had said he wanted some hard money. He had been trying to help the Provincial Congress pay a Canadian debt, and nothing but hard money would do for that. But mentioning a desire for hard money was no crime, and did not constitute a refusal to accept American paper.

Since there had been no sale, the City Committee voted that Alsop had not violated any Provincial Congress resolve. Alsop, who apologized for having talked carelessly, was fortunate to get off without even a reprimand. At the time, a Provincial Congress committee made up of John Jay, Gouverneur Morris, and Comfort Sands was investigating several other rumors of tea-price violation, including stories about Mangil Minthorne, a shopkeeper on Batteau (now Dey) Street, and Andrew Gautier, who ran Ten Eyck and Simmons' store. The fear that they might use the Alsop affair in extenuation of their own actions, if they were guilty, was quickly realized. When Minthorne's case was heard, two weeks after Alsop's acquittal, Minthorne admitted that he had charged too much for his tea. He was declared to be "an enemy of the American cause," and his name was published, at the City Committee's direction, in all the newspapers. His disgrace lasted only eleven days; on June 17, the same newspapers reported that Minthorne had been restored and that his militia commission—he was a captain in the Second New York City Regiment—had been returned to him. Gautier got off even more easily. He admitted that he had told his clerk, Zacharias Sickles, to demand gold or silver for tea. The City Committee found Gautier guilty, since he offered no defense, but before his name was published, the Provincial Congress heard Gautier's appeal. Gautier said he was a good Associator and that his shop had never refused Continental paper for anything except tea. He explained his action on the ground that he had heard that John Alsop was selling his tea for hard money and for hard money only. After deliberation, the Provincial Congress voted to pardon Gautier.

In Philadelphia, General Washington was constantly apprehensive about a British attack on New York. At the end of a week, he had Putnam station several horses at some of the stops on the road between the cities, so that he and his staff, like express riders, could race back in case the alarm came. Washington did not have to use his relays. Though this concern distracted him, the General felt that his conferences with the Continental Congress—mostly with a committee of twelve men especially appointed for the purpose—were going well. He wanted the Continental Congress to send more men to Canada, so the expeditionary force could fight for a position as far down the St. Lawrence as possible from the mouth of the Richelieu

River. The American retreat from Quebec had shocked Washington, but he believed that the defeat could be made up for by redoubled energy and determination. Perhaps the Americans could not possess all Canada, as they had hoped, but, as Washington had written Schuyler, the defeat should not lead to despair, and "a manly and spirited opposition can only ensure success and prevent the enemy from improving the advantage they have obtained." Washington thought a British invasion from the north was possible, but not certain. He wanted to oppose it—if the British were planning it—on the St. Lawrence, not on Lake Champlain, or Lake George, or any point farther south. He also wanted to reinforce in Canada without weakening the defense of New York City.

The Congress, however, had just received the report of Franklin, Carroll, and Chase which told of appalling mismanagement in Canada. The report said that General Wooster was "unfit, totally unfit," for his command, and should be recalled. (He was, on June 6.) Not more than four thousand men were present in Canada, the commissioners reported, and four hundred of them were sick. The soldiers had not been paid, their food was atrocious, and they did not have decent equipment. Nothing could be bought for them locally, since the Army's credit in Montreal was exhausted. The situation, the commissioners said, was "miserable beyond words." No one in Philadelphia, Washington included, thought that the three men were exaggerating, yet Washington managed to continue to believe that what was wrong could be set right. With the help of Mifflin and Gates, the Commander-in-Chief talked the committee of twelve into his own resolute mood; and the committee's report, with minor modifications, became the Continental Congress' strategy. The British were to be fought on the St. Lawrence, and New York was to be defended, and both were to be major efforts, with neither slighted for the other. Thirty thousand more men would be needed, the Continental Congress decided —about twice as many as had already been raised. New Jersey, New York, Connecticut, Massachusetts, Rhode Island, New Hampshire, and Vermont were to supply twenty thousand militiamen, and a flying camp (a mobile reserve, in present-day language) of another ten thousand was to be raised in Pennsylvania, Delaware, and Maryland. The thirty thousand were to serve under Continental Army general officers, but they were not to be Continental soldiers in any formal sense. The Continental Congress still dreaded a large, standing American army, and was certainly not disposed to enlarge the military establishment by something more than 100 percent. It preferred to think of the increase as an emergency call-up—precisely what the militia was for. Congress also approved the hiring of not more than two thousand Canadian Indians to attack the British forts at Niagara and Detroit, if possible, in order to relieve some of the pressure on the Continentals at Sorel. The militia enlistments, once again, were to last only six months, until December 1, 1776. Washington thought they should be at least twice that long, and possibly for the duration, but he feared that if he pressed his point he would only rattle the delegates. He had therefore simply said what he thought, but had not argued.

Still, having persuaded the Congress to order most of what he believed the war needed, Washington was gratified. For himself, he was delighted that, with the Congress' consent, he could offer Joseph Reed the post of Adjutant General, made vacant by Gates's promotion. A colonel's rank and seven hundred pounds a year in salary and perquisites went with the job, and Reed, who had been a lieutenant colonel, was pleased to accept. (Washington had not entirely understood that Reed needed more money than his former assignment had paid. As Reed explained in a letter to his wife, his salary, with allowances, "will help support us till these calamitous times are at an end. Besides, this post is honorable, and if the issue is favorable to America, must put me on a respectable scale. Should it be otherwise, I have done enough to expose myself to ruin.") Washington knew that Reed had had no experience in army administration, but the Adjutant General's duties were not clearly defined. The Commander-in-Chief wanted Reed with him as a staff member whatever his title, as an expert in law, in persuasion, and in understanding how men's minds worked. Although Washington's unaided efforts to deal with the New York Provincial Congress had turned out beautifully, the General felt sure that Reed could help him do even better. Another Philadelphian, Stephen Moylan, who had been an aide and then Mustermaster General, was to take Mifflin's place as Quartermaster General. The appointment of a new military secretary had already been announced on May 16. He was the thirty-year-old Virginian, Robert Hanson Harrison, who had been acting as military secretary, with help, since Reed's departure, and who, after an uncertain start, had become more and more expert at the job.

Every man in Philadelphia who was not talking about Canada was talking about independence. Washington did not enter into that debate. Privately—for instance, in a letter to his brother, John Augustine—Washington expressed his shock at the number of Continental Congress delegates who still thought that reconciliation was possible. In public, since the Continental Congress did not ask his opinion, the General said nothing.

Washington's conferences were finished by June 3. Hancock, who was suffering from an attack of gout and could not see the General off, wrote him a letter of thanks for his help and released him to return to New York. By the afternoon of the sixth, Washington was back at his downtown headquarters, No.

1 Broadway. New York City was quiet, except for the interminable, noisy work on the fortifications. Washington could see some improvements, and he was happy to hear, from Putnam, that the Paulus Hook fort had been started. A few British ships had arrived the day before, raising the total number off Sandy Hook to a dozen or more, including transports. Headquarters, however, did not believe that the arrivals meant anything in particular, and felt no reason to give the alarm. In the letters waiting for Washington there was more bad news from Canada. Schuyler reported another defeat, this time at a place called the Cedars, seventy miles west of Sorel and thirty miles southwest of Montreal. Perhaps the next express rider would bring word that the British had recaptured Montreal itself. There was a report that General Thomas was sick with smallpox, and then, just two days later, on June 8, Washington learned that Thomas had died. With Wooster in the process of being relieved, Sullivan, third in rank, would automatically take over the Canadian command. Washington did not know if Sullivan was up to that responsibility. Washington admired Sullivan's enthusiasm and felt that the expeditionary force needed Sullivan's aggressiveness, and yet, as Washington wrote the Continental Congress, "he has his wants, and he has his foibles. The latter are manifested in a little tincture of vanity and in an overdesire of being popular, which now and then leads him into some embarrassments." Altogether, Washington's appraisal praised Sullivan more than it criticized him—and left the decision to the Continental Congress.

Washington was pleased that the New York Provincial Congress, on its own initiative, had voted to raise two more militia battalions for the city's defense. He told the Congress that New York was to contribute to the new levy of thirty thousand men, and urged it to get started on that right away, too. But New

York's report on the Committee to Detect Conspiracies disappointed him. Washington had hoped to find, on his return, that all the principal Tories were in jail. Not an arrest had been made. Instead of requesting prompt military assistance, the Conspiracies committee was experimenting to see how many of the less dangerous men on the list would come in for questioning in response to summonses. The more dangerous men—those who, the committee assumed, would have to be arrested—were left, for the time being, to local committees. Gouverneur Morris, the chairman of the committee (which now included Colonel Henry Remsen, John Ten Broeck, John Haring, Thomas Tredwell, Colonel Lewis Graham, and Joseph Hallett), explained that this method would save time and money. But in his concern for economy, Morris had lost the element of surprise. The complete list was no longer confidential but had been published—ample warning to any Tory who wanted to escape.

The list itself was obvious to the point of absurdity. Every man on it must have guessed that his name would appear. More than half of the hundred or so were Crown officers, government officials, judges, and Council members, including Governor Tryon, Attorney-General Kempe, and the others on board the *Duchess of Gordon,* along with Mayor Matthews, who was on shore. Most of the rest of the suspected conspirators had simply been copied off old lists. Captain Richard Hewlett, as always, led the index of men in Queens who, the committee thought, would have to be arrested. (But no one, including Heard and Sears, had come close to catching Hewlett.) The Kings County and Richmond County compilations were hardly better than jokes. Only six men were listed for all of Staten Island, and three of them were Heard's old finds, Isaac Decker, Abraham Harris, and Minah Burger, who had already been tried for disaffection and dismissed. The others were Christopher Billop, the island's largest landowner; Benjamin Seaman, a member of the old Assembly, who had supported the protest movement at its beginning, but had changed his mind; and Ephraim Taylor, who was wanted for questioning about supplying the warships.

Washington described New York's performance to John Hancock: ". . . the subject is delicate, and nothing is done in it: we may therefore have internal as well as external enemies to contend with." But, on the bright side, the Conspiracies committee was in being, and New York intended to ask for the Continental Army's help if the summons method did not work; and, although the new list was inadequate, the committee could add names. A fumbling start did not necessarily mean that the effort would fail. Washington was inclined to let New York have a little more time before he interfered. Meanwhile, he ordered Major Peter Schuyler, of the Third New York, to guard the eastern end of Long Island with the three companies of soldiers the area had raised but had never sent on to the Continental Army. Schuyler was supposed to protect Long Island livestock against British raiders, but his orders, dated June 10, also instructed him to watch Suffolk County people. Anyone guilty of supplying the British or of corresponding with the warships, Washington wrote, was to be arrested and brought before the local committee. Since the Provincial Congress had not requested this help—although the Suffolk Committee had—Washington was anticipating, but not, he hoped, by much.

Some New Yorkers, particularly the active members of the Mechanics Committee, were less tolerant than the General was of the Conspiracies committee's slowness. The Mechanics and their "constituents," as they liked to call the New Yorkers who sympathized with their political opinions, continued to be several steps ahead of the Provincial Congress. The Mechanics had petitioned the Congress on May 29 to instruct the New York delegates in Philadelphia to vote for independence, but had received only a polite refusal in reply. On the question of conspiracy, the Mechanics had maintained for months that the principal New York Tories were being treated with far greater consideration than they deserved. Release of the names without simultaneous arrests made them think that the situation had improved only slightly. Judge Richard Morris, Gouverneur Morris' half-brother, was on the Westchester County list, but he was not arrested, and that, some men argued, proved that the Morris committee was less interested in detecting conspiracies than in arranging clearances for conspirators for money. (Judge Morris, in fact, was not a Tory. He had resigned his judgeship on the Court of Admiralty in 1775 because he disagreed with the Crown's policies. But, because he was not an Associator either, New York had stigmatized him as an "equivocal," one degree less bad than an inimical.)

A crowd of impatient New Yorkers collected on the evening of June 10. Someone must have exhorted it to action, but the authorities, afterward, did not say who he was, if they knew. (Colonel Lasher, Peter Van Zandt, John Smith, Joshua Smith, and Abraham P. Lott were suspected.) In any case, the mob agreed that it was time for citizens to do what the Morris committee was failing to do. In a night of stormy rioting, far past the ten o'clock curfew, and to the distress of the military men, who thought, for a time, that their soldiers were causing the trouble, the mob hunted out half a dozen Tories, tarred and feathered two, rode some on rails, beat them, abused them, and paraded them, in a most disorderly fashion, through the streets in the direction of the Commons. Nothing of the sort had happened for more than a year. Two of the victims, Dr. Donald McLean and Theophilus Hardenbrook, an architect and builder, were on the Morris committee list, but the others were not, and just what the mob knew or suspected about them was far from clear. Order was finally restored by Generals Putnam and Mifflin, who arrived at the Commons with enough Continental soldiers to enforce their demands that the rioters disperse. Even so, a small-scale riot of the same sort broke out the next day. Rumors of more rail rides in the offing persisted for a week longer. During the time, as Peter Elting explained gleefully in a letter to his brother-in-law, Captain Richard Varick, "there is hardly a Tory face to be seen. . . ."

The Continental Army was displeased. The defense of New York offered enough problems without adding civilian riots. Putnam and Mifflin complained jointly to the Provincial Congress, which was at least equally displeased. In its resolution on the subject, it said that it "by no means" approved of the rioting, and it assured "the warm friends of liberty" that it was in the process of taking effectual measures against the Tories, and in a proper manner. However, the Provincial Congress did change the composition of the Conspiracies committee once again, adding Philip Livingston, John Jay, Leonard Gansevort, and John Sloss Hobart, and dropping Remsen, Ten Broeck, and Haring—not that it admitted that the work of the old group had been unsatisfactory. And, while Morris remained a member of the committee, the chairmanship pro tem went to Hobart. (Livingston was the Provincial Congress' first, unanimous choice, but he preferred not to accept the job.) Regular hearings were about to start, which meant that the fortnight's experiment in permissiveness might be at an end. If the summonses were not answered immediately, arrests would have to be made, because hearings could not be held without suspects to interrogate. To New York's annoyance, the Continental Congress, responding to Washington's pessimistic comment in his letter to Hancock, took note of the Conspiracies committee's poor performance and, in a special resolution dated June 14, "recommended" that New York "make effectual provision for detecting, restraining, and punishing disaffected and dangerous persons" in the colony—as if New York had not been trying.

The Provincial Congress had received another letter, on June 13, that was almost as irritating as the Continental Congress' gratuitous advice. New York had waited six months for Connecticut to answer the Provincial Congress' complaints about Sears's raid in November. When the reply finally came, it was sly to the point of impudence. After blaming the delay on the Connecticut Assembly, Trumbull wrote: "Your candor in imputing the intrusion of a number of our people into your capital (in the manner they did) to an imprudent though well intended zeal for the public cause, gives me real pleasure; and I can give you the strongest assurance that this Colony by no means approve their conduct, yet a severe censure at this time . . . might be attended with such inconveniences as you will readily apprehend."

A severe censure was not the heart of the matter from New York's point of view; the Provincial Congress had wanted compensation, payable to Rivington, for his printing plant and his type. Trumbull made it clear that Connecticut was not accepting any liability. In happier times, he pointed out, a suit in a court of law would be the place to settle such an argument. Connecticut was not concerned, Trumbull explained, because "the head or leader of the whole transaction was a respectable member of your city and Congress, who we consider as the proper person to whom the whole transaction is imputable, and who belongs, and is amenable to your jurisdiction alone; and, therefore, the affair cannot be considered as an intrusion of our people into your Province, but as a violence or disorder happening among yourselves."

While New York was preparing for its county-by-county elections, scheduled for June 17, the Continental Congress continued to move toward declaring the United Colonies independent of Great Britain. On June 7, Richard Henry Lee, of the Virginia delegation, introduced a motion to that effect, and caught the New York delegation unprepared. Since Jay, Duane, Alsop, and Philip Livingston were all busy in New York City, Robert R. Livingston had become the leader of the New York delegation in Philadelphia; and, though the old instructions (with which Livingston agreed) were not to vote either way, he could see that abstention on Lee's motion would not be quite right. Livingston felt, as did many other men, that the referendum was about to reveal New York's opinion on independence as well as on statehood. Livingston himself favored both. He had given up his hope for a settlement—it had never been great—on hearing of the passage of the Prohibitory Act. But since he had only recently returned to political life from his long, grieving retreat at Clermont—he had been sick after the deaths of his father, father-in-law, and brother-in-law, General Montgomery—he was listening attentively to what his colleagues said. Livingston's temperament, like his radicalism, was moderate. He imagined that independence was inevitable and suitable, but that an immediate declaration might not be advantageous. Suddenly it looked as if Lee's motion might come to a vote before New York even went to the polls. If so, did the Provincial Congress still want the New York delegation to abstain? The other New York delegates in Philadelphia—William Floyd, Henry Wisner, and Francis Lewis—were no more certain than Livingston, so Livingston wrote the Provincial

Congress a letter asking for New York's "sentiments." While waiting for an express rider to return with the answer, Livingston joined Edward Rutledge, of South Carolina, John Dickinson and James Wilson, of Pennsylvania, and one or two others in arguing for delay. Lee could hardly bear waiting, and George Wythe, of Virginia, and John Adams spoke eloquently, with Lee, for prompt action. But at least four other colonies besides New York (Pennsylvania, New Jersey, Maryland, and Delaware), and perhaps a fifth, South Carolina, were not ready to vote yes on the Lee motion. On that account, the Continental Congress decided to put off a decision until July 1. Meanwhile a committee of five men, including Livingston as the representative of the cautious minority, was asked to write a specific declaration and thus add substance to Lee's motion for independence—a text for the Continental Congress to accept, amend, or reject. The others were Thomas Jefferson, of Virginia, John Adams, Benjamin Franklin, and Roger Sherman, of Connecticut.

When Livingston got the Provincial Congress' answer, written June 11, he knew he had taken the proper course. As before, New York did not want its delegation to vote either way on independence. Moreover, as the Provincial Congress saw it, the forthcoming elections were not going to involve the question of independence, but only the issue of statehood. New York felt that it would be "imprudent" to ask simultaneously for the voters' sentiments on independence; it might create divisions and thus have an "unhappy influence" on the vote over statehood. By now the majority in the Provincial Congress definitely wanted New York to consent to the formation of an improved, regular, and independent government; and what had seemed debatable only two weeks earlier now seemed necessary to all but a very few men. As for independence itself, the letter to

Livingston continued: "The earliest opportunity will, however, be embraced of ascertaining the sentiments of this Colony on that important question, and of obtaining their consent to vest the Congress of the Colony, for the time being, with authority to deliberate and determine on this and every other matter of general concern; and to instruct their delegates in Continental Congress thereupon."

The plausible, cooperative ring to that assurance was peculiar. New York was not contemplating a second election of Provincial Congress delegates, and if there was some other way of ascertaining the voters' sentiments, it had never been mentioned. If the Provincial Congress was looking ahead to a determination some time after July 8, when the new Congress was to assemble, that was preposterous. The present house, as its majority was eager to explain to everybody, had no authority to commit the future house to embrace anything.

Jay and Remsen were aware that the Provincial Congress was sliding into a muddle. Right after the answer to Livingston's question was sent, they moved that the purpose of the June 17 elections be enlarged to include, besides the vote on statehood, authority for the Provincial Congress "to deliberate and determine on every question that may concern or affect the interest of the Colony," including, specifically, "the great question of independency."

The Jay-Remsen motion was adopted unanimously, and for a few minutes it looked as if the confusion had been swept away. Then the Provincial Congress made things worse than they had been by amending the resolution: "Agreed, That the publishing of the aforegoing resolves be postponed until after the election of Deputies with power to establish a new form of government."

The amendment destroyed the resolution without rescinding it, which made no sense at all. Since the voters, under the circumstances, could not possibly know what they were voting for, their sentiments were doomed to remain unclear.

Two days later, on June 13, the Provincial Congress read a letter from John Hancock which suggested that New York County might not be able to hold its elections. The Continental Congress, Hancock reported, expected a British attack on New York City within the next ten days—and two days had passed since he had written. For the second time in a week, the Continental Congress asked New York, as it had also asked New Jersey, Connecticut, and Massachusetts, to call out its militia in the emergency. Hancock's second letter to the Provincial Congress sounded as if he thought New York might not be willing to do so, judging by the long argument he saw fit to include:

The important day is at hand that will decide not only the fate of the City of New York, but in all probability of the whole Province. On such an occasion there is no necessity to use arguments with Americans; their feelings I well know will prompt them to their duty, and the sacredness of the cause will urge them to the field. The greatest exertions of vigor and expedition are requisite to prevent our enemies from getting possession of that town; I must therefore again most earnestly request you, in the name, and by the authority of Congress, to send forward the militia, agreeable to the requisition of Congress, and that you will do it with all the dispatch which the infinite importance of the cause demands.

Hancock could have saved his rhetoric: the militia had already been called out in response to the Continental Congress' first request. It was true that New York was not as excited about the imminence of Howe's arrival as was Philadelphia. The Provincial Congress believed, as did Washington, that the ten-day rumor, which had circulated throughout the New York City encampments, had been originated by Governor Tryon and was just a British attempt to unnerve the Americans. In any case,

John Morin Scott had been made a brigadier general and was now in command of the entire New York militia in all parts of the province—a total of three thousand men, the Provincial Congress hoped. Handbills warning of the expected attack had been printed and were being distributed. Marching orders had been worked out, and no one needed to be reminded that keeping the British out of the city was important. On the other hand, the march orders needed improvement. The different militia companies were ordered to start for New York on various days, but those farthest away were to move last instead of first. The New York County men were to parade on the Commons on June 14. The Dutchess, Ulster, and Suffolk men were not to leave their home towns until June 21, and the Albany militia companies not until June 23. Counting those due from New Jersey and Connecticut, the militia calls might produce eighty-five hundred additional men, and that would more than double the size of the Army at New York. Washington's eighteen Continental regiments added up to ten thousand men on paper, but only about sixty-five hundred were present and fit for duty. However many soldiers arrived, the weather was improving, so the men, for the most part, could bivouac in the conveniently expandable Manhattan and Brooklyn campsites.

The New York City militiamen did not parade on June 14. They needed a few more days to get ready, and the formation was put off until June 18. By mid-June, the local defense forces promised to be a bit stronger than had been planned, if the British would allow New York enough time. The City Committee asked all healthy New York men more than fifty years old to volunteer for militia duty despite their age exemption. (Quakers, clergymen, licensed physicians, and firemen of all ages remained exempt.) The old men were asked to form themselves into companies, not for combat, but for garrison duty, and their organization meeting was scheduled for the afternoon of the seventeenth at Mrs. Vandewater's Tavern. In case of invasion, furthermore, the exempt firemen planned to report as a company to Washington and to put themselves under his command. Despite their exemption, many of New York's volunteer fire fighters had enlisted in one regiment or another during the year, and the two fire battalions were down from two hundred men to about one hundred—far fewer than was safe. New York had to worry about fire all the time. While there were fire engines—hand-operated water pumps on wheels—in sheds scattered around town, they were not very powerful. Some men believed that the engines were more trouble than they were worth, and that a fire company would do better to rely entirely on its primary resource, the leather fire bucket. But no matter what the firemen used, there should be no confusion about the deployment of the fire-fighting experts, particularly since it was assumed that the British might use fire as a weapon against the city; and the experts should be under the leadership of the Army in an emergency rather than the command of their own chief, Jacobus Stoutenburgh. Lewis Tibou, the new chairman of the Mechanics Committee, and Theophilus Hardenbrook, who was recovering from having been manhandled as a Tory by the mob, were both firemen. There was no doubt that if flames broke out, they would forget their political differences.

The Provincial Congress arrested two Continental soldiers, Micah Lynch and Thomas Hickey, on June 14. That was unusual because, as far as possible, New York had been leaving military discipline to the Army. (The courts-martial punishments, from fines to reprimands to lashings, were more severe than civil penalties.) But because Lynch and Hickey were suspected of having passed counterfeit money, New York thought that the Conspiracies committee was the proper agency to investi-

gate the charges. Perhaps the soldiers had not been acting alone
but were connected with a ring of some sort—the latest rumor
was that counterfeit Continental money was being printed on
board the *Asia* as part of a conspiracy to increase American
uncertainty about the value of paper money. While awaiting
trial, Lynch and Hickey were locked up in the City Hall jail,
and that put them in with Dawkins, Youngs, and Ketchum. The
meeting of the suspected money passers with the known
counterfeiters was almost unavoidable, however, because the
City Hall jail rooms were about the only secure cells at the
Provincial Congress' disposal—and the number of escapes from
them, even so, had been shocking. On the day Lynch and
Hickey were confined, though not especially on their account,
the Provincial Congress resolved that if any more prisoners
escaped from any of the county jails, including New York
County, and if the jailer's negligence or connivance could be
shown, then the jailer would have to serve out the escaped
prisoner's sentence.

Though New York did not take the attack warnings very
seriously, the reports did revive the Provincial Congress' concern about the safety of the city's and the colony's records. They
were still stored on the Nicholas Bayard estate, but that place
did not seem as safe as it once had. Its distance from the Grand
Battery seemed to have shrunk with the steady growth of the
huge Manhattan bivouac area. Most of the dry ground between Collect Pond and the Bayard mansion was now the
encampment—filled with company streets, duckboards, shacks,
huts, and tents. The built-up area of the city had been enlarged
in this temporary manner by nearly one-third. The Bayard place
may have been beyond the range of naval guns, but it still
seemed too close to the battlefield, if not on it. Some of the
records were priceless. The Provincial Congress was not worry-

ing about the old notes on the Assembly's debates, or about future political history; what mattered were the files of real-estate titles, dating back more than one hundred years, on which substantial fortunes depended. If they were burned or rained on, the litigation over who owned what and where the surveyed boundary lines were might go on for decades.

Happily, James Beekman, a delegate to the Provincial Congress, had obtained the Congress' permission to be absent for a day or two in order to take his family to Kingston by sloop, and the boat was large enough to carry the records, too. Kingston sounded safe. (It was. The foot-by-foot story of New York real estate is available in the library of Manhattan's Hall of Records, at 31 Chambers Street.) The Provincial Congress gladly accepted Beekman's offer to carry the files up the Hudson. Samuel Bayard was to move with the records, and to stay in Kingston with them, continuing his custodian's job under the supervision of a committee of Ulster County men—Dirk Wynkoop, Abraham Hasbrouck, Joseph Gasherie, and Christopher Tappen.

Another old housekeeping detail, the security of the gun parks beyond the King's Bridge, was attended to. The initiative was Colonel Knox's rather than New York's, for since his arrival, Knox, as chief of the artillery, had taken over the whole problem of guns and gun batteries. Quite a few of the New York cannon had been repaired by this time, and there was hope for others. The New York militia had done well enough, after the disaster, at guarding the parks, and no further sabotage had taken place. Nonetheless, the militia party there was reinforced by a Continental Army detachment of a sergeant, a corporal, and twenty soldiers to guard the cannon, and to be "exceedingly careful that no damage is done to them."

The general improvement in the artillery arrangements was marvelous. Knox, a former Boston bookseller who had learned much of what he knew about artillery from reading his own stock, was more of an amateur than most of Washington's colonels, but his ability to get a job done showed at New York as it had at Cambridge. The fourteen main batteries, including Fort Stirling and the new position under construction at Paulus Hook, now contained a grand total of a hundred and twenty-one cannon and nineteen mortars. Many of the guns were fieldpieces that Knox had brought down from Boston. With a few exceptions, the batteries were fully equipped, and at least thirty rounds of ammunition had been made up and were in place near each of the pieces. Captain Alexander Hamilton's New York artillery company was under Knox's command, though technically it was still on provincial, not Continental, service. Hamilton was in charge of the Fort George battery of six guns. Since Lee had torn down the north wall, Hamilton was supposed to be prepared to fire out to sea and also to turn the pieces around to fire up Broadway. Hamilton's company was also responsible for several of the nineteen guns and six mortars at the Grand Battery, adjoining Fort George. The Commons gun park now, as before, contained a lot of guns, but not the guns Hamilton had helped steal from their mounts on the Grand Battery. Those cannon had been emplaced wherever they were most needed. Some were right back where they had come from, at the Grand Battery. The Commons, as a central location, now held Knox's artillery reserves, which consisted of twenty-five field-pieces, mostly six- and twelve-pounders. They were to be "run"—an optimistic word for manhandling them by hand at what was usually a painfully slow rate—to "where the enemy shall make their greatest effort," as Knox phrased it.

Knox's urgent need was no longer for guns or gunpowder but for artillerymen. Since each gun called for a ten-man gun crew, he needed 1,210 cannoneers. (Gun crews, in addition to servic-

ing their cannon, fired the mortars as extra work.) Knox's ten
Continental artillery companies, with Hamilton's men added,
had fewer than half that number. Knox, as usual, had a suggestion to offer, if Washington "should think it proper that all the
artillery should be manned at the same time"—as, of course,
Washington did. Knox pointed out that since most of the infantry battalions were short of weapons, and a man without a
musket would count for next to nothing in combat, the artillery
could borrow soldiers, temporarily, from the Continental infantry companies without reducing their effective strength.
Washington immediately accepted Knox's idea. Four able-
bodied men from each of the companies were to be delivered by
their adjutants to Colonel Knox at the Bowling Green at six
o'clock on the morning of Sunday, June 16. Those who had
"arms, ammunition, and accoutrements," were to leave them
behind for use by their comrades. In a twinkling, Knox had
about doubled his command—the order was calculated to produce six hundred men. True, Knox would have to see that these
new artillerymen got some teaching, but they were a bargain:
for an indefinite time, they were to be continued on their old
regiments' pay and muster rolls.

Washington also acted, perhaps tardily, to rescue the Highlands forts from the administrative mess they were and had
always been in. Putnam, following the General's instructions,
had sent three good men—Stirling, Rufus Putnam, and, as a
substitute for Knox, Captain Winthrop Sargeant, of the artillery—up the Hudson to inspect Fort Constitution and Fort
Montgomery, and their expert and detailed report had indicated that nothing was quite right. Fort Montgomery, which
was supposed to make up for Barnard Romans' error of putting
Fort Constitution in the wrong place, was a serious disappointment. Apart from the fact that Fort Montgomery was open to

attack from dominating ground to its rear, the post was highly inflammable. Lord Stirling thought that perhaps its wooden fascines could be fireproofed with a coating of quicklime and sand, but experiments along that line were just starting. Colonel Nicholl, as commander of the garrisons at both forts, was not doing well. The job appeared beyond the competence of the Provincial Congress' four commissioners. (On top of that, the Committee at New Windsor, six miles north of Fort Constitution, had reported that the wife of Commissioner Jonathan Lawrence was a tea-price violator, and had been using Fort Constitution as a tea storehouse.)

Washington informed the Provincial Congress that he himself—meaning the Continental Army—wanted to take direct control of the Highlands forts, and that therefore the commissioners' services would no longer be required. The Provincial Congress was not disposed to quarrel with Washington's decision. Since most of the soldiers at the forts were Dutchess County men who belonged to Colonel James Clinton's regiment, the Third New York, Washington hardly had to think who should be put in charge. Clinton had a good record, besides—he had taken part in Montgomery's expedition to Quebec. His whole regiment, minus those three controversial Suffolk companies that had never left the eastern end of Long Island, would be with him; and Washington promised, in addition, at least five hundred New York militiamen. Clinton was to take complete command of the entire enterprise. To stress the "infinite importance" of the forts, especially Fort Montgomery, Washington specified that no more than two soldiers from each company were to be given furloughs at any one time, and then only in cases of real necessity.

The results of the New York County elections on June 17 were all that Jay and Remsen could have hoped for. Although the issues were clouded, thanks to the Provincial Congress' unfathomable resolutions, a shift toward independence was discernible, and there was no doubt that the county wanted men who agreed that New York ought to have a new form of government. Seventeen delegates, including all the new men who had won in April, were reelected. The four old men who lost were John Alsop, Jacobus Van Zandt, Comfort Sands, and Joseph Hallett. The exact reasons were, of course, unknown. But Alsop was definitely opposed to independence, and uncertain about the advantages of statehood, too; and his tea troubles had not enhanced his vote-getting ability. Whatever the voters thought, they replaced Alsop, Sands, Van Zandt, and Hallett with delegates of a markedly more radical cast, whose enthusiasm for both independence and statehood were conspicuous: Garrett Abeel, chairman of the City Committee; Abraham P. Lott, who had helped bring the tea-violation charges against Alsop; Robert Harpur, formerly the King's College librarian and still a part-time faculty member who was noted for disagreeing about politics with almost all of his academic colleagues; and Daniel Dunscomb, a member, and a former chairman, of the Mechanics Committee. New Yorkers guessed that the other county results, when they were known, would show that the province, again, had moved noticeably away from cautiousness. That proved to be the case. Two of the Albany County districts, in fact, specifically endorsed independence as well as statehood, although they had not been asked about independence—or, at any rate, were not supposed to know that they had been. The voters in Spencer Town, Albany County, pledged their "lives and fortunes" to the struggle for independence without expressing any particular interest, one way or another, in statehood for New York.

V. June and July, 1776

☆

A LTHOUGH most New York voters were satisfied that the elections had gone well, they were surprised by the speed of political developments in the other middle colonies. Before the New York ballots had all been counted, Pennsylvania's appearance completely changed—a result, partly, of Joseph Reed's months of work against Dickinson's party. First, the Pennsylvania delegation to the Continental Congress was authorized to "concur with the other delegates" in Philadelphia on the independence motion "as shall be judged necessary"; and then, on June 24, it had been instructed to vote for a declaration without any great concern for concurrence and what was or was not necessary. Delaware was expected to follow Pennsylvania's example. And New Jersey had elected a new Provincial Congress and had selected a new delegation—Richard Stockton, Abraham Clark, Francis Hopkinson, and the Reverend Dr. John Witherspoon—to go to Philadelphia. The New Jersey men's instructions were like the first set of orders to the Pennsylvania delegates: Join with the others in a declaration of independence, if it seems wise.

In just one week, as New York understood this news, the minority of colonies still opposed to a declaration had been reduced from five to two—Maryland and New York. Duane's argument against haste had proved wrong. If Maryland also moved into the pro-independence column, as it might, New York would look ridiculous. Yet, given the efficiency with which New York had clipped its own wings, there could hardly be a change in policy until July 8, at the earliest, and then only if the new Congress contradicted all the current Congress had said about lack of authority.

At least equally interesting, from a New York point of view, was New Jersey's action against its Royal Governor, William Franklin. The New Jersey Provincial Congress had ordered Franklin's arrest. That was no more than New York had done about its Royal Governor, William Tryon. One big difference, however, was that Franklin could be arrested—the summons for Tryon had really been *pro forma,* and no one thought the Governor would turn himself in or that he could be taken off the *Duchess of Gordon.* A second difference was that Franklin had been treated by New Jersey with even greater consideration than New York had shown for Tryon. He was Benjamin Franklin's illegitimate son and had been his father's associate for many years. Before his appointment to the governorship, in 1763, when William was only thirty-two years old, he had been the comptroller of the Post Office and clerk of the Pennsylvania Assembly, and had accompanied his father to England, in 1757, on a mission there as agent for Pennsylvania. The New Jersey Provincial Congress had leaned over backward to let William Franklin alone, because his father was a hero to New Jersey's Associators. In fact, New Jersey had been more tolerant of William's Tory opinions than Benjamin Franklin had. Father and son were no longer speaking. Benjamin had argued long and hard with William, who, at first, had seemed to be pro-British out of a simple sense of gratitude to the government that had appointed him to his high office. But the Governor was committed, if primarily for that reason, and Benjamin Franklin's brilliance did not move him. Finally, the father had abandoned his effort, dismissing his son as "a thorough government man."

Nevertheless, when the New Jersey Provincial Congress ordered Colonel Heard to arrest William Franklin for scheming, as Tryon had, to reconvene the old Assembly, it hoped that Franklin would make things easy for himself. If he would just promise to behave—to do nothing—New Jersey would be happy to release Franklin on his own parole. There was a blank in the arrest form, so Franklin could decide to stay where he chose—at Princeton, Bordentown, or Rancocas, not far south of Burlington, where he had a farm. The one place New Jersey did not want Franklin to stay was where he was—at Amboy, close to Tryon and the British fleet. When Heard, with a detachment of soldiers, appeared on Franklin's doorstep, however, Franklin was as prickly as a porcupine. He would not sign, he would not talk, he would promise nothing. He did comment, Heard later reported, "It is your turn now, but it will be mine another day."

Franklin's intransigence embarrassed New Jersey, but not enough to change the Provincial Congress' mind. It ordered Heard to escort Franklin to Burlington, where the Provincial Congress was sitting. The Governor was locked up. While he was busy scolding everybody by letter, warning of the "traps of independency and republicanism," and inveighing against the "desperate gamesters" who were plunging America into war and leading the American people away from "the sweets of British liberty under a British constitution," New Jersey decided that if the Continental Congress approved, it would deport Franklin to Connecticut—assuming that Governor Trumbull was willing to accept him as a charge.

On Tuesday, June 18, the day Heard started from Amboy to Burlington with Franklin, New York gave a dinner party. It was something the New York Provincial Congress had wanted to do ever since General Washington had returned from Phila-delphia: a feast at Fraunces' Tavern for the Commander-in-Chief, his staff, and the commanding officers of all his regi-ments. The Provincial Congress had resolved that it would pay the check. New York wanted to thank the Continental Army, and Washington most particularly, for what it was doing. There had been a little trouble about setting the date for the dinner, and one postponement; and, on that account, Washington had already received New York's formal commendation in writing. President Woodhull had handed it to him on June 8—a letter of appreciation "for the important services he has rendered to the United Colonies, and for the attention he has paid to the interest and civil authority of this Colony, and that he be assured of the readiness of this Congress to afford him all the aid in their power to enable him to execute the important trust reposed in him." For that matter, Washington had immediately ac-cepted the honor in a polite reply:

GENTLEMEN:

I am extremely obliged for the high sense you entertain of my services, and for your promise of every possible assistance in the dis-charge of my important duty.

You may rest assured that every attention to the interest and happiness of this Colony shall not be wanting, nor my regard to its civil authority remitted, whilst I am honored with the command I now hold.

The dinner's ceremonial purpose had been accomplished be-fore the guests sat down, but that did not spoil the occasion. It was a great, good-humored success, and the total number of toasts drunk came to thirty-one, which may have accounted for the fact that General Putnam suddenly became indisposed and had to retire to his quarters.

By the end of the week, the Conspiracies committee, now

under John Jay's chairmanship, was at last working as hard as it had been promising to work ever since its formation. The number of men it needed to question was immense. As one shocking clue led to another, Jay realized that there was enough material for at least two simultaneous investigations, and so he split the committee into two parts. With Livingston and Morris, Jay held daily hearings in City Hall, usually in the courtroom. The second part of the committee—Joseph Hallett, Thomas Tredwell, Lewis Graham, and Leonard Gansevort—conducted parallel hearings. When there was no room available in City Hall, they moved the proceedings to Scott's Tavern on Wall Street, just a few doors away.

One name that emerged quickly from the testimony was that of Gilbert Forbes, the well-known gunsmith, proprietor of the shop The Sign of the Sportsman, at No. 18 Broadway. Forbes, a short, stocky man, was famous for the quality of his guns, and he had played a modest role in city affairs. He lived in the West Ward, where he had been an elected assessor, and he had worked for the city at various times. It was Forbes who, under contract, had built the fence around the oval park at Bowling Green. He was mentioned first by Isaac Ketchum, the counterfeiter. Ketchum wanted to get out of the City Hall jail. Besides petitioning the Provincial Congress for a compassionate release so that he might look after his six children (like the one Isaac Gidney had obtained), Ketchum was trying to ingratiate himself with the New York authorities in every possible way. He had been talking in jail to Hickey and Lynch, the suspected counterfeit passers, who had been raging and bragging about their own disloyalty. As Ketchum informed the Provincial Congress, Hickey and Lynch were swearing that they would never fight for America. Both young men said that they had secretly enlisted with the British, and that hundreds of others had done the same—not just ghostly figures in Long Island swamps, but soldiers at present serving in the American regiments on Manhattan Island and Brooklyn Heights. Lynch and Hickey, according to Ketchum, had named Forbes as the man who had recruited them. (Ketchum called Forbes "Horbush," confusing the Conspiracies committee considerably, until it realized that he meant to say "Forbush," and that Forbush was a variant of Forbes.) What raised Ketchum's tale to the pitch of horror was Hickey's status—something that had been realized soon after the soldier's arrest. Hickey was not just an ordinary infantryman, but a member of Washington's guard, all supposedly handpicked men of absolute loyalty.

A day or two later, a mass of corroboration was added to what Ketchum said Lynch and Hickey had said. Jay and Morris questioned an Orange County man named William Leary. (It was mere coincidence that his name was the same as the Town Major's.) Leary had come to New York City looking for a runaway indentured workman, William Benjamin, who had disappeared from Erskine's Bigwood Ironworks, near Goshen. Unless he had enlisted in the Continental Army and was therefore immune from arrest, Benjamin was subject to arrest as a contract breaker—and Leary, if he could manage the arrest, would get a bounty from Erskine for bringing the runaway back.

Leary had found and arrested Benjamin, all right, but had lost his prisoner as they were starting back for Goshen. Benjamin had escaped near the Paulus Hook Ferry slip, at the foot of Cortlandt Street. Somehow—Leary did not explain the details—Captain John J. Roosevelt, of the First New York Militia Regiment, sized up Benjamin's predicament, and before Leary could intervene, Roosevelt had sworn in Benjamin as a private in Roosevelt's company.

A short while later, when Leary was walking around town

regretting the loss of his man, he ran into another former Big-wood Ironworks employee, James Mason, who was not a run-away, but who had been fired from his job some time earlier. Mason told Leary that there were at least three other Bigwood Ironworks men in the city, and asked Leary whether he, like them, had run away. Leary, hoping to make up for losing Benjamin by finding one of the others and arresting him, lied to Mason and said he had. And did Leary, Mason asked, intend to do what he, Mason, and the other Goshen men had done? Without knowing what that was, Leary said he did.

His answer, Leary testified, had led him a certain distance into a British recruiting conspiracy—until the other Goshen men became suspicious of Leary's intentions and stopped confiding in him. Leary had seen and heard enough, he said, to believe that Mason, Benjamin, and the others had sworn to join the British and to go aboard the *Asia* at the earliest opportunity. An agent in New York City—possibly it was more than one—was manag-ing the recruiting, promising bounties, administering oaths, ar-ranging temporary lodging for recruits, and providing them with food and money until transport to the man-of-war could be arranged.

Jay and Morris put Mason on the witness stand, and he added considerably to the information Leary had given. The British were not in any hurry to move the recruits to the war-ships, Mason said, since there was no room for them. Instead, prospective enemy soldiers were sheltered in rented rooms and lodging houses throughout the city. James Houlding's beer house in Tryon Row, opposite the gate to the Upper Barracks, was one place recruits stayed. Mason named three other taverns as favorites of the conspirators: the Sign of the Highlander, at Broadway and Beaver Street, run by Thomas Mason (not a relative); Lowrie's Tavern, just off Broadway and what is now

Cedar Street; and Corbie's Tavern, near General Washington's Richmond Hill headquarters. James Mason implicated nine or ten men, besides the tavern owners. Peter McLean, the shoemaker at the foot of Broad Street, who had done much of the repair work for those aboard the *Duchess of Gordon* when commerce between the city and the British ships was still legal, who owned a boat, and who had been known for years as an enthusiastic fisherman, was accused of carrying recruits to the British ships; and Mason said that a silversmith named Feuter, who had been mauled with the other suspected Tories by the mob on the night of June 10, was involved in the recruiting plot, along with his brother; and so were William Forbes (no relation to Gilbert Forbes), a tanner, who owned a house near Goshen but was living, for the time being, at New York; and John Clarke, a painter and glazier, of Blooming Grove, near Goshen, who had been boasting, Mason said, that he had recruited sixty men.

Mason testified that he believed that William Hickey, of Washington's guard, had indeed sworn to go over to the British, and that Hickey was by no means the only, or even the principal, traitor in that élite company. Mason thought that William Green, a drummer in the guard, had sworn Hickey, James Johnson, a fifer, and a soldier named Barnes; and that Green had then authorized them to take other soldiers' oaths; but that Green was the most important agent in the unit, said to be getting a bounty from the British of one dollar per enlistment.

On the next level above all these minor agents, Mason said, was Gilbert Forbes, the gunsmith. It was Gilbert Forbes who had sworn Mason. It was Gilbert Forbes who paid out the subsistence money, ten shillings a week, to enlistees—and who was trying to get the British to raise the amount to twelve shillings, because ten was too little. Governor Tryon, it almost went without saying, was the head of the whole apparatus. Mason's most upsetting revelation—although it had been mentioned by others as a possibility—was the name of Gilbert Forbes's superior, the go-between who transmitted the money from ship to shore, and Forbes's reports from shore to ship: Mayor David Matthews. The Mayor's brother, James Matthews, Mason believed, was at least aware of what was going on, and was letting the conspirators use his town house as a message center.

Without waiting to hear any more from any of the other scheduled witnesses, the Conspiracies committee went straight to Washington with all this information. Hickey and Lynch had already been returned to the Army's jurisdiction for trial because, after thinking for two days, the Provincial Congress had decided that New York lacked competence in their cases. The Congress was not a court of law, and the New York courts, insofar as they were functioning, derived their authority from the Crown. It seemed wrong to try Continental Army soldiers before a British, or at least a quasi-British judge. Now that Hickey had been accused of treason as well as of passing counterfeit money—Lynch had not been mentioned as a recruiting agent—his case, as well as the whole question of subversion of the Headquarters Guard, was clearly a matter for Washington to deal with.

But the Conspiracies committee wanted the Continental Army's help in arresting Matthews, Forbes, and all the other men—the civilians who had just been implicated and the men on the June 5 list who had not yet appeared voluntarily. (That large category included both Mayor Matthews and McLean, the shoemaker.) Washington had been waiting since the middle of May to be asked for such help. He promptly ordered General Greene to have Matthews arrested by "a careful officer," and specified that the time of the arrest should be one o'clock on the morning of June 22 when, presumably, Matthews would be off guard. This tactical notion was useless. Matthews was not exactly awaiting Greene's men, but he had not left his Flatbush house, and since he had known he had been subject to arrest for ten days or more—whenever the "reasonable time," after June 5, for him to come in voluntarily had expired—he had clearly prepared carefully for the occasion. Greene's men searched diligently throughout the house and were unable to find any papers of any kind, much less incriminating evidence. Gilbert Forbes was arrested that same night and taken to be questioned by Jay, Morris, and Livingston at a late hour. Forbes refused to testify, and so he was locked up in the City Hall jail, as was Matthews. At the same time, the provost marshal's men, with fixed bayonets, were routing out all the members of Washington's guard who had been mentioned as turncoats and taking them into custody. The total haul of suspects, in three days' time, was almost forty men.

The Conspiracies committee charged Matthews with "dangerous designs and treasonable conspiracies against the rights and liberties of the United States of America." ("States" instead of "Colonies" was a departure from the usual form; evidently Livingston, Jay, and Morris thought the New York election results gave them the right to call New York a state.) Considering the gravity of the accusation, Matthews, when he testified on June 23, was wonderfully self-possessed. He admitted that he had carried money—more than a hundred pounds—from Tryon to Gilbert Forbes, but, as Matthews explained his role, he was a reluctant go-between rather than the master plotter. It had all started six or seven weeks earlier when the Mayor, with General Putnam's permission, had visited the *Duchess of Gordon* to arrange a safe exit for the ship that was to take Lord Drummond to Bermuda. When that business was done, as Matthews was about to leave the ship, Tryon had taken him into his cabin and had put "a bundle" of paper money into his hands. Tryon had told Matthews to take out five pounds and to give it to the prisoners in the New York City jails. The rest of the money was to go to Gilbert Forbes. Tryon had explained that it was in payment for some guns Forbes had made, and for some other guns Forbes was going to make. Matthews was also to tell Forbes that Tryon did not want any more guns.

This errand, Matthews said on the witness stand, greatly worried him. He did not tell Tryon he would not do it. (Since the Mayor was Tryon's appointee, the Conspiracies committee could see that, if his story were true, Matthews would have been in a quandary.) Matthews said he had been surprised to hear that Forbes was making guns for the British, and, at the same time, he felt that Tryon was putting "a matter on my shoulders which might bring me into some difficulty." Nevertheless, Matthews had taken the money and had come ashore.

Then, Matthews said, he had consulted a friend about what to do. Matthews did not name him, but the Conspiracies committee learned that Matthews' friend was Alderman George Brewerton, who, like Matthews, was on the June 5 list and had failed to appear voluntarily. Brewerton had agreed, Matthews said, that Matthews' position was unfortunate. Brewerton did not want to pay Forbes on Matthews' behalf, but Brewerton had agreed to look up Forbes, question him, and find out whether he was really the man Tryon had been talking about.

While Brewerton was doing that, Matthews testified, he had decided the best thing he could do was to delay. He had received the money, and there was nothing he could do about that. But as long as he did not pay Forbes, Matthews thought, he would look only half guilty in case he was found out. But Forbes, having learned from Brewerton that Matthews was holding his money, came right to Matthews' house and demanded it. Matthews pretended that he did not yet have the money and that he expected to receive it soon. And, according to Matthews, the conversation went:

MATTHEWS: Is it possible that you have been sending guns on board the Governor's ship?

FORBES: Yes.

MATTHEWS: You will be hanged if you are found out. If you have any regard for your own safety, you will not go on with such schemes. . . .

(Matthews' testimony was a little weak at that point; he had said he was supposed to tell Forbes that Tryon did not want any more guns.)

FORBES: I can send the guns on board in a way that nobody can find out. I send them in a canoe or a boat covered with a straw bed and two or three old chairs on top of it.

Forbes had left without his money, but, Matthews said, the gunsmith had returned several times, and each time Forbes had confessed a little more. According to Matthews, Forbes said that he had a number of recruits he wanted "to send down" to the Governor; that he was thinking of raising a whole company of men and wondered whether Matthews could get him a captain's commission from Tryon; that he, Forbes, was in a position to enlist a number of soldiers who were serving in General Washington's guard. Matthews said that he had begged Forbes to give up all such ideas or the gallows would surely be his end.

As Forbes pressed harder for his money, Matthews said he had taken to spending more time in Flatbush instead of New York, and that when Forbes had taken to calling on him at Flatbush, Matthews had moved out to Polhemus, a town four miles from Jamaica; but that finally, "finding there was no way to get rid of him," Matthews had returned to New York and had paid Forbes.

Matthews said he had seen Forbes once more, the next day, and then only to tell him that he must never come into the Mayor's office again. But that even so, against Matthews' desires, a small procession of men had been presenting themselves to Matthews—including a soldier in uniform who said he belonged to Washington's guard—and asking how to get to the British warships to sign up with the British forces. In every case, Matthews testified, he had told the callers that he had nothing to do with British enlistments, and he had urged them to forget the idea and go home—or, in the case of the guardsman, "to return to his quarters."

Livingston, Jay, and Morris could not tell exactly how candid Matthews was being with them. They had no proof that the Mayor had done more than he admitted, but that alone was enough, the Provincial Congress decided, to keep Matthews in jail. The Conspiracies committee suspected, as did Washington, that Matthews had played a more important part than he said, and it feared that some of the material that had emerged from Matthews' testimony—schemes that Forbes had mentioned to Matthews—might be significant. Forbes had casually mentioned a plot to capture one of the New York batteries as soon as the British fleet arrived, and had added that he had been able to inspect all the gun positions without any interference from the sentries who had been guarding them. Forbes, Matthews said, had also mentioned a plan to cut down the King's Bridge.

Right after his arrest, Gilbert Forbes himself had refused to say anything, but early on the morning of the next day, the Reverend Mr. John Henry Livingston, Robert R. Livingston's thirty-year-old first cousin, visited Forbes in prison and advised him to confess to save his soul, since, Livingston thought, Forbes had no more than three days to live. Soon after that visit, Forbes began to testify before the Conspiracies committee. His account more or less confirmed what the earlier witnesses had said, the great difference being that Forbes described himself as a small second-rank figure in the plotting rather than the leader the other witnesses had made him out to be. Forbes traced all his troubles back to a night in April, a day or two after General Washington's arrival from Boston, when he had met William Green, the drummer in Washington's guard. Forbes had been drinking with some friends, and Green had come in and offered a toast to the King's health. Forbes had drunk to that, and Green, in Forbes's words, "supposed I was his friend." Green had proposed the enlisting scheme, and Forbes had gone along with it reluctantly, and only after "repeated applications." Green had handed Forbes lists of the names of men recruited, including William Hickey's, but Forbes's own activity, Forbes insisted, had been that of a go-between. The money he got from Mayor Matthews, Forbes said, was not for guns at all but for the men who had been recruited. Still, Forbes admitted that he had sold guns to Tryon—a total of twenty. But the nine rifles included in that number, Forbes added, were bad ones that would not shoot straight.

The several other schemes—capturing a battery, cutting down the King's Bridge, and so on—had not gone beyond conjecture, according to Forbes. (Some of them, apparently, were no more than ideas that had occurred to Governor Tryon on board the *Duchess of Gordon.*) But New York's rumor factory, seizing on scraps of information that leaked out of the Conspiracies committee's sessions, magnified the recruiting plot, which was bad enough, to include all kinds of spine-chilling projects. It was widely believed that the conspirators had planned to murder Washington, Putnam, and, possibly, Greene. The number of men implicated was raised to seven hundred in one story. Some had heard that the plotters' idea was to blow up the powder magazine and set fire to the city, and there were those who had it on good advice that the King's Bridge cannon were about to be respiked. The New York newspapers did not help restrain the popular imagination. "A most wicked, unnatural, and treasonable conspiracy . . . has, we hear, been discovered," said Holt's *Journal* in the issue of June 27, "and proper measures will, no doubt, be taken to circumvent the design, which appears similar to that of Rome for the restoration of the Tarquin family and tyranny. As soon as a particular account can be collected, it will be inserted."

None of these rumors was wholly absurd (except the number seven hundred), but Washington's immediate concern was less with a nebulous assassination plot than with the state of his guard. On June 26, even before the Conspiracies committee had finished taking testimony on the recruiting scandal as a whole, a military court-martial proceeded to try Thomas Hickey. There was nothing against Lynch beyond Ketchum's report of what Lynch had said—except, of course, the suspicion of passing counterfeit money. The drummer, William Green, was accused of worse crimes than Hickey, but Green, in contrast to Hickey, was eager to cooperate with the authorities and tell everything. His excuse for himself was that he had taken money from the Tories to cheat them and, as a self-appointed counter-intelligence agent, to find out what they were up to. Hickey would not talk, and the case against him was airtight, and so he was picked as the one soldier out of at least three, and perhaps as many as eight, to be court-martialed as an example to the rest of the Continental Army.

Hickey was a solidly built man, about five feet six inches tall, with a dark complexion. He had lived in Weathersfield, Connecticut, for some years. It was believed that he had been born in Ireland, and that, years earlier, he had deserted from the British Army. He was a private sentinel in the guard. The formal charge accused him "of exciting and joining in a mutiny and sedition, and of treacherously corresponding with, enlisting among, and receiving pay from the enemies of the United Colonies." Hickey pleaded not guilty.

Colonel Samuel H. Parsons, taking his turn as president of the General Court-Martial, which was one of a regimental commander's duties, ran the proceedings efficiently. There were twelve officers on the court besides Parsons—a lieutenant colonel, a major, and ten captains—and it sat at Washington's downtown headquarters, No. 1 Broadway. The four witnesses against Hickey were Green, Gilbert Forbes, Isaac Ketchum, and William Welch, who testified that Hickey had tried, unsuccessfully, to recruit him. They all spoke their pieces as expected. Green established the fact that Hickey had accepted money to enlist—Green had handed it to him—and said that the amount was two shillings. Forbes testified that he had paid Hickey an additional half-dollar. Ketchum repeated some of the hearsay evidence with which he had inspired the entire investigation.

Then Hickey took the stand. He had no witnesses on his behalf, and no evidence to offer. The best he could do was to explain that he had engaged in the scheme at first for the sake of "cheating the Tories"—the extenuation Green had just offered. Afterward, Hickey said, he "had consented to have his name sent aboard the man-of-war in order that if the enemy should arrive and defeat the Army here, and I should be taken prisoner, I might be safe." This reasoning did not help his case.

The courtroom was cleared. The officers considered the evidence for a time and voted unanimously that Hickey was guilty as charged. The sentence was also unanimous: "that the prisoner, Thomas Hickey, suffer death for said crimes by being hanged by the neck until he is dead."

Washington and his Council of General Officers (Heath, Spencer, Green, Stirling, Mifflin, and Scott), who met the fol-

lowing day, June 27, reviewed the transcript of the Hickey trial
and confirmed the results. Washington ordered the provost
marshal to execute Hickey at eleven o'clock on the morning of
June 28. Though Washington's army and all the civilians in
the city were talking about little except the infernal conspiracy
and Hickey's court-martial, the Commander-in-Chief and his
advisers were largely concerned with other subjects. All the
news from Canada was bad. The Continental Congress had
chosen Horatio Gates to assume command there—a better choice
than Sullivan, in Washington's opinion, though he had preferred not to say so—and Gates, who had left New York on
June 25, was well on his way to Albany. But while the Continental Congress had been deciding on Gates for the assignment,
the American military situation in Canada had deteriorated.
General Thompson had attacked the British at Three Rivers,
and had been beaten. Fifty men were killed, and Thompson,
along with about two hundred and fifty of his officers and men,
had been taken prisoner. The Americans had been forced to
evacuate Montreal. Arnold, with his three hundred men, was
retreating to Ile-aux-Noix, at the north end of Lake Champlain.
Sorel had to be abandoned, too. The main body of the Continental Army's expeditionary force, under Sullivan, was with-
drawing to the south, down the Richelieu River.

    Canada, in fact, was lost. The question was now where Gates
should try to halt the British invasion. Ile-aux-Noix might be too
far north for the Americans to defend. It was possible that Sullivan and Arnold should be ordered to retreat all the way to Crown
Point, 150 miles south of Sorel—for, from the scraps of intelligence Washington had received, he believed that the British had
been reinforced at Three Rivers and Sorel. Washington guessed
that General John Burgoyne's army, or some of its leading ele-
ments, had probably reached the mouth of the Richelieu River.
And although the Continental Congress, on June 25, had once

again resolved to send more men to the Northern Department—
four thousand this time—and had even authorized a ten-dollar
bounty for three-year enlistments without Washington's having
had to put in a word in favor of long enlistments, the men in
Philadelphia were still unrealistic about the difference between
voting and producing large numbers of effectives. (No exact
tally was available, but the Continental Congress' resolution calling for thirty thousand additional militiamen had been widely
ignored. The number of militiamen present at New York and
ready to fight was about one thousand.) For the moment, counting only the men present, Sullivan's force, with Arnold's men
included, added up to about seven thousand officers and men, of
whom perhaps thirty-five hundred were well enough to be
called "fit for duty." Even if Gates could reorganize the Northern Department, and restore its morale, his defensive mission
might be more than he or any other commander could handle.

As for the New York front, Washington and his Council of
Generals were well aware that if General Burgoyne had had
time to move from Halifax to Sorel, General Howe had had
time to move from Halifax to Sandy Hook. They expected
word of a sighting at any moment. Two or three British transports had joined the little fleet off the Hook on the twenty-fifth,
and two more had arrived on the twenty-sixth. While the
comings and goings of the British ships had not meant anything
so far, these latest arrivals might. No one on Long Island had
seen the invasion fleet or any part of it, but there was an unconfirmed rumor that Howe's flagship had been sighted off the
Massachusetts coast on June 20. Lieutenant Colonel Tupper's
squadron was keeping watch, and Tupper, on June 21, had made
a brave but unsuccessful effort to destroy the Sandy Hook lighthouse. His landing party had carried some field artillery ashore
and had worked their way to within 150 yards of the building.

Then Tupper and one of his officers had advanced close enough to talk to the British there, hoping to persuade them to surrender. The British commanding officer replied by firing several shots at Tupper. Tupper and his escort had returned, unwounded, to their position, and the American guns had bombarded the lighthouse for an hour. The walls were too thick and strong for Tupper's light artillery, and Tupper had withdrawn, thinking that he might attack again with some different plan; but Washington, much as he admired Tupper's initiative, ordered him "to desist . . . as it seems dangerous and not to promise success." So, while waiting for the British, the only new defense preparations the Council of Generals could think of to add to those already going on was to urge the owners of livestock on Staten Island and the south shore of Long Island, as they had been urged before, to move their animals as far inland as possible, out of the reach of the hungry invaders.

The gallows for William Hickey's execution was constructed, by Washington's order, in a field off the Bowery Road not far north of the Commons. Hickey was marched there by a ceremonial guard of eighty soldiers with fixed bayonets. A tremendous crowd had gathered—one of the newspapers reported later that it numbered twenty thousand, but it could hardly have been that large—including all the off-duty soldiers from the four regiments encamped nearest the scene: Heath's, Spencer's, Stirling's, and Scott's. The artillery surgeon, Dr. William Eustis, was a spectator. It was Eustis' impression that Hickey appeared "unaffected and obstinate to the last, except that when the Chaplain took him by the hand under the gallows and bade him adieu, a torrent of tears flowed over his face." But then, Dr. Eustis reported, Hickey had wiped away his tears with his hand, and had regained his "indignant, scornful air" and his "confident look." Hickey's last words were something about how Green had better be cautious or the design would be worked against him yet. It was not clear whether Hickey meant General Greene, a possible assassination victim, or the drummer Green, witness for the prosecution. At a few minutes past eleven o'clock, Hickey was dead.

In the hours immediately before Hickey's execution, Washington, who was not going to attend it, had written a letter to the Continental Congress reporting on the whole British recruiting scheme and on Hickey's trial. Washington's version—especially by comparison with the sensational accounts other men were writing—was matter-of-fact: "Congress, I doubt not, will have heard of the plot that was forming among the many disaffected persons in this city and government for aiding the King's troops upon their arrival. No regular plan seems to have been digested, but several persons have enlisted and sworn to join them. The matter, I am in hopes, by a timely discovery, will be suppressed and put a stop to. Many citizens and others, among whom is the Mayor, are now in confinement."

Washington said that the plot had been traced up to Governor Tryon, and that he thought Mayor Matthews had been Tryon's "principal agent, or go-between." Members of his guard had been engaged in the plot, but Washington made it plain that he considered Tryon the villain, rather than any of his own soldiers, and that, with the execution of Hickey, he considered the incident closed: "The others are not tried. I am hopeful that this example will produce many salutary consequences, and deter others from entering into the like traitorous practices."

While Washington was still working on this report, a messenger delivered a letter from one of Tupper's subordinates, Lieutenant Joseph Davison, who was serving on board the *Schuyler*. Part of Davison's news was good: the *Schuyler* and the *Montgomery* had managed to retake the four American ships that had been captured by the British. They were two brigs from Nantucket carrying oil, a schooner from Cape Ann carrying molasses and sugar, and a sloop from Rhode Island with a cargo of flour and lumber. The rest of his news was bad. The *Schuyler* had taken some British sailors in the course of recovering the ships, and one of the prisoners had said that General Howe, aboard the *Greyhound*, with a fleet of 130 ships, had left Halifax for New York on June 9. Given that information, Lieutenant Davison thought he could identify a warship the *Schuyler* had sighted on June 24: it had been the *Greyhound* sailing past on a course that would take her to Sandy Hook.

Washington believed Davison's letter, and for at least a few hours, the General was filled with uncharacteristic pessimism. It seemed to him that all his defensive preparations were inadequate and that his army was too small. He had copies of Davison's letter made, and included one with his own letter to the Continental Congress:

I could wish General Howe and his armament had not arrived yet, as not more than a thousand militia have yet come in, and our whole force, including the troops at all the detached posts, and on board the armed vessels, which are comprehended in our returns [Washington was also sending Philadelphia a return of his forces at New York], is but small and inconsiderable when compared with the extensive lines they are to defend and most probably the army that he brings.

Washington also wrote immediately to Massachusetts and Connecticut, and had Reed write to New Jersey, begging all three provinces to send their militia to New York without losing "a moment's time," and telling them that, in all probability, Howe was already at Sandy Hook. Washington thought that Howe would attack quickly, perhaps without even waiting for his full force to arrive, when he learned the weakness of New

York's defenses—a subject on which, as everybody in New York realized after the recent revelations before the Conspiracies committee, Tryon could brief him in great detail. Connecticut had suggested that a brigade of light horse might be useful, and offered to lend one. Washington, in general, was an enthusiast for mounted troops, although he did not have any, and he wanted to encourage the formation of such units. According to Governor Trumbull, Connecticut could send Washington three regiments—perhaps five hundred men—under the command of Colonel Thomas Seymour. (There was no mention of the fact that some of the troopers had been in New York earlier.) The prospect of five hundred additional men was attractive, but the army officers' mounts, the working horses, and the artillery horses were already consuming all the forage on Manhattan Island. If the Connecticut light horse mounts could be supported at all, the expense would be enormous, and Washington asked whether, for the emergency, he could have the men without the horses—at least until Connecticut sent militiamen to relieve them.

Early the next morning, Saturday, June 29, the lookouts on the roof of No. 1 Broadway saw that the Staten Island signal flags were up: the British fleet was in sight. During the morning forty-five ships arrived and dropped anchor off Sandy Hook—a relief of a minor sort, because it had occurred to Washington that Howe's fleet might come straight through the Narrows into the harbor immediately. Ships kept coming in all afternoon. By the time darkness fell, the count was up to 110, and according to General Greene's outposts on Long Island, still more were following. Even though the British invasion had been threatened for so long, and rumored or imagined so often, the reality of so many ships gathered together was awesome. No one in New York had ever seen such an armada, because none so big had ever been assembled in American waters. One Continental Army private, Daniel McCurtin, wrote afterward: "I was upstairs . . . and spied as I peeped out the Bay something resembling a wood of pine trees trimmed. I declare, at my noticing this, that I could not believe my eyes . . . I thought all London was afloat." Many of the British transports had marvelously winning names, such as *Friendship, Felicity, Amity's Admonition, Good Intent,* and *Father's Good Will,* but no one on shore regarded the British Navy's style of nomenclature as a sign of amiability.

Yet since they were powerless to react in any effective way, the men in New York, soldiers and civilians alike, went on doing what they had been doing before, without any public demonstration of fear or surprise. Washington's spirits improved. In the general orders for the day, after announcing the formation of a special corps of carpenters, armorers, blacksmiths, and other skilled workmen, Washington wrote:

The General expects that all soldiers who are intrusted with the defense of any work will behave with great coolness and bravery and will be particularly careful not to throw away their fire; he recommends to them to load for their first fire with one musket-ball and four or eight buckshot, according to the size and strength of their pieces. If the enemy is received with such a fire, at not more than twenty or thirty yards distance, he has no doubt of their being repulsed.

And, in reporting the morning's events to the Continental Congress, Washington sounded more like his usual, determined self: "I suppose the whole fleet will be in within a day or two. I am hopeful, before they are prepared to attack, that I shall get some reinforcements; be that as it may, I shall attempt to make the best disposition of our troops, in order to give them a proper reception, and to prevent the ruin and destruction they are meditating against us."

Washington made arrangements for his wife to go back to

Virginia, and again he sent word to the neighboring colonies to speed their militia to New York. (Reed in person took the message to General William Livingston, commanding the New Jersey forces.) Washington wrote Colonel Clinton in the Highlands to warn him in case the British fleet should attempt to sail past the New York City batteries, and on up the Hudson toward a junction with the forces of Carleton and Burgoyne. And he called another meeting of his General Officers Council to review everything that had been done.

Even though the British fleet had arrived, the Conspiracies committee continued to hear testimony on inimicality, as if there was all the time in the world to round up dangerous men. Actually, the committee was working about as fast as it could; it had simply started too late. Jay, Livingston, and Morris had been spending most of their time on the Matthews-Forbes case, while the other section of the committee—Hobart, Tredwell, Graham, Randall, and Gansevort—had been trying to work its way through the names on the June 5 master list. It had had limited success. Most of the most dangerous men could not be found, and even among the "equivocals"—those men who, the Provincial Congress had hoped, would answer their summonses without needing to be arrested—there were quite a few missing persons. James Jauncey, Jr., a member of Tryon's Council, had vanished. Oliver De Lancey, also a Council member, Charles Ward Apthorpe, and Major Robert Bayard could not be found because they were on board the *Duchess of Gordon*. On the night of June 19 the three men had sailed down to Sandy Hook in a canoe, starting from Apthorpe's estate on the Hudson. (The Apthorpe mansion was on the Bloomingdale Road, now Broadway, not far south of Striker's Bay, an indentation in the shoreline at what is now Ninety-sixth Street and Riverside

Drive.) Howe had arrived ahead of his fleet, on June 25, just as Lieutenant Davison had thought he might (one of the "transports" whose arrival was reported that day was, in fact, the *Greyhound*), and since then, the newcomers—De Lancey, Apthorpe, and Bayard—along with Tryon, and the other long-term residents of the *Duchess,* had been explaining New York's political and military situation to the General.

Still, a large number of the men wanted for questioning were right where they were expected to be. If they had not come in voluntarily, neither had they made a serious effort to get away. The group included Judge Whitehead Hicks, the former mayor; Councillor William Axtell; Supreme Court judges Thomas Jones and George D. Ludlow; Captain Archibald Hamilton, of Flushing, Queens; Dr. Samuel Martin, of Far Rockaway; and Theophylact Bache, the President of the New York Chamber of Commerce, who owned houses in both New York City and Flatbush and, through a clerical error, had the doubtful distinction of appearing on the list twice. Hicks, one of the first of the Crown officers questioned, was asked, as all the men were, to give evidence that he had been "a friend to the American cause." Hicks replied, truthfully, that he was not *for* the "so-called" American cause, but that he had never done anything *against* the United Colonies. He could not sign the Association oath, Hicks explained, because, as an honest man, he could not promise anything he did not mean to perform. Most of the others who had stood their ground like Hicks recited similar pieces, and most of them were allowed to go free, some on bonds and some without bonds, if they would swear, negatively, not to do anything to oppose the measures of the Continental and New York Provincial Congresses. William Axtell was almost alone in refusing to promise that much. Most of his property, Axtell pointed out, was in Great Britain and the

British West Indies. He was willing to swear that he would not take an active part against the American cause, and he was willing to move from Flatbush and take his family up the Hudson River to stay in the country, but he felt that the parole as it stood might be construed "on the other side of the water" as an overt act that would result in the confiscation of his overseas properties. There was nothing for the Conspiracies committee to do, under the circumstances, except to keep Axtell in jail, at least until the Provincial Congress could debate his unusual case.

By and large, the Conspiracies committee was willing to give non-Associators the benefit of the doubt. It accepted a number of paroles without requiring bonds. (The case of John Willett, of Jamaica, Long Island, was the conspicuous exception. Willett was not let go until he had posted the extraordinarily large sum of two thousand pounds.) The shortage of jail space explained, at least in part, the committee's kindness. Throughout the year Crown officers had been treated with respect. Even the Mechanics Committee and the New York mob had not molested them, and, while the members of the Governor's Council may not have been popular, they had not been harassed. The arrival of the British invasion fleet was a tense moment, certainly, but the Conspiracies committee, reflecting the prevailing New York City view, was inclined to accept the words of many of the best-known Crown officials and sympathizers on the ground that they were men of integrity. Washington's General Officers Council, on the other hand, felt that New York was far too trusting, and that too many disaffected inhabitants were released, after their arrests, too casually. The generals urged Washington to ask the Provincial Congress "to take some more effectual method of securing the good behavior of those people." It was thinking of such methods as imprisonment or deportation. Washington did

not disagree with his Council. He asked the Provincial Congress
to reconsider this question. In the meantime, the roundup continued, not only in the New York City area but throughout the
province. At Albany, the haul of inimicals and equivocals was
particularly large. On June 26, the Albany Committee reported
to the Provincial Congress that it was sending six of its recalci-
trant residents—Abraham Cuyler, Henry Cuyler, Stephen De
Lancey, John Duncan, Benjamin Hilton, and John Monier—as
prisoners to Hartford, Connecticut. At New Windsor, the men
arrested included Cadwallader Colden, Jr., the Lieutenant Governor's oldest surviving son. (Two younger sons, David and
Richard Colden, had been arrested and heard in New York, and
released on parole; but Cadwallader, Sr., had been omitted
from the wanted list. He was now eighty-nine years old, in poor
health, and confined—without any action on New York's part—
to his house in Flatbush.) New Windsor, like New York City,
was uncertain about the propriety of treating with an outright
Tory like Cadwallader, Jr., who was not charged with any
inimical act, but who could not show that he was a friend to the
American cause because he was not. The local committee had
released young Colden temporarily and, as New Windsor reported to the Provincial Congress, uneasily; New Windsor
planned to question Colden at greater length, and hoped that he
would reappear when he was wanted.

   The Provincial Congress assumed, as it had for some time,
that it had better plan to leave City Hall and move away from
Manhattan entirely, to make certain that it could continue to
meet after the shooting started. Nevertheless, the Congress sat,
and the Conspiracies committee took testimony—Gilbert Forbes
was back, adding a few details to his previous accounts—
throughout Saturday, the twenty-ninth, as the waters off Sandy
Hook filled with enemy sails. Jay and Livingston, thinking that

Washington might be especially interested in the balance of what Forbes had to say, had invited the General to attend. Washington, in a polite note, thanked them cordially, but explained that he was "so exceedingly hurried at this time" he could not make it. Washington did hope, however, that when the Conspiracies committee had finished with Forbes it would send him over to Headquarters—any time after four o'clock in the afternoon—so that he could have one or two of his officers question Forbes. Washington thought that it might be useful to compare two sets of Forbes's answers to see how truthful the man was.

The Conspiracies committee had planned a busy week of hearings. Twenty equivocals were scheduled to appear between Monday, July 1, and Saturday, July 6, and summonses were out for an additional fourteen. The committee meant to question at least that many men, and perhaps more. Washington's soldiers had found only a few of the immediate-arrest names on the June 5 list—Captain Hewlett, for example, remained at large—but they had arrested many more dangerous suspects than had been on the list, mostly men who had been mentioned during the hearings. One of Greene's officers, Lieutenant Colonel Cary, had led a detachment into Captain Hewlett's sanctuary, the swampy wilderness near Rockaway, and, after a short, sharp skirmish, had captured twenty of the men hiding there. All were presumed to be British Army recruits, and a few were willing to admit it. Several had gunpowder, which, they said almost boastfully, had come from the *Asia*. The Conspiracies committee intended to proceed with its work, at maximum speed, until it was interrupted.

The interruption came, however, on the next day, Sunday, June 30, when the Provincial Congress voted to adjourn for just one day, Monday, in order to move to White Plains. The

British fleet at Sandy Hook had done nothing more ominous than arrive, and both Orange and Kings counties were opposed to moving. Despite their opposition, the resolution passed easily:

Whereas there is great reason to apprehend that an attack will soon be made upon this city: And whereas during the tumult and confusion incident upon such attack it may be difficult to assemble a sufficient number of members to form a Congress: And whereas the minutes and other necessary public papers and records of this Colony ought to be removed from this city: And whereas the present or future Congress of this Colony, as well by reason of the removal of the papers aforesaid as for other causes and considerations, will be unable to deliberate and determine in this city on the several important matters submitted to their consideration:

Resolved, therefore, that the Treasurer and Secretaries of this Congress . . . are directed to repair . . . unto the White Plains, in the county of Westchester.

The Provincial Congress had in mind, of course, those papers and records beyond the files that had already gone to Kingston. Gouverneur Morris turned over all the Conspiracies committee's papers, sealed, to Secretary Robert Benson, as a security measure for the move. Zebediah Mills was empowered to impress teams, carriages, and boats to transport not only the Provincial Congress files and the money in Peter Van Brugh Livingston's treasury, but also all the lead, powder, and other military stores that belonged to New York rather than to the Continental Army. The Provincial Congress decided that fifty dollars was enough to pay for its entire physical removal. (The thirty delegates present out of a hundred and two members were expected to arrange for their own moves.) Packing may have reminded New York that its own supply of lead, for all the year-long attempt to persuade people to mine more, was much too small. At any rate, the Provincial Congress authorized

Daniel Dunscomb and Samuel Prince, as a committee of two, to collect all the lead in the city—lead window-sash weights, for instance, and everything else except the small lead weights used on shopkeepers' scales—to be melted and molded into bullets and shot. Careful accounts were to be kept so that, at some indefinite future time, the owners could be compensated.

Before adjourning, the Provincial Congress authorized General Washington to take over all, or any part of, the New York militia for New York's defense. And, in response to the general officers' complaint about New York's easy treatment of Tories, which Washington had passed along, the Provincial Congress also gave the Commander-in-Chief blanket authority "to take such measures for apprehending and securing dangerous and disaffected persons as he shall think necessary." The Conspiracies committee did not intend to stop functioning, although it was going to be handicapped by Philip Livingston's departure for Philadelphia. (Jay was also under pressure to rejoin the New York delegation to take part in the debate on the independence resolution. The draft text of a resolution had been reported on June 28. Rutledge of South Carolina, relying on Jay to oppose a declaration, wrote that Jay's presence was "absolutely necessary." Jay had been opposed to a declaration, but he was becoming more and more amenable to one; he was also inclined to think that the work he could do at White Plains was more important than his place in the Continental Congress—at least for the next week or two.) In any case, until the Conspiracies committee was back in session after its move, Washington needed at least emergency power to cope with what he had carefully agreed was primarily a New York responsibility.

One of the problems that could not be solved satisfactorily—at least not overnight—was the fate of the city's prison population. It would be inhuman to keep the prisoners locked up during a bombardment, since the likelihood of a fire was so great. Morris felt that, under the circumstances, all prisoners ought to be released on their paroles, even though some of them would certainly escape to the British anchorage. The Tories in jail, as well as their friends who were outside, had been showering the Provincial Congress with letters making that same suggestion, but the majority of the delegates thought the idea too liberal. Many Tories had already been sent to prisons in Ulster and Orange counties, and there was room for more. The difficulty was a lack of guards to serve as escorts. The question was therefore put over, for the time being, in the hope that the Provincial Congress could figure something out before Howe's shells began to fall.

Compared to the night of August 23, when the *Asia* had fired, and the several other occasions when, for less substantial reasons, New York had panicked, the city was calm. Howe's arrival had been thoroughly advertised, and a prompt order from Washington's headquarters forbidding anyone to ride the ferries without a special pass from General Stirling, who had been named New York "commandant," ruled out any rush to take refuge in New Jersey or Long Island. Even so, the sight of the British fleet appeared to arouse more interest than terror. The weather, which had been dry, had become extremely hot, and no one exerted himself unless he had to. New York took it for granted that Manhattan Island was Howe's target, but seemed less agitated than the New Jersey shore towns, Amboy, Elizabeth, Woodbridge, and Monmouth. In all those places, the residents suddenly realized that British interest in New York City was only an American assumption, and New Jersey men began to doubt that it really made sense to lend New Jersey militiamen to New York, as promised, and leave New Jersey defenseless. Queens County felt menaced. The Queens Committee met, thought about the state of Queens' defenses, and resolved, in view of the chance of the county's "being plundered by the ministerial troops," to raise a special fund of two hundred pounds for self-protection. Twenty-one of the residents of Cortlandt Manor, Westchester, where New York's emergency provisions depots had been established in two large warehouses, saw Cortlandt Manor as a prize the British might value highly, and they wrote the Provincial Congress asking for two fieldpieces to defend the stores.

In New York, reveille on Monday morning, July 1, was at 5 A.M. The Continental soldiers were allowed one hour for breakfast. Their work on the fortifications started at about six o'clock. At nine o'clock the alarm flags flew, the alarm guns fired, and every soldier, as he had practiced, ran for his battle post. British sails were up. The vessels were getting under way, and they were heading toward the Narrows.

The alarm, in a sense, was false. Having been briefed by his bevy of informants, William Howe was ready to put part of his 9,300-man force ashore in Brooklyn, but he was far from ready to attack New York City. Inconceivable as it was to New York, Howe's ships—113 in all—were the smaller part of the complete British expeditionary force, and Howe meant to wait for his brother, Richard, Admiral Viscount Howe, who was expected from England any day with 150 more ships and about 20,000 more men. General Howe also believed that General Clinton, with his 2,500 men, might soon arrive from what Howe hoped had been a victory at Charleston, South Carolina. (Clinton, who had talked too much for his mission's security, had been beaten at Charleston on June 28. General Charles Lee, three regiments of Continentals, six regiments of South Carolina militiamen, and seven South Carolina artillery companies had been waiting for him. So had a well-organized, though only half-completed, fort on Sullivan's Island, at the mouth of the

Charleston harbor. Clinton had suffered a good many casualties, and had withdrawn without coming close to breaking the city's defenses. He planned to leave Charleston for New York, but he was going to arrive considerably later than Howe imagined.) There was still another reason that General Howe would not attack immediately, though no one on shore understood it. Both William and Richard Howe still took themselves seriously as "peace commissioners." They did not realize that their negotiating power, which was no more than a power of pardon, was, from every colony's point of view, far too limited. Howe's purpose on July 1 was only to move somewhat more than half his fleet to Gravesend Bay, with the intention of establishing a camp in and around the village of Gravesend, now part of the Bensonhurst section of southwest Brooklyn.

That section of shore was General Greene's responsibility, but Greene's forces were stretched thin. A British reconnaissance party came ashore and was fired on. Greene called for help. Before the afternoon was over, five hundred of Spencer's men arrived on the scene. By that time, the British landing party had returned to its ship.

The Americans in Brooklyn spent an uneasy night wondering what might happen the next morning and worrying about the fire power the British ships could bring to bear on the shore. The *Asia*, sixty-four guns, was still the biggest vessel in sight, but the *Centurion* and the *Chatham* both carried fifty guns, the *Phoenix* forty, the *Greyhound* thirty, and even the troop and supply transports mounted at least a pair of cannon. Greene's men might get a few fieldpieces into position to use against the British, but the nearest American guns of any size were at the mouth of the Narrows, where a battery of nine-pounders had been established close to what is now the Brooklyn end of the Verrazano Bridge. That was too far away to help Gravesend.

But, during the night, General Howe decided against establishing a British camp at Gravesend because it would have to have a strong perimeter guard against the possibility of an American attack from Brooklyn Heights, and Howe did not like the description he had of the terrain. He did like what he had heard about Staten Island, so he decided to follow his alternate plan and camp there.

Early Tuesday morning, July 2, three of the British warships led the way into the Narrows ahead of the first group of transports, carrying the grenadiers and the light infantry. The American battery fired vigorously, but could not hit anything. The ships anchored at the Watering Place, and the troops landed without opposition. As Howe reported to London a few days later, his arrival filled the Staten Islanders—"a most loyal people, long-suffering on that account under the oppression of the Rebels stationed among them"—with great joy. And, on discovering that the American troops charged with the defense of Staten Island did not intend to fight, Howe summoned all the rest of his men and ships to follow. By late Wednesday, July 3, most of the British troops were on Staten Island, and by the end of July 4, the transfer was complete, with most of the ships anchored along Staten Island's north shore in the Kill van Kull, or the Kills, as it was commonly called, the waterway between Newark Bay and New York Bay. The last ship to move, bringing up the end of the line, was the *Asia*. As she entered the Narrows on her way to her new anchorage, the American ninepounders blazed away. (All they had hit, so far, was the rigging of a small tender, killing one sailor and wounding nine others.) The gunners missed the *Asia*, but the *Asia*, unlike the other British ships, returned the fire with a blast from several of her twenty-four-pound starboard guns. The *Asia* missed the American battery. One round of solid shot tore into a Mr. Bennet's house and stuck in the wall, and three rounds crashed into the property of Mr. Bennet's neighbor, Denyse Denyse. One hit his house, one hit his barn, and the third carried away his garden fence, opposite his front door.

Washington could do nothing to prevent the British occupation of Staten Island or even to make it uncomfortable for Howe's regiments, unless the Staten Island militia, who were outnumbered by at least twenty to one, decided to fight. General Orders for July 2—which reached the troops everywhere except on Staten Island—contained what was, for Washington's headquarters, a most unusual three-paragraph section of exhortation:

The time is now near at hand which must probably determine whether Americans are to be freemen or slaves; whether their houses and farms are to be pillaged and destroyed, and they consigned to a state of wretchedness, from which no human efforts will probably deliver them. The fate of unborn millions will now depend, (under God) on the courage and conduct of this army. Our cruel and unrelenting enemy leaves us no choice but a brave resistance or the most abject submission. This is all we can expect. We have, therefore, to resolve to conquer or die. Our Country's honor calls upon us for a vigorous and manly exertion; and if we now shamefully fail, we shall become infamous to the whole world. Let us, therefore, rely upon the goodness of the cause and the aid of the Supreme Being (in whose hands victory is) to encourage and animate us to great and noble action.

The eyes of all our countrymen are now upon us; and we shall have their blessings and praises if happy we are in being the instrument of saving them from the tyranny meditated against them. Let us therefore animate and encourage each other, and show the whole world that freemen contending for liberty on their own ground is superior to any slavish mercenaries on earth.

The General recommends to the Officers great coolness in time of action, and to the soldiers a strict attention and obedience, with a becoming firmness and spirit.

Every spyglass on Manhattan was trained on Staten Island, and it was possible to make out the British formations in brilliant uniforms marching precisely along the shore roads and up the hill toward Fresh Pond (now the Silver Lake reservoir) to the cadence of their drums. One watcher noticed the slow pace of these movements, as if Howe's men were not in any hurry to get wherever they were going. That was an accurate observation. Despite the abrupt change in Howe's plan, the Staten Island occupation had been carefully worked out in advance with the help of several prominent Richmond County men who, like De Lancey, Apthorpe, and Bayard, had lost no time getting down to Sandy Hook to offer their assistance to Howe. Richard Lawrence had been one of them—a dismaying fact because, while he had not been reelected, he was a member, in good standing, of the current Provincial Congress. (But then so was Richard Conner, whose anti-Association comments had driven Colonel Heard to arrest him.) The British troops were to be billeted in private houses, which meant that Howe needed to spread his force out over the entire island. The headquarters troops were to be near the center, at the town of Richmond. The Fourth Brigade was assigned to the Amboy road, which ran diagonally across the island. The First and Third Brigades were to share the houses along the north shore; the Second Brigade was to be on the west; the Fifth Brigade on the east, and the Sixth Brigade on the south. Since artillery was hard to move and, in Howe's estimation, would not be needed elsewhere, almost all the guns and the artillery companies were to stay in the vicinity of the Watering Place, where they had come ashore. The British were confident that the Americans could not oppose them successfully if they tried, and so the elaborate deployment was going ahead slowly and carefully. The soldiers had orders to be on their best behavior; they were to treat Staten Islanders politely, and they were not to steal or commandeer provisions, but to buy them. Two British infantrymen quickly discovered that Howe meant what he said. They found that no one was guarding Justice Peter Mersereau's wine cellar. Mersereau, a member of the Richmond County Committee, had fled from his place on the north shore, facing Newark Bay, and, like several other Staten Island Associators, had taken refuge in New Jersey. The soldiers broke into the cellar, drank a bottle or two of wine, and were arrested and held for a summary court-martial. Before long, Tryon and his friends from the *Duchess of Gordon* came ashore, along with General Howe. Adrian Bancker made a considerable fuss because, of all the handsome houses along the north shore road, Howe decided he wanted to occupy Bancker's for his personal use. Bancker objected strenuously. Howe had him moved to a cabin on one of the British warships.

None of the details of the Staten Island invasion reached New York City immediately, although it was evident, from the lack of the sound of musket fire, that no battle was taking place. Washington was puzzled. He had expected a fast attack directed at Manhattan, even if it came by way of Long Island or Westchester. New Jersey's anxieties grew, for Staten Island seemed to be a perfect stepping stone to New Jersey, not New York. And Washington, acknowledging that there might be something to New Jersey's argument, released the colony from its promise to send militia and dismissed those New Jersey men who had already reported to him, except for the Morris County companies, so that General William Livingston could guard the New Jersey coast from Elizabethtown to Amboy. And the Morris County militiamen, with some Continental troops to help them, were posted in New Jersey, at Bergen Point. Colonel William Prescott, commanding the Seventh Continental Regiment on Governor's Island, with one of the best views of Howe's fleet, suddenly realized that a British attack on his position would undoubtedly be made on an incoming tide and with a southerly wind, and under those conditions reinforcements from

Manhattan Island would find it impossible to reach him. On the other hand, Prescott thought, Washington could very well send many more men to Governor's Island on a contingency basis. If the British attacked elsewhere—Manhattan, say—Governor's Island could reinforce handily, because Prescott's troops would have the same advantage of wind and tide as the enemy. So Prescott asked General Heath to ask Washington for at least two thousand men, two and a half times as many as the Colonel had. As a hero of the battle of Breed's and Bunker's hills—many of the veterans insisted that Prescott, not Putnam, had been the actual field commander that day—Prescott could expect that his tactical notions would get a hearing. Still, with only twelve thousand effectives on hand, Washington was not likely to place twenty-eight hundred of them on Governor's Island. The long-awaited Connecticut militiamen—seven battalions commanded by Brigadier General James Wadsworth, Jr.—were finally marching to New York, with the head of the column expected on July 5, and they were needed, though not particularly for the defense of Governor's Island.

All New York wondered what had been happening in Philadelphia. Robert R. Livingston had come up to New York over the weekend to attend the last City Hall session of the Provincial Congress, and he had brought his friends up to date on the Continental Congress news. Livingston liked the text of the Declaration of Independence as it stood, but, he explained, he and Sherman had had nothing to do with writing it. They had left that entirely up to the other three committee members, Franklin, Adams, and Jefferson.

Jefferson had written the first draft. He had worked quickly, leaning heavily (in his own phrase) on the language of earlier statements as he remembered them, especially Virginia's newly adopted "Declaration of Rights." Although Jefferson had taken pains with his style, he had not tried to write anything markedly original. The Declaration was intended to be a consensus statement on which all the colonies—if not all the citizens in all the colonies—could agree. It was meant to prove to the whole world that the Continental Congress and the United Colonies were doing something much more principled than engaging in a "rebellion," and, furthermore, that they were well justified in doing it. For proof of that, Jefferson had relied, like Paine, on a list of the King's wicked acts, going far, far back in time. Adams and Franklin had carefully edited Jefferson's draft. Adams had found the language, here and there, unnecessarily flamboyant. Franklin had made several word changes to tighten Jefferson's sentence structure. By and large, these minor improvements had left Jefferson's version intact. One section, however, worried Franklin and Adams, especially Adams. In his catalog of King George's misdeeds, Jefferson had written: "he has waged cruel war against nature itself, violating its most sacred rights of life & liberty in the persons of a distant people who never offended him, captivating & carrying them into slavery in another hemisphere, or to incur miserable death in their transportation thither. . . ." Adams hated slavery at least as much as Jefferson, but, remembering the number of slave owners who were sitting in the Continental Congress, he thought that that particular royal offense might be eliminated, lest the Continental Congress embark on a long debate about slavery instead of independence. But, with Livingston and Sherman agreed, the subcommittee had decided to take that risk. As the edited draft had been submitted, Jefferson's antislavery passage stood, with the word "captivating" changed to "capturing."

New York did not hear that the Lee resolution had been adopted until the evening of July 4. As so often before, the

Coffee House patrons had the news as a rumor ahead of everyone else; and, as so often before, the rumor was a little bit
garbled. It confused the passage of the Lee motion to absolve
the United Colonies from all allegiance to the British Crown,
and to dissolve all political connection between them and the
State of Great Britain with the adoption of the Declaration
itself. And the rumor was also premature: it summarized the
result of the vote of July 1 when, technically, the Lee resolution
had not been adopted until July 2. What had actually happened
on the first was that the Continental Congress, sitting as a committee of the whole, had taken what was later declared to be a
"preliminary" vote. The New York delegates had explained
that they were compelled to abstain. Then the other twelve
colonies had passed the resolution, but by a disappointingly
divided vote of nine in favor to two opposed. Delaware could
not be counted either way, because two of her three men disagreed, and the third, Caesar Rodney, who could have broken
the tie, was absent. South Carolina was unanimously opposed.
Pennsylvania was opposed, five to two.

Rutledge, of South Carolina, felt that, since the resolution
had passed, the record would look better if it passed unanimously. He had argued that a final vote by the Congress proper,
not the Congress as a committee of the whole, should be postponed for twenty-four hours—a strong hint that he and his
eleven South Carolina colleagues might vote differently on July
2. The Rutledge motion to postpone was accepted. On the
second, in the final vote, South Carolina favored the Lee resolution, twelve to nothing. Pennsylvania had changed its vote, too.
Dickinson and Robert Morris could not bring themselves to vote
yes, but they had been persuaded to stay away, and Benjamin
Franklin, using all his diplomacy, had talked James Wilson into
changing his vote. Pennsylvania was recorded as "yea" by three

to two. Rodney, who had been in Dover, Delaware, eighty miles from Philadelphia, on the first, rode almost all night, and arrived on the second in time to break the Delaware tie. And so, officially, the Lee resolution had passed unanimously, with one state abstaining.

The New York delegates—those present were George Clinton, Henry Wisner, William Floyd, Francis Lewis, and John Alsop—were unhappy about New York's unique position, and on July 2, before the formal vote, they were already worried about what part New York should play after the Lee resolution passed. As Wisner pointed out in a letter to the Provincial Congress, which had not yet resumed its meetings, every act of the Continental Congress that New York joined in henceforth could be "considered as in some measure" acceding to the vote for independence, and therefore, perhaps, a violation of the New York delegation's instructions.

Indeed many matters in this new situation may turn up in which the propriety of our voting may be very doubtful; though we conceive (considering the critical situation of public affairs, and as they respect our Colony in particular, invaded or soon likely to be by powerful armies in different quarters) it is our duty, nay, it is absolutely necessary, that we should not only concur with, but exert ourselves in forwarding military operations. The immediate safety of the Colony calls for and will warrant us in this. Our situation is singular and delicate, no other Colony being similarly circumstanced, with whom we can consult. We wish, therefore, for your earliest advice and instructions, whether we are to consider our Colony bound by the vote of the majority in favor of Independency, and vote at large on such questions as may arise in consequence thereof; or only concur in such measures as may be absolutely necessary for the common safety and defense of America, exclusive of the idea of Independency. We fear it will be difficult to draw the line; but, once possessed of your instructions, we will do our best endeavors to follow them.

Wisner, who was writing for the whole New York delegation, could not expect a prompt reply to his nice question. The New Yorkers knew, however, that their instructions were to abstain from the debate over the text of the Declaration, which started on July 3. The day was extraordinarily hot—Philadelphia and New York were sharing the same heat wave—and the great chamber in the Philadelphia State House was uncomfortable, even though its tall windows were open. The Congress voted to sit as a committee of the whole, with Benjamin Harrison presiding instead of John Hancock. Copies of the draft Declaration had been passed around, and it was read aloud until someone— more than fifty men were present, including the New Yorkers— had an objection or a suggestion, whereupon he interrupted and explained his idea; then it was debated, and accepted or rejected by a majority vote. The draft was four pages long, with about thirty-five lines to a page, and while the first two or three paragraphs went through fairly easily, from there on, the interruptions came fast, and some of the debates were furious. The author sat near the back of the room, with Franklin beside him, in agony over what was being done to his prose, writing in the changes and marking the deletions on his copy of the subcommittee's original. Franklin tried to cheer Jefferson up, reminding him of the joke about John Thompson, the hatter, who planned a beautiful sign—a picture of a hat with the words, "Here John Thompson makes all kinds of fine hats for gentlemen." After Thompson's helpful friends had finished criticizing redundancy and unnecessary explicitness, nothing was left of the proposed sign except the picture of the hat. Adams did his best to defend the text as submitted—"fighting fearlessly for every word," Jefferson later described it—but with limited success. The process continued all afternoon and into the evening, until everyone was exhausted, and it went on through much of the following day, Thursday, July 4. By the time the last sentence was approved, Jefferson's master copy was almost illegible; he had had to write in sixty changes, some quite elaborate, and delete nearly five hundred words. Jefferson felt that his statement had been ruined, and that, for the sake of his literary reputation, he would have to make copies of his original and send them to all his friends so they could see how the congress of editors had destroyed his prose. As soon as he had the chance, he did.

Congress had indeed eliminated or altered a number of Jefferson's favorite phrases. The reference to slavery had been taken out. (To Adams' surprise, the argument over that point had taken no longer than some of the other emendations.) After editing, the text became less fiery and less flowery. In any case, literary values aside, all the delegations, including New York's, liked what the Declaration said. It was adopted in the late afternoon by a vote of twelve to none, with New York abstaining. The Continental Congress resolved that a formal copy should be engrossed on parchment decorated with a seal of the United States of America, and that the individual delegates should all sign it. The United States, of course, having just come into being, did not have a seal; Jefferson, Franklin, and Adams were promptly appointed a committee of three to design one.

Printed copies would do for immediate distribution to all the legislatures, state governments, committees of safety, commanding officers, and others who needed a text. The manuscript was taken to the Continental Congress' official printer, John Dunlap. His press worked all night, and the copies were ready the next day, July 5. These all had to be signed by President John Hancock and by the Continental Congress' secretary, Charles Thomson, and Hancock wrote covering letters—most of them began with the sentence, "The Congress, for some time past, have had their attention occupied by one of the most interesting and important subjects that could possibly come before them or any other assembly of men"—explaining that the Continental Congress wanted the news proclaimed in every one of the newly free and independent states. The letter to Washington asked him to make the announcement to the Continental Army in whatever way he thought proper. Writing these letters took another day, and the official printed copies did not leave Philadelphia until the morning of Saturday, July 6. Washington received his on Monday morning, July 8, and New York's copy reached White Plains a few hours later. By then the New York *Gazette* was on sale in the city with the news that independence had been declared, but without any of the text.

The General was pleased with the Declaration. Besides agreeing with it, he thought it would inspire his soldiers. There had been no changes in the military situation at New York, but by Monday, Washington had learned that Admiral Howe was bringing a huge second part of the British invasion force to New York; and he now had several eyewitness reports from Staten Island, some from Americans, and some from British Army deserters. General Howe's intentions remained mysterious, partly because Washington's intelligence was incorrect: more British defensive digging on Staten Island had been reported than was going on. Washington would have liked to know if many Americans had gone to Staten Island to join the British forces. Some had, but their number was small. Sixty men had arrived from New Jersey, and about an equal number had come by boat from hiding places along the south shore of Long Island. Added to the recruits who had been waiting on board the warships when Howe arrived, the total, as Howe reported it to Germain, was two hundred—a great disappointment, since the British General had expected several thousand. On the other hand, in just three days, Governor Tryon had accomplished more with an overt effort on Staten Island than in all the months of covert recruiting; he had signed up the whole Staten Island militia. Tryon had spoken to the men as they returned to their homes after hiding during the first hours of the British occupation, and persuaded them to take an oath of allegiance and fidelity to His Majesty. The oath would not make them regular British soldiers, but something preferable: they would be entitled to British Army pay but they would not have to serve anywhere except on Staten Island. On July 6, in a mass ceremony at Richmond, Tryon had administered the oath to four hundred men—almost all the militia Staten Island had raised at its high point of Association patriotism.

The New York Provincial Congress' move from City Hall to the courthouse in White Plains had taken longer than one day, because so many of the New York, Westchester, Queens, Kings, and Suffolk delegates needed to make last-minute arrangements for their families and their properties. There had not been a legal quorum on July 2, or the third, or the fourth; and by the middle of the week, since the new Congress was to assemble on the eighth, it did not seem to matter much whether the old Congress sat for another session or two. There was still no quorum on Monday, July 8, but only a man or two more were needed. The following morning, July 9, thirty-eight delegates, representing more than a majority of counties and therefore constituting a legal quorum, gathered at the courthouse. The first business was an embarrassment, for, somehow, three delegations—from New York, Albany, and Charlotte counties—had mislaid or forgotten their certificates of election. But the delegates all knew each other, and the election results were equally well known. Moreover, the sense of excitement in the Congress was tremendous. There was some contention about seating men without credentials, but no one wanted to postpone the first meeting of the new Congress any longer. The New York,

Albany, and Charlotte delegates swore that they would produce their certificates just as soon as they could find them, and the session proceeded.

General Nathaniel Woodhull, of Suffolk County, who had been President since December, was reelected—a tribute to the fair-minded solemnity with which he had wielded his gavel. Then John McKesson and Robert Benson, neither of whom was a delegate, were reelected secretaries. Next, on John Jay's motion, the Reverend Mr. Abraham Keteltas, a delegate from Queens, was given special permission to be absent whenever "godliness" required it. Keteltas was concerned because there had been many Sunday sessions recently, and he feared that there might be more. Keteltas, the only clergyman in the Provincial Congress, was noted for his long-winded speeches of overwhelming dullness, and Jay's motion to give him Sundays off was unopposed.

Altogether, it was a great day for Jay. He and his friends had been working for nearly a month on plans for transforming New York Province into New York State. (Their work had made the Mechanics Committee apprehensive; its members feared that Jay's group might write a constitution and persuade the Provincial Congress to adopt it without letting the inhabitants comment or vote on the document.) Jay was well prepared, and he was the dominating delegate on the floor—a delightful responsibility, inasmuch as there was no opposition to statehood.

But Jay and his tacticians had not anticipated what had come in the mail: Henry Wisner's letter of July 2, asking for instructions on how to vote after independence had been declared, and two copies of the Dunlap printing of the Declaration itself—one from Hancock and the other forwarded by the New York delegates.

The new Provincial Congress was not competent to vote on independence—or so some men thought—because the voters had not yet been informed that independence had been an issue in the last election. (The amendment to the Jay-Remsen resolution had not specified when New York was to be told what it had done.) No one was in a mood to remind the Congress of all that, however. As the noontime recess for lunch was approaching, both Wisner's letter and the Declaration were read out loud, and referred to a five-man committee (Jay, Yates, Hobart, Brasher, and William Smith, of Suffolk, not to be confused with Councillor William Smith, of New York, who was suspected of equivocality, but had not yet appeared before the Conspiracies committee) for immediate action. A few minor matters were raised: Colonel Reed, writing for General Washington, expressed concern about the number of prisoners still confined in New York City, and hoped the Provincial Congress could move them. Reed also suggested that, since White Plains was so far from Bowling Green, it might be useful to set up a small committee of the Provincial Congress to stay in the city and "regulate such matters of internal concern as daily present themselves." Reed's letter was referred to another committee (Van Cortlandt, Gansevort, and Graham). Then the Provincial Congress adjourned for lunch.

By the time the delegates were back in their seats, the Jay committee's report, in Jay's handwriting, was ready, and the heading at the top of the page—"In Convention of the Representatives of the State of New York, White Plains, July 9, 1776"—suggested the rest of it. The report proposed four short resolutions. The first declared for statehood and independence in fifty-eight words: "Resolved, that the reasons assigned by the Continental Congress for declaring the United Colonies free and independent States are cogent and conclusive; and that while we lament the cruel necessity which has rendered the measure unavoidable, we approve the same, and will, at the risk of our lives and fortunes, join with the other Colonies in sup-

porting it." (After passage, unopposed, a fifty-ninth word—
"unanimously"—was inserted after the word "resolved.")

The second and third resolutions concerned administrative
details: five hundred copies of the Declaration of Independence
were to be printed as handbills, and they were to be distributed,
along with the announcement that New York had become a
state, in every district of every county. The fourth resolution
instructed the New York delegates to the Continental Congress
to vote for anything they chose—"all such measures as they may
deem conducive to the happiness and welfare of the United
States of America."

Everyone regretted—New York most of all—that the July 4
vote of the Continental Congress could not be changed retro-
actively to include New York's "yea" with the votes of the other
twelve states. That was impossible. However, since New York's
abstention had been erased only five days later, the Continental
Congress thought it proper to change the title of the document
from "A Declaration by the Representatives of the United
States of America in General Congress Assembled," as Jefferson
had called it, to "The Unanimous Declaration of the Thirteen
United States of America." In August, when the parchment
copy, with a handsome seal, was ready, that was how the title
was worded, under the dateline, "In Congress, July 4, 1776."
Four New York delegates signed—William Floyd, Philip Livingston, Francis Lewis, and Lewis Morris—exactly as if they
had voted on July 4. And, for the sake of appearances, New
York decided to predate its transformation from a province to a
state. Instead of the real date, July 9, the New Yorkers voted to
use May 27, the day the previous Provincial Congress had voted
to hold county-by-county elections on the issue. In time, perhaps,
it would look as if New York had declared itself free and independent at the same time as the other twelve states.

Whatever elation the men at White Plains felt about their

unanimous vote, they went on working. They voted Lewis Morris permission to leave Philadelphia to attend to his daughter, who was ill; they decided that all the sheriffs in the state should keep all prisoners in custody for the time being, with the exception of debtors, who could be released if their creditors agreed; they set up a committee to make recommendations about supporting the New York City poor, who were suffering more than usual on account of the many dislocations the war was causing. Reed's suggestion, or something like it, was adopted. New York voted to combine the Conspiracies committee with the special committee that had been maintaining liaison between Washington's headquarters and the Provincial Congress. Hobart, Morris, Graham, Randall, and Remsen were to be its members, and although the Convention did not say where the new group would meet, the implication was that it would have to keep in close touch with the Commander-in-Chief. New York believed that the combined committee could relieve the General and his staff of the burden of examining and securing Tories—the responsibility the old Provincial Congress had thrust upon Washington on June 30. (New York wished it had not been quite so cavalier in giving Washington authority over New York inimicals, but the resolution merely offered to help, with no suggestion that the state was trying to take that authority back.) The new committee was to have broad powers over all the present and future prisoners in New York. If it wanted, it could appoint a commissary to feed them. It could also remove them to a proper place, or places, of safety. (Just where they might go, or how the committee could guard the prisoners in transit, New York did not say.)

In New York City, July 9 had been a day much like all the other days of the past week. The Americans had constantly watched the long line of British warships filling the Kills, but there had been no signs of unusual activity in the fleet, and soldiers and civilians had gone about their work. The sight and the idea of the British presence were familiar, and New York took the ships for granted, as it had taken the *Asia* and the *Duchess of Gordon* for granted during most of the year. Though each additional hour of calm was welcome, no one imagined that Howe's ambitions had been satisfied by taking Staten Island.

Washington had had the Declaration of Independence copied in longhand for each of his brigades. The copies had been handed to the brigade majors, along with their copies of the General Orders, during the morning. Retreat was to be half an hour earlier than usual—at six o'clock instead of six thirty—because Washington wanted every man in his command to hear the "grounds and reasons" for what the Continental Congress had done. The Army was to form up by brigades, each brigade on its own parade ground—a much more formal retreat ceremony than most nights when the end of the day was usually marked by a company-sized, or, at most, a regiment-sized, retreat parade. The General said, in his orders, that he hoped "this important event will serve as a fresh incentive to every officer and soldier to act with fidelity and courage, as knowing that now the peace and safety of his country depends (under God) solely on the success of our arms, and that he is now in the service of a state possessed of sufficient power to reward his merit, and advance him to the highest honors of a free country."

Headquarters had turned out a lot of letters. Among them was Washington's note to Governor Trumbull trying to assuage any hurt feelings Connecticut might be developing over the horses of the Connecticut light horse. That brigade, following the seven regiments of Connecticut militia, had arrived in the city on July 8. Somehow Washington's request that the troopers leave their mounts behind had not been attended to. Forage was as scarce as before, and the only solution, as Washington explained to Trumbull, had been to send the mounts up to Westchester. (Because his wife was about to have a baby, Colonel Seymour had not been able to ride with his unit, and so missed his cavalry's second humiliation in New York.) The General was happy to have the cavalrymen, on foot, in town, and the Barracks Master was finding accommodations for them. "I would not have it understood," Washington wrote, ". . . that I think their coming forward was a wrong step. I think it is a step which is highly advisable, and am much pleased to see with what cheerfulness and dispatch your orders were executed. . . ." Some of that cheerfulness had worn off. With their mounts turned out to pasture eleven or twelve miles away, the troopers felt themselves hardly better than infantrymen.

Washington had also written Governor Cooke, of Rhode Island, congratulating him on the arrival of a ship at Providence with a cargo that included flints, small arms, and canvas, and reminding Cooke that, by order of the Continental Congress, Cooke was supposed to forward the flints to New York City. Washington wanted the canvas, too, if it was suitable for tenting; if not, Rhode Island could keep it. In another letter, the Commander-in-Chief had assured the Massachusetts Assembly that he believed that Boston need not worry, for the time being, about a British attack. Washington had also written General Artemas Ward, commanding at Boston, ordering him to send his three "fullest" regiments to Fort Ticonderoga to reinforce Gates.

Shortly before six, Washington and his aides mounted their horses and rode toward the Commons. The companies there were finishing the complicated drill of taking position and straightening out their files and ranks. (The Commons was the only site properly leveled and planted for a military parade ground; all the other brigades were using the nearest plausible open field.) Mifflin's two regiments, Shee's and Magaw's Pennsylvanians, were drawn up near King's Bridge. Greene's regiments—Varnum's, Hitchcock's, Little's, and Hand's—were on Brooklyn Heights. Prescott's and Nixon's regiments were on Governor's Island. Heath's brigade (Learned's, Reed's, Bailey's, and Baldwin's regiments) was on the west side of the main camp on Manhattan, now called The Grand Camp. Spencer's brigade (Parson's, Arnold's, Huntington's, Ward's, and Wyllys' regiments) was in the center. Stirling's brigade (Ritzema's, McDougall's, and Webb's regiments, with several Virginia and Maryland rifle companies) was on the east. Since Knox's artillery was scattered, his companies had fallen in with whichever brigade they happened to be near. The New York and Connecticut militia—Scott's brigade, which included Lasher's, Malcolm's, and Drake's regiments, and Wadsworth's brigade (Silliman's, Gay's, Bradley's, Sage's, Selden's, Douglas', Chester's, and Seymour's regiments)—were drawn up on the Commons. One full brigade was a large formation; the two brigades on the Commons, while they were not up to full strength, were almost more than the parade ground could contain. (The field was at the south end of what is now City Hall Park, and it extended below the Park's present limits, into the traffic lanes where Broadway and Park Row now intersect.) A considerable number of civilians had been attracted by the unusual stir, and they partly filled the adjoining streets. Washington and his aides rode into the hollow square of men and joined Scott and Wadsworth, who with their aides and staff were waiting for them on horseback. There was a hullabaloo of shouting as the company officers reported to their regimental commanders that all men were present or accounted for. Regimental commanders reported to brigade commanders, who reported to the Commander-in-Chief. Then the formation was ordered to stand at ease, and it was quiet.

On all the other parade grounds—on a smaller scale, and without the excitement of General Washington's presence—the drill was the same. Within minutes of each other, the brigade adjutants were stepping forward a pace to read, as loudly as they could, the announcements for the day—appropriate paragraphs from the General Orders, together with whatever the brigade commanders wanted to add.

Routine announcements came first. Two soldiers, one from McDougall's and one from Ritzema's regiment, had been court-martialed for desertion and had been found guilty. General Washington had approved their sentences: thirty-nine lashes each. The form of the passes required to ride the New York ferries had been changed. The Continental Congress had voted that each of the regiments should have its own chaplain (as many already had), paid for by the Continent at the rate of thirty-three and one-third dollars a month.

With those matters out of the way, one of Washington's aides, in the loudest voice he could raise, then read the special announcement:

When in the Course of human events, it becomes necessary for one people to dissolve the political bands which have connected them with another, and to assume among the Powers of the earth, the separate and equal station to which the Laws of Nature and of Nature's God entitle them, a decent respect to the opinions of mankind requires that they should declare the causes which impel them to the separation.

We hold these truths to be self-evident, that all men are created equal, that they are endowed by their Creator with certain unalienable Rights, that among these are Life, Liberty, and the pursuit of Happiness. That to secure these rights, Governments are instituted among Men, deriving their just powers from the consent of the governed, That whenever any Form of Government becomes destructive of these ends, it is the Right of the People to alter or abolish it, and to institute new Government, laying its foundation on such principles and organizing its powers in such form, as to them shall seem most likely to effect their Safety and Happiness. Prudence, indeed, will dictate that Governments long established should not be changed for light and transient causes; and accordingly all experience hath shown, that mankind are more disposed to suffer, while evils are sufferable, than to right themselves by abolishing the forms to which they are accustomed. But when a long train of abuses and usurpations, pursuing invariably the same Object evinces a design to reduce them under absolute Despotism, it is their right, it is their duty, to throw off such Government, and to provide new Guards for their future security.— Such has been the patient sufferance of these Colonies; and such is now the necessity which constrains them to alter their former Systems of Government. The history of the present King of Great Britain is a history of repeated injuries and usurpations, all having in direct object the establishment of an absolute Tyranny over these States. To prove this, let Facts be submitted to a candid world.

He has refused his Assent to Laws, the most wholesome and necessary for the public good.

He has forbidden his Government to pass Laws of immediate and pressing importance, unless suspended in their operation till his Assent should be obtained; and when so suspended, he has utterly neglected to attend to them.

He has refused to pass other Laws for the accommodation of large districts of people, unless those people would relinquish the right of Representation in the Legislature, a right inestimable to them and formidable to tyrants only.

He has called together legislative bodies at places unusual, uncomfortable, and distant from the depository of their Public Records, for the sole purpose of fatiguing them into compliance with his measures.

He has dissolved Representative Houses repeatedly, for opposing with manly firmness his invasions on the rights of the people.

He has refused for a long time, after such dissolutions, to cause others to be elected; whereby the Legislative Powers, incapable of Annihilation, have returned to the People at large for their exercise; the State remaining in the mean time exposed to all the dangers of invasion from without, and convulsions within.

He has endeavoured to prevent the population of these States; for that purpose obstructing the Laws of Naturalization of Foreigners; refusing to pass others to encourage their migration hither, and raising the conditions of new Appropriations of Lands.

He has obstructed the Administration of Justice, by refusing his Assent to Laws for establishing Judiciary Powers.

He has made Judges dependent on his Will alone, for the tenure of their offices, and the amount and payment of their salaries.

He has erected a multitude of New Offices, and sent hither swarms of Officers to harass our People, and eat out their substance.

He has kept among us, in times of peace, Standing Armies without the Consent of our legislatures.

He has affected to render the Military independent of and superior to the Civil Power.

He has combined with others to subject us to a jurisdiction foreign to our constitution, and unacknowledged by our laws; giving his Assent to their acts of pretended legislation:

For quartering large bodies of armed troops among us:

For protecting them, by a mock Trial, from Punishment for any Murders which they should commit on the Inhabitants of these States:

For cutting off our Trade with all parts of the world:

For imposing taxes on us without our Consent:

For depriving us in many cases, of the benefits of Trial by Jury:

For transporting us beyond Seas to be tried for pretended offences:

For abolishing the free System of English Laws in a neighbouring Province, establishing therein an Arbitrary government, and enlarging its Boundaries so as to render it at once an example and fit instrument for introducing the same absolute rule into these Colonies:

For taking away our Charters, abolishing our most valuable Laws, and altering fundamentally the Forms of our Governments.

For suspending our own Legislatures, and declaring themselves invested with Power to legislate for us in all cases whatsoever.

He has abdicated Government here, by declaring us out of his Protection and waging War against us.

He has plundered our seas, ravaged our Coasts, burnt our towns, and destroyed the lives of our people.

He is at this time transporting large armies of foreign mercenaries to compleat the works of death, desolation and tyranny, already begun with circumstances of Cruelty & perfidy scarcely paralleled in the most barbarous ages, and totally unworthy of the Head of a civilized nation.

He has constrained our fellow Citizens taken Captive on the high Seas to bear Arms against their Country, to become the executioners of their friends and Brethren, or to fall themselves by their Hands.

He has excited domestic insurrections among us, and has endeavoured to bring on the inhabitants of our frontiers, the merciless Indian Savages, whose known rule of warfare, is an undistinguished destruction of all ages, sexes and conditions.

In every stage of these Oppressions We have Petitioned for Redress in the most humble terms: Our repeated Petitions have been answered only by repeated injury. A Prince, whose character is thus marked by every act which may define a Tyrant, is unfit to be the ruler of a free People.

Nor have We been wanting in attention to our British brethren. We have warned them from time to time of attempts by their legislature to extend an unwarrantable jurisdiction over us. We have reminded them of the circumstances of our emigration and settlement here. We have appealed to their native justice and magnanimity, and we have conjured them by the ties of our common kindred to disavow these usurpations, which would inevitably interrupt our connections and correspondence. They too have been deaf to the voice of justice and of consanguinity. We must, therefore, acquiesce in the necessity, which denounces our Separation, and hold them, as we hold the rest of mankind, Enemies in War, in Peace Friends.

We, therefore, the Representatives of the United States of America, in General Congress, Assembled, appealing to the Supreme

Judge of the world for the rectitude of our intentions, do, in the Name and by Authority of the good People of these Colonies, solemnly publish and declare, That these United Colonies are, and of Right ought to be Free and Independent States; that they are Absolved from all Allegiance to the British Crown, and that all political connection between them and the State of Great Britain, is and ought to be totally dissolved; and that as Free and Independent States, they have full Power to levy War, conclude Peace, contract Alliances, establish Commerce, and to do all other Acts and Things which Independent States may of right do. And for the support of this Declaration, with a firm reliance on the Protection of Divine Providence, we mutually pledge to each other our Lives, our Fortunes and our sacred Honor.

A chaplain then read parts of the Eightieth Psalm. Scott's and Wadsworth's brigades, on command, gave three loud cheers, and the troops were dismissed, except those who had guard duty that night, who were to be inspected by the commander of the guard and marched to their respective posts. The crowd dispersed. Most of the soldiers and civilians walked south on Broadway. They were serious rather than jubilant. In Philadelphia, there had been considerable rejoicing on both July 2 and July 4; and at Baltimore, the enthusiasm for the Declaration, which was read to the public, had been riotous, with gun shots and artillery salutes added to the cheers of the population. New Yorkers liked bonfires, and had lit one on the Commons at every opportunity in the past. Now, a fire at night, like the boom of cannon or the peal of church bells, could have been mistaken for a signal—the alarm that battle had begun.

A sizable crowd of strollers accumulated at Bowling Green, as they did on any pleasant evening before curfew. On this occasion, more people than usual were out—men, women, children, and off-duty soldiers. Someone remembered that the equestrian statue of George III, which stood in the grassy oval and looked as if it were made of gold, was gilded lead—a wealth of potential bullets that the Dunscomb-Prince committee had overlooked. Several agile New Yorkers, with ropes and crowbars, climbed over the railing around the statue and scrambled onto its marble pedestal. Pulling and prying, they tipped the figure over, and as it crashed to the ground—it was said to weigh four thousand pounds—it cracked in several places. A man with a crowbar jimmied off the King's head. That symbolic act brought no cheers. One spectator, a captain of a Pennsylvania company, was surprised that the crowd was cold and indifferent. But, after all, the New Yorkers with tools were not demonstrating but working. For some time they continued to break the statue into sections small enough to cart away in the morning.

Sources

☆

BOOKS, PAMPHLETS, AND ARTICLES

Abbott, Wilbur C., *New York in the American Revolution,* Scribner's, New York, 1929

Adams, Samuel, *The Writings of Samuel Adams,* vol. III, Harry A. Cushing (ed.), Putnam's, New York, 1907

Alden, John R., *General Charles Lee: Traitor or Patriot?* Louisiana State University Press, Baton Rouge, 1951

Alexander, E. P., *James Duane of New York: A Revolutionary Conservative,* Columbia University Press, New York, 1938

Andrews, Charles M., *The Colonial Background of the American Revolution,* Yale University Press, New Haven, 1931

Armstrong, John, *Life of Richard Montgomery,* Library of American Biography, vol. I, series 1, Jared Sparks (ed.), Hilliard, Gray, Boston, 1834

Augur, Helen, *The Secret War of Independence,* Duell, Sloan & Pearce, New York, 1955

Bailyn, Bernard, *The Ideological Origins of the American Revolution,* Harvard University Press, Cambridge, 1967

———, *The Origins of American Politics,* Knopf, New York, 1968

Bakeless, John, *Turncoats, Traitors, and Heroes,* Lippincott, Philadelphia, 1959

Bancroft, George, *The History of the United States,* vol. III, Little, Brown, Boston, 1834–1874

Beach, Stewart, *Samuel Adams: The Fateful Years 1764–1776,* Dodd Mead, New York, 1965

Beardsley, E. E., *Life and Correspondence of The Right Reverend Samuel Seabury, D.D.,* Houghton Mifflin, Boston, 1881

Becker, Carl, *The Declaration of Independence,* Knopf, New York, 1942

———, *The Eve of the Revolution,* Yale University Press, New Haven, 1920

———, *The History of Political Parties in the Province of New York, 1760–1776,* University of Wisconsin Press, Madison, 1909, 1960

Bird, Harrison, *Attack on Quebec,* Oxford University Press, New York, 1968

Boatner, Mark M., *Encyclopedia of the American Revolution,* McKay, 1966

Bonomi, Patricia U., *A Factious People: Politics and Society in Colonial New York,* Columbia University Press, New York, 1971

Boorstin, Daniel J., *The Americans: The Colonial Experience,* Random House, New York, 1958

Bridenbaugh, Carl, *Cities in Revolt: Urban Life in America, 1743–1776,* Knopf, New York, 1955

Broome, John, "The Counterfeiting Adventure of Henry Dawkins," *American Notes and Queries,* vol. VIII, no. 12, March, 1930

Brown, Gerald S., *The American Secretary: The Colonial Policy of Lord George Germain, 1775–1778,* University of Michigan Press, Ann Arbor, 1963

Burnett, Edmund G., *The Continental Congress,* Macmillan, New York, 1941

Callahan, North, *Flight from the Republic: The Tories of the American Revolution,* Bobbs-Merrill, Indianapolis, 1967

———, *Royal Raiders: The Tories of the American Revolution,* Bobbs-Merrill, Indianapolis, 1963

Conway, Moncure D., *The Life of Thomas Paine* (2 vols.), Putnam's, New York, 1892

Dangerfield, George, *Chancellor Robert R. Livingston of New York, 1746–1813*, Harcourt, Brace, New York, 1960

Dawson, Henry B., *The Park and Its Vicinity in the City of New York*, privately printed, New York, 1867

——, *The Sons of Liberty in New York*, privately printed, New York, 1859

Decatur, Stephen, "The Conflicting History of Henry Dawkins, Engraver," *American Collector*, vol. VII, no. 12, January, 1939

Delafield, Joseph L., *Chancellor Robert R. Livingston of New York and His Family*, American Scenic and Historic Preservation Society, New York, 1911

Delafield, Julia, *Biographies of Francis Lewis and Morgan Lewis*, Anson D. F. Randolph, New York, 1877

Dictionary of American Biography, Allen Johnson and Dumas Malone (eds.), (21 vols.), Scribner's, New York, 1943

Duer, William Alexander, *The Life of William Alexander, Earl of Stirling, Major General in the Army of the United States During the Revolution*, New York, 1847

Dunlap, William, *History of the American Theatre*, J. & J. Harper, New York, 1832

——, *History of the New Netherlands* (2 vols.), privately printed, New York, 1839–1840

Dunshee, Kenneth H., *As You Pass By*, Hastings House, New York, 1952

Flexner, James T., *George Washington* (4 vols.), Little, Brown, Boston, 1965–1970

Flick, Alexander C. (ed.), *History of the State of New York*, Columbia University Press, New York, 1933–1937

——, *Loyalism in New York during the American Revolution*, Columbia University Press, New York, 1901

Forbes, Esther, *Paul Revere and the World He Lived In*, Houghton Mifflin, Boston, 1942

Fox, Dixon R., *Yankees and Yorkers*, New York University Press, New York, 1940

Freeman, Douglas S., *George Washington: A Biography* (7 vols.), Scribner's, New York, 1948–1957

Graydon, Alexander, *Memoirs of His Own Time, with Reminiscences of the Men and Events of the Revolution*, Lindsay and Blakiston, Philadelphia, 1846

Guttmacher, Manfred S., *America's Last King*, Scribner's, New York, 1941

Hall, Edward H., *An Appeal for the Preservation of City Hall Park, New York*, American Scenic and Historic Preservation Society, New York, 1910

———, *The Catskill Aqueduct and Earlier Water Supplies in the City of New York*, chaps. 3 and 4, New York, 1917

Hammond, Bray, *Banks and Politics in America from the Revolution to the Civil War*, Princeton University Press, Princeton, 1957

Harrington, Virginia D., *The New York Merchant on the Eve of the Revolution*, Columbia University Press, New York, 1935

Hawke, David, *A Transaction of Free Men: The Birth and Course of the Declaration of Independence*, Scribner's, New York, 1964

Haywood, Marshall D., *Governor William Tryon and His Administration in the Province of North Carolina 1765–1771*, Raleigh, 1903

History of Queen's County, New York, compiled by the publisher, W. W. Munsell, New York, 1882

Horsmanden, Daniel, *The New York Conspiracy*, Thomas J. Davis (ed.), Beacon, Boston, 1971

Humphreys, David, *An Essay on the Life and Times of the Honorable Major-General Israel Putnam*, Hartford, 1788

Hunt, Louise L., *Biographical Notes Concerning General Richard Montgomery*, Poughkeepsie, 1876

Jay, William, *The Life of John Jay* (2 vols.), J. and J. Harper, New York, 1833

Johnston, Henry P., *The Campaign of 1776 Around New York and Brooklyn*, Long Island Historical Society, New York, 1878

Jones, Thomas, *History of New York During the Revolutionary War and of the Leading Events in the Other Colonies of That Period* (2 vols.), New-York Historical Society, New York, 1879

Knollenberg, Bernhard, *Origin of the American Revolution, 1759–1766*, Macmillan, New York, 1960

Kouwenhoven, John A., *The Columbia Historical Portrait of New York*, Doubleday, New York, 1953

Labaree, Leonard W. (ed.), *The Autobiography of Benjamin Franklin*, Yale University Press, New Haven, 1964

———, *Conservatism in Early American History*, New York University Press, New York, 1948

Lacey, Dan, *The Meaning of the American Revolution*, New American Library, New York, 1964

Leake, Isaac Q., *Memoir of the Life and Times of General John Lamb*, Albany, 1850

Leder, Lawrence H., *Robert Livingston and the Politics of Colonial New York*, University of North Carolina Press, Chapel Hill, 1961

Lee, W. Storrs, *The Yankees of Connecticut*, Holt, New York, 1957

Lossing, Benson J., *The Pictorial Field Book of the Revolution* (2 vols.), New York, 1851

———, *The Life and Times of Philip Schuyler* (2 vols.), New York, 1860–1873

Malcolm, David, *A Genealogical Memoir of the Most Noble and Ancient House of Drummond*, Edinburgh, 1808

Malone, Dumas, *Jefferson and His Time* (3 vols.), Little, Brown, Boston, 1948–1962

Mark, Irving, *Agrarian Conflicts in Colonial New York*, Columbia University Press, New York, 1940

Martin, George C., *The Shark River District, Monmouth County, New Jersey*, Martin and Allardyce, Asbury Park, 1914

Miller, John C., *Sam Adams, Pioneer in Propaganda*, Little, Brown, Boston, 1936

———, *Origins of the American Revolution*, Little, Brown, Boston, 1943

———, *Triumph of Freedom, 1775–1783*, Little, Brown, Boston, 1948

Mitchell, Broadus, *Alexander Hamilton: Youth to Maturity, 1755–1788*, Macmillan, New York, 1957

Montross, Lynn, *The Reluctant Rebels*, Harper, New York, 1950

Morris, Richard B., *The American Revolution*, Van Nostrand, New York, 1955

Morrison, Hugh, *Early American Architecture*, Oxford University Press, New York, 1952

Nelson, William H., *The American Tory*, Oxford University Press, New York, 1961

Nettels, Curtis P., *George Washington and American Independence*, Little, Brown, Boston, 1951

———, *The Emergence of a National Economy, 1775–1815*, Holt, 1962

———, *The Money Supply of the American Colonies*, University of Wisconsin Press, Madison, 1934

Nevins, Allen, *The American States During and After the Revolution, 1775–1789*, Macmillan, New York, 1924

Nye, Russell B., *Cultural Life of the New Nation 1776–1830*, Harper, New York, 1960

Onderdonk, Henry (ed.), *Queens County in Olden Times: Being a Supplement to the Several Histories Thereof*, Charles Welling, Jamaica, N.Y., 1865

Paltsits, Victor H., *John Holt, Printer and Postmaster*, New York Public Library, New York, 1920

Phillips, A. V., *The Lott Family in America*, Trenton, N.J., 1942

Plumb, J. H., *England in the 18th Century*, Penguin, London, 1950

Roche, John F., *Joseph Reed: A Moderate in the American Revolution*, Columbia University Press, New York, 1957

Rossiter, Clinton, *Seedtime of the Republic: The Origin of the American Tradition of Political Liberty*, Harcourt, Brace, New York, 1953

Sabine, Lorenzo, *Biographical Sketches of Loyalists of the American Revolution*, Little, Brown, Boston, 1864

Scharf, J. Thomas (ed.), *The History of Westchester County, New York, Including Morrisania, Kings Bridge, and West Farms*, (2 vols.), L. E. Preston, Philadelphia, 1886

Scheer, George F., and Rankin, Hugh F., *Rebels and Redcoats*, World, New York, 1957, 1972

Schlesinger, Arthur M., *The Colonial Merchants and the American Revolution, 1763–1766*, Barnes & Noble (reprint), 1939

————, *Prelude to Independence: The Newspaper War on Britain 1764–1776*, Knopf, New York, 1958

Scott, Kenneth, *Counterfeiting in Colonial America*, Oxford University Press, New York, 1957

Seabury, William J., *Memoir of Bishop Seabury*, Gorham, New York, 1908

Smith, Frank, "New Light on Thomas Paine's First Year in America, 1775," *American Literature*, January, 1930, Durham, North Carolina

Smith, J. H., *Our Struggle for the Fourteenth Colony: Canada in the American Revolution* (2 vols.), Putnam's, New York, 1907

Smith, William, *Historical Memoirs of William Smith from 16 March 1763 to 9 July 1776*, William Sabine (ed.), New York Public Library, New York, 1956

Sparks, Jared, *The Life of Gouverneur Morris* (3 vols.), Gray & Bowen, Boston, 1832

The Spirit of 'Seventy-Six, Henry S. Commager and Richard B. Morris (eds.), Harper, New York, 1967

Stephenson, Orlando W., "The Supply of Gunpowder in 1776," *American History Review*, January, 1925

Stiles, Henry B., *History of the City of Brooklyn* (2 vols.), Brooklyn, 1867

Swiggett, Howard, *The Extraordinary Mr. Morris*, Doubleday, New York, 1952

Thomas, Isaiah, "The History of Printing in America," vols. V and VI, *Proceedings of the American Antiquarian Society*, Albany, 1874

Thomas, Milton H., "The King's College Building," *New-York Historical Society Bulletin*, January, 1955

Trevelyan, George O., *The American Revolution*, Richard B. Morris (ed.), McKay, New York, 1964

Valentine, Alan, *Lord George Germain*, Oxford University Press, London, 1962

Van Doren, Carl, *Secret History of the American Revolution*, Viking, New York, 1941

Van Schaack, Henry C., *Life of Peter Van Schaack*, Appleton, New York, 1841

Van Tyne, Claude H., *Loyalists in the American Revolution*, Macmillan, New York, 1902, 1929

Wall, A. J., "Samuel Loudon, 1727–1813," *New-York Historical Society Bulletin*, October, 1922

Ward, Christopher, *The War of the Revolution* (2 vols.), Macmillan, New York, 1952

Wecter, Dixon, "Thomas Paine and the Franklins," *American Literature*, Durham, North Carolina, November, 1940

Wells, William V., *The Life and Public Services of Samuel Adams* (3 vols.), Little, Brown, Boston, 1865

Wertenbaker, T. J., *Father Knickerbocker Rebels*, Scribner's, New York, 1948

Whittemore, Henry, *The Abeel and Allied Families*, privately printed, New York, 1899

Willcox, William B., *Portrait of a General: Sir Henry Clinton in the War of Independence*, Knopf, New York, 1960
Wilson, James G. (ed.), *The Memorial History of New York* (2 vols.), New-York History Co., New York, 1892

MANUSCRIPTS AND DOCUMENTS

Alsop, John, 1775 papers, The New-York Historical Society Bancroft Collection, New York Public Library
A Biographical Congressional Directory 1774–1911, Government Printing Office, Washington, D.C., 1913
Burnett, Edmund C. (ed.), *Letters of Members of the Continental Congress*, vol. I, The Carnegie Institution, Washington, D.C., 1921
Deane, Silas, papers, Charles Isham (ed.), New-York Historical Society Collections, vols. XIX–XXIII.
Duane, James, papers 1767–1795, New-York Historical Society
Fernow, Berthold (ed.), *Documents Relating to the Colonial History of the State of New York* (15 vols.), Weed, Parsons, Albany, 1853–1887
Force, Peter (ed.), *American Archives: Fourth Series* (6 vols.), Washington, D.C., 1837–1846
The Papers of Alexander Hamilton, Harold C. Syrett (ed.), vol. I, Columbia University Press, New York, 1961
The Correspondence and Public Papers of John Jay, Henry P. Johnston (ed.), New York, 1890
Journals of the Provincial Congress, Provincial Convention, Committee of Safety and Council of Safety of the State of New York 1775–1777, Thurlow Weed, Albany, 1842
Lamb, John, papers, New York Public Library
The Charles Lee Papers (4 vols.), Collections of the New-York Historical Society, New York, 1871–1874
Manuscript Books and Papers of the Commission of Enquiry into the Losses and Services of American Loyalists, Public Record Of-

fice of England, transcribed for New York Public Library, 1899

McDougall, Alexander, papers 1775–1776, New-York Historical Society

Minutes of the Committee and First Commission for Detecting Conspiracies in the State of New York, vol. I, New-York Historical Society, 1924

Minutes of the Common Council of the City of New York, 1675–1776, vol. VIII, Dodd Mead, New York, 1905

New York City During the American Revolution, The Tomlinson Collection, privately printed, New York, 1861

Olson, Edwin, *Negro Slavery in New York*, Ph.D. dissertation, New York University, New York, 1947

Shannon, Anna M., *General Alexander McDougall, Citizen and Soldier, 1732–1786*, Ph.D. dissertation, Fordham University, New York, 1957

Stirling, Lord (William Alexander), papers, New-York Historical Society

Stokes, I. N. Phelps, *The Iconography of Manhattan Island*, New York, 1915–1928

Letter Book of John Watts, Merchant and Councillor of New York, January 1, 1762–December 22, 1765, Dorothy C. Barck (ed.), Collections of the New-York Historical Society, New York, 1928

Correspondence and Journals of Samuel Blachley Webb, Worthington C. Ford (ed.), (3 vols.), Burnett, New York, 1894

NEWSPAPERS

John Anderson, *The Constitutional Gazette*, August 1775–May 1776, Wednesdays and Saturdays

Hugh Gaine, *The New York Gazette and Weekly Mercury*, January 1776–July 1776, Mondays

John Holt, *New-York Journal or The General Advertiser*, June 1775–July 1776, Thursdays

Samuel Loudon, *The New York Packet and the American Advertiser*, January 4, 1776–July 1776, Thursdays

James Rivington, *Rivington's New-York Gazetteer or Connecticut, Hudson's River, New Jersey, and Quebec Weekly Advertiser*, June 1775–November 1775, Thursdays

Notes

☆

PART I

Page

1   *twenty thousand persons:* Within the built-up area. The population of Manhattan Island (New York County) was 21,863 in 1771, according to Tryon's Report to the Crown, June 11, 1774, and had increased about 10 percent by 1775.

4   *ordered Colonel Lasher to commit:* Journals of the Provincial Congress, July 25, 1775.

5   *members of the New York Provincial Congress, the New York City Committee, . . . and a few ministers:* Jones, *History of New York.*

6   *Bunker's Hill:* Or Bunker Hill, or even Buncker's Hill. The monument is the Bunker Hill Monument, but I am following the Boston Committee of Safety and, I think, the prevailing style in 1775.

6   *the* Asia *had joined the* Kingfisher: Holt's *Journal,* June 1, 1775.

8   *a substantial number:* Jones, *History of New York.*

10   *hummed a tune:* Smith, *Historical Memoirs,* June 25, 1775.

14   *Washington and Lee were eager:* GW to the Continental Congress, 5:00 P.M., June 25, 1775. Force, *American Archives.*

15   *the seizing of a Governor:* GW to Schuyler, June 25, 1775. Force, *American Archives.*

17   *the biggest public demonstration:* Freeman, *George Washington,* vol. III, p. 463.

27   *one of the earliest New York Sons of Liberty: Dictionary of American Biography.*

28   *Sears had replaced:* Journals of the Provincial Congress, June 9, 1775.

30   *a full complement of officers:* Holt's *Journal,* July 20, 1775.

31   *a position paper . . . early in July:* Adopted June 27, forwarded June 29, acknowledged July 6, 1775. Journals of the Provincial Congress.

33   *meant to replace:* Journals of the Provincial Congress, August 5, and August 9, 1775.

35   *Tryon had learned:* Capt. Vandeput to Mayor Hicks, Journals of the Provincial Congress, August 24, 1775.

39   *go on supplying the* Asia: Journals of the Provincial Congress, August 29, 1775.

40   *in domestic service:* Olson, *Negro Slavery in New York.*

42   *McDougall's decision:* McDougall to Schuyler, November 14, 1775. McDougall papers.

46   *order his arrest:* Smith, *Historical Memoirs,* October 10, 1775.

53   *imposingly large man:* Beardsley, *Life and Correspondence of The Right Reverend Samuel Seabury, D.D.*

53   *two hundred worshipers:* Seabury, *Memoir of Bishop Seabury.*

56   *his second wife's . . . Elizabeth:* Thomas, *The History of Printing in America.*

57   *to the* Kingfisher: Stokes, *Iconography,* May 10, 1775.

57   *model of gentlemanliness:* Dunlap, *History of the American Theatre.*

59   *give Rivington another chance:* Rivington's *Gazetteer,* June 8, 1775.

60   *tenants who rented property:* Journals of the Provincial Congress, October 25, 1775.

62   *"all" the inimicals:* Dawson, *The Sons of Liberty in New York.*

65   *lifted off her cap:* Seabury's memorial to the Conn. General Assembly, December 20, 1775. Stokes, *Iconography.*

PART II

Page

72　*wiped out Falmouth:* GW to the New York Provincial Congress, received November 2, 1775. Journals of the Provincial Congress.

77　*come to the realization:* Report by the Committee on the Highlands Fortifications, December 18, 1775. Journals of the Provincial Congress.

78　*by drawing beautiful plans:* Force, *American Archives,* September 19, 1775.

82　*joined by the* Phoenix: Stokes, *Iconography,* December 25, 1775.

85　*Sears's description might be correct:* GW to Reed, January 4, 1776. Force, *American Archives.*

87　*a courtesy rank:* George Moore, *The Treason of Charles Lee,* in vol. IV, *The Charles Lee Papers.*

89　*would not cost much:* GW to Reed, March 3, 1776. Force, *American Archives.*

90　*of running down Tories:* Lee to Morris, January 3, 1776. *The Charles Lee Papers.*

96　*Jay had a suggestion:* Jay to McDougall, December 23, 1775. *The Correspondence and Public Papers of John Jay.*

97　*Hamilton had noticed:* Hamilton to Jay, December 31, 1775. *The Correspondence and Public Papers of John Jay.*

97　*with great seriousness:* In the Committee's language: ". . . let no time be lost in taking every necessary care and pains to secure their election." Journals of Provincial Congress, January 4, 1776.

99　*all been excellent:* Except that, by macabre coincidence, an Albany rumor of Montgomery's death and the Americans' total defeat had circulated a week or more before they happened; and Schuyler had written the Continental Congress to explain that the lies had been contrived by inimicals in Albany. Force, *American Archives,* December 26, 1775.

100 *belonged to the First New York:* Ward, *The War of the Revolution,* p. 191.

103 *now called the Varian Homestead:* Scharf, *The History of Westchester County,* vol. I, p. 753.

104 *New Jersey minutemen:* Stirling to Hancock, January 18, 1776. Force, *American Archives.*

104 *the shoemaker, was given a pass:* Journals of the Provincial Congress, January 18, 1776.

111 *had brought them out:* Trumbull to Lee, January 12, 1776. *The Charles Lee Papers.*

119 *would be "politic":* Journals of the Provincial Congress, January 27, 1776.

120 *on a stretcher:* Lee to GW, February 5, 1776. *The Charles Lee Papers.*

120 *which overlooked the Commons:* Hall, *An Appeal for the Preservation of City Hall Park,* p. 20. (Among other spellings of the lady's name are Montagnie, Montagne, Montayne, and Montaine.)

126 *an oddity:* Lee to Captain Ledlie, February 8, 1776. *The Charles Lee Papers.*

129 *a reconnaissance for future reference:* Wilcox, *Portrait of a General,* p. 71.

130 *next in line:* Malcolm, *A Genealogical Memoir of the Most Noble and Ancient House of Drummond.*

135 *more prudence:* Smith, *Historical Memoirs,* February 4, 1776.

148 *with admirable speed:* Holt's *Journal,* February 22, 1776 (in a story dated February 12).

PART III

Page

157 *what should have been good news:* Robert Morris to Lee, February 17, 1776. *The Charles Lee Papers.*

162 *leave Great Britain by April 7:* Valentine, *Lord George Germain,* p. 129.

163 *a hundred thousand copies:* Conway, *The Life of Thomas Paine,* p. 69.

163 *in the fall of 1774:* It may have been as late as December, 1774. Smith, *New Light on Thomas Paine's First Year in America.*

173 *the queer situation:* Journals of the Provincial Congress, March 2, 1776.

176 *Lee also had word:* Lee to the Provincial Congress, March 4, 1776. Journals of the Provincial Congress.

180 *received Lee's orders: The Charles Lee Papers,* March 5, 1776.

182 *several complaining letters:* For instance, Gale to McKesson, February 29, 1776. Force, *American Archives.*

185 *The Provincial Congress' one recourse:* Journals of the Provincial Congress, March 7, 1776.

187 *had left him a fortune:* Duer, *The Life of William Alexander, Earl of Stirling.*

188 *watching the sheriff sell it:* Stirling to Philip Livingston, October 27, 1775. Stirling papers.

190 *began on March 15:* Stirling to Hancock, March 14, 1776. Force, *American Archives.*

192 *213,400 separate bills:* Journals of the Provincial Congress, March 5, 1776.

194 *was a failure:* Journals of the Provincial Congress, March 11, 1776.

197 *"a gentleman" living some distance from New York:* He was Charles Inglis, D.D., assistant rector of Trinity Church, and he lived right in New York.

199 *Loudon immediately complained:* Loudon's memorial to the Committee of Safety, March 20, 1776. Journals of the Provincial Congress.

202 *of a sanguinary despot:* Holt's *Journal,* April 4, 1776.

206 *more military assistance:* John Varick, Jr., to Richard Varick, April 1, 1776. Stokes, *Iconography.*

208 *except forty women and children:* Heath to Hancock, April 3, 1776. Force, *American Archives.*

208 *overcoats and white shirts:* Loudon's *Packet,* April 4, 1776.

208 *a present to welcome Howe:* Tryon's report to Germain, April

6, 1776. *Documents Relating to the Colonial History of the State of New York.*

214 *and a shrewd businessman:* Too shrewd, according to some. Boatner, *Encyclopedia of the American Revolution,* p. 320.

214 *an agent of the United Colonies:* Ralph V. Harlow, *The Dictionary of American Biography.*

219 *the Mortier house was ready:* Freeman, *George Washington,* vol. IV, p. 89.

227 *the shocking testimony:* April 17, 1776, the Committee of Safety sitting. Journals of the Provincial Congress.

232 *his good friend James Duane:* April 14, 1776. Alexander, *James Duane of New York.*

PART IV

Page

237 *using the structure as a fort:* Tryon to Germain, April 18, 1776. Stokes, *Iconography.*

250 *Peter Puillon . . . was arrested:* Chambers to GW, May 5, 1776. Force, *American Archives.*

254 *ready in a few days:* Journals of the Provincial Congress, May 9, 1776.

256 *management of Cornelius Bradford:* Stokes, *Iconography,* May 1, 1776.

260 *in the May 16 issue:* Following a very brief account in Anderson's *Constitutional Gazette,* May 11, 1776.

260 *to return immediately:* Gaine's *Mercury,* May 13, 1776.

261 *six shillings a pound:* Gaine's *Mercury,* May 6, 1776.

262 *bad news from Canada:* Schuyler to GW, May 17, 1776. Force, *American Archives.*

264 *with the Continental troops:* GW to the Provincial Congress, May 17, 1776. Force, *American Archives.*

265 *a long memorandum:* GW's instructions to Putnam, May 21, 1776. Force, *American Archives.*

280 *the Conspiracies committee was experimenting:* Journals of the Provincial Congress, June 5, 1776.

285 *would not be quite right:* Dangerfield, *Chancellor Robert R. Livingston,* pp. 75–78.

286 *asking for New York's "sentiments":* Journals of the Provincial Congress, June 10, 1776.

286 *representative of the cautious minority:* Hawke, *A Transaction of Free Men,* p. 142.

292 *the artillery arrangements:* Henry Knox, "A Return of the Disposition of the Cannon, etc.," June 10, 1776. Force, *American Archives.*

296 *Seventeen delegates . . . were reelected:* Holt's *Journal,* June 20, 1776.

PART V

Page

298 *leaned over backward:* Van Doren, *Secret History of the American Revolution.*

300 *came to thirty-one:* Holt's *Journal,* June 20, 1776.

302 *questioned an Orange County man:* Force, *American Archives,* June 20, 1776.

310 *Washington, Putnam, and, possibly, Greene:* Peter Curtenius to Richard Varick, June 22, 1776. *The Tomlinson Collection.*

312 *Hickey took the stand:* General Court Martial Proceedings, June 26, 1776. Force, *American Archives.*

314 *a brave but unsuccessful effort:* Tupper to GW, June 21, 1776. Stokes, *Iconography.*

316 *a letter from . . . Lt. Joseph Davison:* Force, *American Archives,* June 27, 1776.

324 *it might be useful to compare:* GW to John Jay, June 29, 1776. *The Correspondence and Public Papers of John Jay.*

324 *adjourn for just one day:* Journals of the Provincial Congress, June 30, 1776.

328 *Howe meant to wait:* Howe to Germain (from Staten Island), July 7, 1776. Force, *American Archives.*

336 *Coffee House patrons had the news:* Hazard to Gates, July 5, 1776. Force, *American Archives.*

341 *the whole Staten Island militia:* Tryon to Germain, July 8, 1776. *Documents Relating to the Colonial History of New York State.*

341 *forgotten their certificates:* Journals of the Provincial Congress, July 9, 1776.

348 *the hollow square:* Lossing, *Pictorial Field Book of the American Revolution.*

353 *serious rather than jubilant:* Graydon, *Memoirs of His Own Time, with Reminiscences of the Men and Events of the Revolution.*

353 *as they did on any pleasant evening:* Freeman, *George Washington,* vol. IV, p. 134.

Index

☆

Abeel, Garrett, 296
Abingdon, Earl of, 152
Adams, John, 157, 286; and Declaration of Independence, 286, 334, 335, 338, 339; letter from, to Washington on medal, 218; in Naval Committee, 235; Washington asks his advice on New York expedition, 89
Adams, Samuel, 233; and Paine's "Common Sense," 163, 165–166
Aitken's *Pennsylvania Magazine*, 163
Alamance, Battle of the, 10
Albany 13–14, 41, 216; army recruiting, 154–155; militia, 289; Tories (inimicals) from, 323
Albany County, 30, 177, 296, 341–342
Alfred (American Navy ship), 236
Allen, Andrew, 174; in Congress committee on Lee, 118–120, 139; and Drummond's peace plan, 134
Allen, Thomas, 92
Allen, William, 104
Alner, Capt. James, 156, 213
Alsop, John, 98, 127, 230, 285, 296, 336; Provincial Congress committee report on Tories, 271–272; in tea trade, charges against him, 273–275, 296
Amboy, N.J. (Perth Amboy), 123, 145, 237, 266, 299, 327, 333
Amity's Admonition (British Navy ship), 319
Amusements, 17

Anabaptists, 18
Anderson, Mr. and Mrs. Alexander, 246–247
Anderson, John, *Constitutional Gazette*, 56
Anderson's bookshop, 163
Andrea Doria (American Navy ship), 236
Anglicans (Church of England), 18, 53, 55
Antil, Sgt. Edward, 98
Apthorpe, Charles, 145, 195, 320, 321, 332; estate, 320
Army, *see* Continental Army
Arnold, Benedict: in Canadian expedition, 99, 100, 156; retreat from Canada, 313, 314
Arnold's regiment, 348
Artillery, 292–294; *see also* Cannon
Asia (British Navy ship), 6, 26, 29, 44, 62, 82, 104, 107, 140, 144, 206–209, 211, 226, 303, 324, 329, 346; American prisoners on, 150, 228; boat of, captured and destroyed, 32–33, 39; counterfeiting on, rumored, 291; fires on New York, 35–39, 121, 327; moved to outer harbor, 212; provision ships seized by, 159–161, 172–173; Puillon delivers provisions for, 250–251; spies visiting, 228; in Staten Island landing, 330; Tryon protected by, 46–48
Assembly, *see* New York Assembly
Association, *see* Continental Association

72 73 8 7 6 5 4 3 2 1

A South West View of the City of

Taken from the Governours Island at